# Burgess and Maclean

# Burgess and Maclean

## A NEW LOOK AT THE FOREIGN OFFICE SPIES

## John Fisher

ROBERT HALE . LONDON

© *John Fisher 1977*
*First published in Great Britain 1977*

ISBN 0 7091 6479 3

Robert Hale Limited,
Clerkenwell House,
Clerkenwell Green,
London EC1R 0HT

Printed in Great Britain by
Willmer Brothers Limited, Birkenhead, Merseyside

# Contents

# Illustrations

### PICTURE CREDITS

Popperfoto: 2, 5, 8, 9, 10, 15
Keystone Press: 1
Syndication International: 3
Associated Press: 4, 6, 17
Press Association: 7
Camera Press: 11, 12, 13, 14, 16
London Express: 18

# Acknowledgements

This book, so far as it has been possible to ascertain from a highly placed, though unofficial adviser, in no way endangers national security. Nevertheless it has been compiled under a government headed by a Prime Minister who has shown himself indifferent, if not hostile, towards the freedom of the Press and at the same time favourable towards government by camouflage, if not by stealth. Meanwhile the ridiculous Official Secrets Act remains in force.

I have not therefore felt free to express my thanks in detail to those who, in off-the-record interviews, have helped me to arrive at a fresh interpretation of the Burgess–Maclean affair. I hope they will accept this collective expression of my gratitude to them for their enlightened comments.

When first approached to write this book, I wondered at first whether I should be able to add much to what earlier writers had achieved. But the mere passage of twenty-five years has lent new significance to what happened—just as it has led people to talk a little more freely than they were willing to do at the time. Some of what is new is unpalatable. What emerges is a chronicle of human weakness, of evasions on the part of friends, relatives, officials and politicians—above all of politicians.

Earlier writers were, of course, working without the advantage of hindsight. Thus Cyril Connolly's engaging tract *The Missing Diplomats* appeared in 1952 when Melinda Maclean and her children were still this side of the Iron Curtain, and no one knew for sure where Burgess and Maclean might turn up. Equally, both Geoffrey Hoare's *The Missing Macleans* and the *Daily Express* account *The Great Spy Scandal* were published before Burgess and Maclean had re-appeared in Moscow, and Tom Driberg's biography of Guy Burgess was published before the connection between Burgess and Philby had been established.

Today we know a good deal more—for instance about Donald Maclean's sudden marriage in Paris and his escape with his bride at the time of the fall of France. We can now realize just how Maclean's drinking exploits in Cairo came to be hushed up through what amounted to a semi-official conspiracy; we know the name of the distinguished—and blameless—woman psychiatrist who treated Maclean after his breakdown, and why, despite evidence to the contrary, the Foreign Office believed Maclean had recovered from it. In addition we know the reason why he was then appointed Head of the American Department. We can appreciate the conflict of evidence between what emerged publicly at the time of Maclean's escape and what is available today. And we are entitled to wonder how Melinda's mysterious two-day visit to Paris in 1951 was never reported at the time.

Burgess emerges as a far more accomplished agent than had hitherto been realized and we learn about the trunkful of information he left behind him, containing particulars of the political beliefs and potential vulnerability of his Cambridge friends. We now know also the true explanation, that Harold Macmillan felt unable to give, of how Burgess was recruited into the Foreign Office, and how he came to be posted to the British Embassy in Washington, an episode that could have occurred only in the Britain of twenty years ago or in the pages of Evelyn Waugh.

But no account of the flight of the missing diplomats can afford to neglect what has already been written by earlier pioneers. Thus the late Tom Driberg's *Guy Burgess, A Portrait With Background* is specially valuable for the anecdotes of Burgess as a schoolboy and undergraduate—a period covered in *Philby, The Spy Who Betrayed A Generation* by Bruce Page, David Leitch and Phillip Knightley as also by Patrick Seale and Maureen McConville in *Philby, the Long Road to Moscow*. No one who wishes to understand the psychology of Guy Burgess can afford to miss Professor Rees's elegantly written and entertaining rationalization of the man who, in Britain, if not overall, turned out to be the senior partner in the Burgess–Maclean conglomerate. And even though one may be permitted to have some reservations about the highly favourable account which the late Geoffrey Hoare gave in *The Missing Macleans* of Melinda's motives and character, yet most if not all the details he gives—particularly those on Melinda's early life, her sojourn in Cairo and the preparations which she made for her flight to Moscow, have the stamp of authenticity. The late Eleanor Philby in *Kim Philby, the Spy I Loved* throws some invaluable side-lights on the Maclean family's somewhat drab existence in Moscow.

My special thanks are due to Beaverbrook Newspapers for their kindness in allowing me to examine their extensive assembly of cuttings on the Burgess and Maclean story and for their permission to reproduce the text of their front page story which first put the world on the track of the missing diplomats.

The text of the White Paper on Burgess and Maclean (Report Concerning the Disappearance of Two Former Foreign Office

Officials, Cmd. 9577) is used with the permission of the Controller of Her Majesty's Stationery Office.

I am grateful to Sir John Colville and to Messrs Collins for their permission to quote from *Footprints in Time* the anecdote of Donald Maclean at the débutantes' dance. I am also indebted to Mr Leo Muray for a number of useful leads and introductions.

Grateful acknowledgement is made to the following authors and publishers for permission to reproduce copyright material: *Headlines All My Life*, by Arthur Christiansen, William Heinemann Limited; *Diaries and Letters 1945–1962*, by Harold Nicolson, William Collins Sons & Company Limited; *The Missing Macleans*, by Geoffrey Hoare, Cassell & Company Limited; *The Missing Diplomats*, by Cyril Connolly, Queen Anne Press Limited; *Born 1900*, by Gyula Hay, Hutchinson & Company Limited; *The Real Spy World*, by Miles Copeland, George Weidenfeld & Nicolson Limited.

My thanks are also due to the Staffs of the London Library, the British Museum Reading Room and the West Sussex Library (Chichester) for their help, to Miss Anne Hoffmann for her researches and to Mrs Irene Thrower for her meticulous typewriting.

# 1

# Springtime In Paris

The disappearance of Burgess and Maclean, the two Foreign Office diplomats, which was to astonish the world and their friends for more than a quarter of a century became known to the public on Thursday 7th June 1951. The news—a world scoop—was embodied in the *Daily Express* in a short item of only 164 words, across two columns at the top of page one.

'YARD HUNTS TWO BRITONS' said the main headline above it. ' "ON WAY TO RUSSIA" ' the paper added below, between quotes indicating that this piece of information was still an unconfirmed opinion. A further sub-heading read 'FROM FOREIGN OFFICE?'.

The story was unsigned and bore the anonymous byline 'Express Staff Reporter', usually an indication that its contents came from several sources and had been put together in London. It said:

> Scotland Yard Officers and French detectives are hunting for two British Government employees who are believed to have left London with the intention of getting to Moscow.
>
> According to a friend, they planned the journey to 'serve their idealistic purposes'.
>
> One report says that the two men were employed by the Foreign Office, and there is a possibility that they may have important papers with them.
>
> News of their plan was given to the authorities by the friend, who said they expected him to go with them. They were to go to France as if on holiday, and then make their way behind the Iron Curtain. The friend backed out.
>
> All French airports and frontiers are being watched. Plain-clothes men are searching the Montmartre area of Paris, where it is easy for anyone to hide. It is understood the police are watching visitors to the Soviet Embassy in Paris.

Sometimes, editors, when they have a story they believe to be exclusive, purposely withhold it from the early editions of their paper. For if it appears in an edition printed early enough to reach readers in Cornwall, then rival editors who manage without too much difficulty to pirate copies of early editions before they go away on the newspaper train, can then overtake the story, and print it in their final edition for distribution in London where so many of the top people live.

On this occasion, however, the *Daily Express* cherubic editor Arthur Christiansen had no such intention. His trouble was to make the story firm enough to run at all. The first hint of it came to London from a soft-spoken heavy built bespectacled American, Larry Solon, who was then the *Daily Express* correspondent in Paris.

On Wednesday of that first week of June, Solon, by himself, decided to have dinner at a restaurant in the Bois de Boulogne. Soon after he had sat down, however, the telephone rang. A voice asked to speak to the American. Solon was surprised. He was not expecting to be rung, and as far as he was aware no one knew where he was eating. He picked up the receiver. 'This is Solon,' he said. A voice with what might have been a German accent answered with a question: 'Am I speaking to the Chef de Bureau of the *Daily Express* Paris office?' Solon replied that this was indeed the case. Then came a warning from the stranger not to 'go round asking questions about missing persons who, in any case, were not in France'. The caller refused to say who he was or to give the names of the missing persons. But he added that if Solon was looking for trouble he would find it. Then he rang off.

And here, if we try to discover why Solon should have been warned, we are already in the gloaming half-world of spies and counter-spies.

First of all, the warning probably came from a Russian or satellite source. No Westerner—the French police for example—would expect an experienced reporter like Solon to pay any regard to such an approach. Indeed it could safely be assumed that he would become far more interested in the story after the warning than he was before he received it.

Did the Russians—if indeed the warning came from them—believe their threat would be heeded or did they *want* the story published to humiliate the British? They could release it without risk if the missing persons were already dead or in custody. Searching Paris, with its abundance of airlines, its profusion of embassies and its streets of communist 'safe houses' (where escapees could be hidden for weeks at a time as they had been during the German occupation) would keep the allied counter-intelligence services busy—fruitlessly —for months, and make the Western alliance look still more ineffective. But, in that case, why tell Solon that the missing persons were not to be found in France?

Another possible explanation: if the French Government came to believe that its territory had been used by foreign agents to contrive the escape of wanted persons, there could be a danger that it would expel those agents. And who would want a thing like that to happen? Not the Russians or the Czechs, to take two examples.

Meanwhile Solon, predictably, pursued his investigations. A few days earlier, an informant had told him that a routine query had been made by the British police to the French police about two members of the British Foreign Service who had landed in France. No names were given and it was hinted that they had come over to France 'on a spree'. Obviously they had not kept in touch with the British Embassy in Paris.

And since this was a matter engaging the police forces of two countries Solon arranged to see the Head of the International Police Organization, Interpol, the following day.

At eight thirty in the morning, the official was surprisingly genial—but uncommunicative about the Foreign Office diplomats. Interpol dealt only with civil crime he said. Kidnapping, it would look into, but political escape was a different kettle of fish.

'But I said nothing about political escape,' Solon countered.

'Ah then, I've misunderstood you,' said the official blandly.

He added that as Interpol was not involved, he knew nothing about the case to which Solon referred, and that it would be a matter for the British Government.

As he returned to his table at the restaurant, Solon reflected that he must have been followed there by someone who knew about his visits to Interpol. The story, then, must be far more important than at first it had appeared. He also recalled how, earlier in the day, a friend at the American Embassy over a pre-lunch drink had asked him if he had been following any hot clues lately and had shut up like a clam when Solon asked what clues he ought to be following.

But where could he pick up the trail of the missing Foreign Office diplomats? Leaving his dinner half eaten, Solon walked to the nearest taxi rank and gave the driver the address of a small bistro in Montmartre where he could expect to find another informant, a former police employee who had specialized in anti-smuggling work. He perhaps would know of the most likely way in which two diplomats could be spirited out of France undetected by police who were searching for them, perhaps in a private plane sent to fetch them. But the informant said there was no need for this. The Russians had plenty of money, he said, and could use ordinary air routes for their protégés.

So Solon telephoned 'Vincent', a trusted police contact, and met him on the way back to the office at the bar of the Scribe Hotel, near the Opéra, which was still a traditional meeting place, in those days, for expatriate newspapermen. But 'Vincent' wanted no part of the affair. The French police were clearly furious with the British for not having called on their services earlier while the trail was still hot. And a big row between the two forces was brewing.

But how to run the story without knowing even the names of the diplomats or whether they were still missing? Solon's next move was to contact Georges Gherra, the crime reporter of the Paris evening paper *France-Soir*, with which the *Express* had a special relationship in so far as it rented two rooms in the *France-Soir* building. Georges, under pressure, was able to produce two names but they were in Franglais and without spelling. Translating these sounds into surnames that could be verified was a matter of some difficulty. It was well on in the evening of Wednesday before Solon with the help of Joan Harrison, his golden-haired, resourceful assistant, had fined down the possibilities of two names Guy Burgess and Donald Maclean.

One final call remained: to a high official of the British Embassy. 'Do the names Guy Burgess and Donald Maclean mean anything to you?' Solon asked. 'So the story's out, is it?' the official gasped. By then it was ten o'clock and high time to telephone the *Daily Express* in London with the story as Solon had it. Already, the first edition of Thursday's paper was being rolled off, crammed tight with readable copy. Half of page one was already filled with the account of a siege of a house in Symons Avenue, Chatham, where a nineteen-year-old youth, Alan Poole, was holding 200 armed police at bay after having shot dead a policeman earlier in the day.

Against this competition Solon's story was still worth a lead—but no editor could afford to run it without some more definite confirmation from a British source. Accordingly the Chief Sub-Editor was sent to the *Express* library for the Foreign Office list which did indeed contain the wanted names, and a call was rushed to Percy Hoskins, the *Express* Chief Crime Reporter. Meanwhile Derek Marks, a leviathan of a man who later became editor of the paper, was asked to make enquiries of the Foreign Office. Hoskins was a seventeen-stone crinkly-haired Pickwickian figure who had helped the police more than once to get their man.

In 1924 he was inquiring into the mysterious disappearance of Miss Elsie Cameron who had vanished after telling her parents that she was going to spend the weekend with her fiancé, a chicken farmer called Norman Thorne. Hoskins interviewed Thorne and asked him if he was bothered by the police. 'I don't mind what they do as long as they don't disturb my chickens,' Thorne said. Later the police, who were getting nowhere, asked Hoskins what he thought of the case. 'You'll find Elsie Cameron in the chicken-run,' he said. They did—under spadefuls of earth. Thorne was executed.

Later, in 1957 Hoskins reported the case in which an Eastbourne practitioner, Dr John Bodkin Adams, was accused of poisoning one of his women patients. He took the view that Adams was being tried by newspaper innuendo and refused to allow the *Daily Express* to follow the line taken by some other reporters. On the day Adams was declared 'not guilty' Hoskins got a telegram from Lord Beaverbrook, proprietor of the *Daily Express*. 'TWO MEN WERE ACQUITTED TODAY', it said, 'ADAMS AND HOSKINS'.

On the night of the Burgess and Maclean story, Hoskins rang his contact at Scotland Yard's Special Branch. The man he wanted was out to dinner and could not be reached.

Marks was then the *Daily Express* Lobby Correspondent, the man who lobbies MPs, forecasts Cabinet changes and the like, and, because the *Express* had none too much time for diplomatic niceties, he covered the Foreign Office as a secondary job. Doubtless he rang the Foreign Office switchboard for the number of the member of the News Department currently on night duty. And it is probable that the News Department in turn rang the Foreign Office Duty Officer who occupies a flat in the Foreign Office building off Downing Street. And the Duty Officer, in turn, may have telephoned an official dealing with Security Matters who preferred to save anything he had to say until he had the facts before him in writing and could consult his colleagues.

What Hoskins eventually discovered, as we can see from the final story, was vital. He confirmed that Scotland Yard was indeed interested in the whereabouts of two government employees, in other words they had not returned and were away on something more than a spree. It was also clear that one of their friends had got in touch directly or indirectly, or been consulted by the police about their absence and put forward a theory to account for their disappearance, namely that they had gone to Moscow 'to serve their idealistic purposes'.

This, and also the fact that the two men were listed as members of the Foreign Office Service was closely in line with what Larry Solon had discovered in Paris. The possibility of their having important Foreign Office papers with them greatly added to the readability of the affair and helped to account for the interest taken by the police in the whereabouts of the two idealists.

The identity of the 'friend who had backed out' remained undisclosed for the moment and the *Express* also decided not to identify Burgess and Maclean in their story. No doubt the lawyer pointed out that enormous damages would be payable if it turned out that no important papers were missing from the Foreign Office, especially if the men had not, after all, gone to Moscow. Yet any story with Moscow and the Foreign Office in it was of great news value. Also, by keeping the names Burgess and Maclean to themselves for the time being, the *Express* would have a head start on other papers when gathering news on the following day.

It was well after midnight when Hoskins, having run his man to ground, reported his findings, and the first story of the 'missing officials' appeared in the 1 a.m. edition.

'When I got home about 2.30 a.m.,' Christiansen afterwards wrote in his recollections *Headlines All My Life*, 'I did not sleep. Panic seized me and I lay groaning with fear, convinced that I had acted precipitately and foolishly. A whole day's consideration should have been given to a story of this dimension, I thought as I lay there sweating. Why rush into print after a couple of hours' work which had produced only the flimsiest confirmation? A copy of the 1 a.m. edition was on the floor at the side of my bed, and I picked it up to read again the sensational headlines of the paragraphs of dynamite which would blow me out of my job if they were wrong. I looked at my watch. It was 4.30 a.m., and within five minutes the presses would have completed their task of printing four million copies, every one of which could sink me. . . . When with the arrival of daylight, confidence returned, or at any rate a resigned acceptance of fate, come what may, I found myself sitting on the biggest news block-buster I had been called upon to handle since the blitz on London.'

# 2

# Melinda's Story

The same morning, Thursday 7th June, the Foreign Office, pressed with telephone inquiries, issued its own official statement: 'Two members of the Foreign Service have been missing from their homes since 25th May. One is Mr D. D. Maclean, the other Mr G. F. de M. Burgess. All possible inquiries are being made. It is known that they went to France a few days ago. Mr Maclean had a breakdown a year ago owing to overstrain, but was believed to have fully recovered. Owing to their being absent without leave, both have been suspended with effect from 1st June.'

The announcement was received with some scepticism in Fleet Street. For example, if it was known for certain that the two diplomats went to France why, it was asked, was the date and place of their departure not given and why was there no hint of the means of travel which the missing diplomats used? Were they being accompanied when they left Britain—or pursued?

Again, the statement noted that Maclean had suffered a breakdown through over-work and said he was believed to have recovered. But this titbit about Maclean's private life would hardly have been released unless it was intended to convey that there could have been a recurrence of over-strain. Did the Foreign Office really believe this?

If so, why were both men regarded as being absent without leave and why were they suspended with effect from 1st June? Was it because papers were missing or because they had idealistic plans to go to Moscow?

Newspaper staffs worked hard through that day and new leads to the story sprouted like beanstalks. It was learned, for example, that although Guy Francis de Moncy Burgess, aged 40, was merely a Second Secretary, Donald Duart Maclean at thirty-eight was Head of the American Department. So if any papers were missing, they probably were important.

Telegrams from both Burgess and Maclean were received that day in the U.K. but none of them had been despatched by the fugitives themselves. Burgess's message was addressed to his mother, a widow who had re-married and was living in considerable style as the wife of Lieutenant-Colonel John Retallack Bassett in a flat on the second floor of Arlington House, a block which was inhabited at the time by Lord Beaverbrook and which was also adjacent both to the Ritz Hotel and the fashionable Caprice Restaurant.

The message from Burgess read: 'TERRIBLY SORRY FOR MY SILENCE. AM EMBARKING ON LONG MEDITER-RANEAN HOLIDAY DO FORGIVE GUY.'

It had been handed in at a Post Office in Rome.

Maclean too had sent messages. One to his mother, Lady Maclean, was signed 'Teento', the family nickname by which he was known, and read 'AM QUITE ALL RIGHT. DON'T WORRY. LOVE TO ALL.'

Maclean's other telegram was to his wife Melinda and his two small sons living at Tatsfield, Surrey. It ran: 'HAD TO LEAV UNEXPECTEDLY. TERRIBLY SORRY. AM QUITE WELL NOW DONT WORRY DARLING I LOVE YOU. PLEASE DONT STOP. LOVING ME. DONALD'. But although the two texts were in Donald's style, the handwriting on the forms handed over the counter was not his and had probably been scripted by a foreigner unfamiliar with English.

Thus in both telegrams Maclean was spelt 'MAC LEAN' and in the message to Melinda 'Leave' was spelt 'LEAV'. An unwanted full stop had been inserted after 'STOP'.

Both the Maclean telegrams had been handed in on the night of 6th June at the all-night telegraph office, 8 Place de la Bourse, Paris—a mistake if the Russians wanted to take the heat off Paris—a sound move if the diplomats had never been there.

The other piece of sensational news was that Donald Maclean had left his family at a time when his wife was expecting a baby which would have to be delivered by a Caesarean operation. The baby was due the following month.

These facts led colour to the belief that Maclean had not left the country for idealistic reasons but had been forced to do so in one way or another—unless, of course, he had had another mental breakdown.

Diplomats at a French Embassy party that week hazarded a guess that the whole operation was an elaborate attempt by the British Secret Service to plant two agents inside the Soviet Union. News-papers and news agencies redoubled their efforts to trace the fugitives. 'Europe scoured by 15,000 police and counter-agents. Two Diplomats Stay Silent' ran one headline. The 21,000-ton vessel *Sovietsky Sojus* which sailed to a home port from Antwerp on 1st June came under suspicion. So did the very much smaller Polish ship *Warmia* which sailed from Dunkirk on 30th May, bound for Gdynia, for it was thought likely that Maclean at least would avoid travelling to Paris where he was comparatively well known. One reviewer came to the conclusion that they were, after all, on the spree and had been knifed to death in a sailors' brawl in Brest. But none of these solutions crystallized. Deauville, it appeared, was another possibility put forward no doubt by reporters who had no objection at all to spending a few June nights there. Romania and even South America were under surveillance according to some newspapers. *Sie und Er* believed that the missing men might be in Switzerland, the *Brisbane Telegraph* favoured Queensland, the *Iraq Times* had glimpsed them in Baghdad, and the *Advocate* was sure they were hiding in Barbados.

After a full month had passed without further news from the fugitives, the *Daily Express* offered a reward of £1,000 for information which would establish their whereabouts. 'Burgess,' the wanted notice said, 'was born on 16th April 1911. He was 5 ft 8 ins tall, thick-set, slightly bald, with hair grey at the temples. Walks with toes turned in. He is invariably untidily dressed, talks a great deal and is fond of discussing politics, philosophy and the arts. Fluent in French', the description ran. Maclean's notice said he was born on 25th May 1913. It gave his height as 6 ft 2½ ins and notes: 'Hair brushed back and parted on the left. Incipient baldness, slightly round-shouldered. Long thin legs. Tight-lipped mouth. Good features. Chain-smokes. Carelessly but well dressed. Speaks French but not perfectly.'

A year later the *Daily Express* engaged Colonel Oreste Pinto ('the Spycatcher') who had run a counter-espionage service for General Eisenhower in the Netherlands, to follow the trail. His first conclusion was that the two men were not behind the Iron Curtain since Britain was their only source of marketable information. Later, however, Colonel Pinto pursued his investigations abroad and eventually proved almost as hard to trace as his quarry.

Guy Burgess's friends were more easily reached than Burgess. Many leading political writers, authors and columnists belonged to the Reform Club, Pall Mall, which Burgess had joined in 1937, and one of Osbert Lancaster's cartoons showed a brooding genius, and, underneath the caption: 'My dear, he's feeling rather low as he's the only intellectual in London who's not yet been asked for his reminiscences of either Burgess or Maclean.'

Late one evening, Donald Seaman, a reporter on the *Daily Express*, was typing what he hoped would be his last story of the day, a report on the weather, when the Night News Editor called over to him: 'Can you speak Italian?' Seaman, who thought he might have to deal with a brawl in Soho or something similar, was cautious. He admitted, however, that he had picked up a few words when he was serving in Italy during the war.

A day or two later he found himself in a smoke-filled café in the village of Forio, on the Island of Ischia, telephoning his story to London. He had been interviewing Wystan Auden, the poet, who in the twenties at Oxford had already earned for himself a reputation of a kind by receiving even his daylight guests in a darkened room and walking abroad carrying a cane and wearing an eye-glass. Since then he had earned a considerable prestige as a serious writer of powerfully evocative poems. W. H. Auden and Louis MacNeice in *Letters from Iceland* had printed a satirical Last Will and Testament in which Burgess, amongst others, was left a keg of whiskey. At this juncture Auden possessed a villa in the Via Santa Lucia in Ischia.

Auden said: 'I have known Guy Burgess for twenty years, since our undergraduate days. He was an open Communist in the 1930s.' Auden explained that his own sympathies with the Communists had ended when the Russians signed their alliance with Hitler in 1939 and that he had nothing to do with them now. He did say, however, that when in New York (he had become an American citizen) he met Burgess several times. 'While he was at the British Embassy in Washington, Burgess was still pro-Communist,' Auden said. 'We met in March this year [1951]. . . . I asked him whether he was screened and Burgess spoke of diplomatic immunity.'

Auden's theory was that Burgess and Maclean had been forced to leave England and had been kidnapped, murdered or compelled to hide. 'I feel sure that if Burgess was free in Europe, he would have contacted a friend, someone like myself.' He thought it was fantastic to suppose that Guy Burgess had gone to Russia.

Tom Driberg, the original William Hickey on the *Daily Express* and later a Left Wing MP and Life Peer, writing his diary on 8th June 1951 expressed the hope of his close friends that the whole thing had been played up 'disproportionately' and that the escapade might turn out to be just a trip for fun with no ideological implications.

On 10th June *The Observer* carried an interview with Stephen Spender, also a poet and a close friend at Oxford of Auden. Spender had been caught up in the political movements of the thirties and in 1937 had published a work entitled *Forward from Liberalism*. Dazzled by the prospect of a classless society and repelled by the evils of capitalism he joined the Communist Party for a short period. He was even prepared to sacrifice his own freedom in the sacred cause of revolution. But he was not prepared to deny freedom to others and he detected the urge for power which lay beneath Communist idealism.

Spender said it was difficult to believe that Guy Burgess had Communist sympathies. He pointed out that very shortly before his disappearance, Burgess had rung up to praise Spender's autobiography *World within World* which expressed many criticisms of Communism.

*The Observer* interview was followed up, however, by two reporters from the *Daily Express* to whom Spender incautiously showed—and lent—a letter from a close friend, John Lehmann.

Lehmann, a contemporary at Eton of such individualists as Ian Fleming, author and reviewer Cyril Connolly, and George Orwell, had had a romantic love affair with pre-Hitler Vienna, was the correspondent there of the French Communist newspaper *Le Feu* and of the *New Statesman*, and a courier of the Austrian Communist underground at about the same time as Kim Philby, the master spy.

He, like many of his generation, foresaw Hitler's war and was convinced that the Soviet Union was the only government which had made plans to fight it. He also believed that World War II could be the first act of a social revolution in his own country. But that was before Stalin made a pact with Hitler. Later he philosophized, 'It was better late than never to realize that we had been walking beside someone whose features we had never discovered till then'. In the meantime he had become a distinguished publisher.

Lehmann had known Burgess in the late thirties and had found him intelligent and endowed with a boisterous sense of mischief and a malicious turn of phrase, and in his letter he told Spender that 'someone you know very well' had just told him that she had worried for years about Guy owing to a piece of information that had come her way during the war.

Lehmann's letter also added that 'someone else we both know' had the same kind of suspicions about Donald Maclean and 'had seriously thought during the last few months of denouncing him'. Lehmann added that if these two surmises were correct it would not be long before the news broke.

Not surprisingly the reporters wanted to know the names of the two 'someones', and, equally understandably, John Lehmann was not forthcoming with them. Pressed to reveal the name of his woman informant 'in the interests of national security', he said that she had already put her knowledge at the disposal of the security services.

The first 'someone' was in fact John Lehmann's sister Rosamund, who, at the time she was married to Wogan Phillipps, often invited Spender for weekends at Ipsden House in the Chilterns. Rosamund, thinking back on all that she could remember of Guy during the years before 1945 when she saw a lot of him, had become convinced that he had become a Communist agent from motives of idealism and since become trapped, and had been compelled to fly when he felt the net was closing round him. The second 'someone' was author

Humphrey Slater, whose novel *The Conspirator* was inspired by a Maclean-like situation. Slater, too, was unnamed by Lehmann.

But, as so often happens, those interviewed underestimate their own news value, and, next day, the headlines ran: 'DIPLOMATS— The Secret "known to two people in England". Mystery Woman phones MI5.'

Anthony Blunt, the distinguished art historian and later Keeper of the Queen's Pictures, a friend of Burgess's since Cambridge days, was also questioned, much to his distress.

Christopher Isherwood, friend of both Auden and Spender, to whom he had introduced the original Sally Bowles in Berlin, was interviewed in the United States, and the gist of his replies published. 'Burgess was a crazy man,' Isherwood said. Did he consider it likely that the couple had gone off on a kind of Rudolf Hess, 'stop-the-cold-war' mission? Answer: 'Well I can't honestly think that they were the type for that, do you? But they are so impulsive that they may have thought they were.'

Guy's relatives were somewhat less voluble than his friends. Colonel Bassett, acting as spokesman, loyally accepted the text of Guy Burgess's telegram, and declared his belief that the missing diplomats had gone away on holiday. But he also threw into the pot the news that his stepson suffered from sinus trouble and had had very bad concussion the previous year.

The Special Branch and the investigating staff of the Intelligence Services had, of course, a star witness in Donald Maclean's wife, Melinda, but preferred that her interrogation should be conducted exclusively by their own men. A police guard was placed on the gates of Beacon Shaw and the front gates padlocked and Melinda's mother, Mrs Melinda Dunbar, answered the telephone.

A bargain seems to have been struck with the establishment by which Mrs Maclean undertook to co-operate with the authorities, and to refrain from giving interviews or making public statements, in return for which she was to be protected from 'harassment'.

Melinda, as it happened, was the last person of consequence to talk to Donald Maclean before he disappeared. But her account of Donald's last evening at home only added to the general air of mystery. It centred round two indisputable facts. One was that she had already arranged for the birth of her third child to take place by Caesarean operation on 14th June; the other that Donald's thirty-eighth birthday fell on Friday 25th May. The Caesarean problem had already been taken care of. Melinda's mother, Mrs Dunbar, had promised to arrive in England about a fortnight before the operation and to take Melinda's two boys, Fergus and Donald Junior away on holiday while Melinda was recovering. Yet for some days before 25th May Donald had been fussing. He asked Melinda several times exactly when her mother would be arriving. It was as though he wanted to make sure that there would be someone to look after Melinda if he should have to leave her suddenly.

In addition, a family celebration had been arranged for Saturday 26th May—the day after Donald's birthday. Donald's sister Nancy and her American husband and Mrs Mary Maclean, widow of an elder brother killed in the war were expected for the weekend. And so, on Friday morning Melinda baked a birthday cake and cooked a ham according to her special Virginia recipe. Even as early as that there had been a hint of trouble. Donald told her on Thursday that a friend of his named Roger Styles of whom she had never previously heard would be coming down to dinner on Friday evening which Melinda had been counting on spending *à deux* with Donald. Melinda was displeased. With the birth of her baby less than three weeks away she did not feel like entertaining a stranger. Fergus and Donald Junior were both down with measles and her only prop was a woman who came up from the village by the day as household help. However, Donald had arranged to take the Saturday morning off and would be on hand to help prepare for the house party.

On the evening of Friday 25th May, Donald, according to Melinda, 'caught his usual train, the 5.19 from Victoria to Oxted', and arrived home around six o'clock ahead of his guest. He took the opportunity to explain to Melinda that, after dinner, 'Roger and I would have to go and see someone on business' and that he would take a few things 'in case we have to spend the night'. Melinda took this news badly. She followed Donald into his dressing-room where he had already begun to pack his things, including a silk dressing-gown and shaving-kit, into a briefcase and registered a strong protest. She complained that he had already spoilt their birthday dinner by asking a stranger to join them and now he was preparing not only to desert her for the evening but for the night as well. Who was going to help her, Melinda asked, to put up beds in the spare rooms for their guests, clean out the cupboards so that they would have somewhere to put their clothes and organize their entertainment programme? Couldn't Donald discuss his problems with Roger Styles at home? But Donald said unfortunately not. He would have to go out that evening. Melinda flounced out of the room and went downstairs. The voices of the parents raised in argument woke up Fergie, and years afterwards, he remembered getting out of bed and running in to see his father. 'Why are you going away, Daddy?' he asked. 'Can I stand at the window and watch you go?'

'Get back into bed, you little scamp,' his father said. 'I'm not going far. I'll be back soon,' words that Fergus remembered when his father, for some unexplained reason, was not back soon or indeed ever.

Roger Styles arrived at the house about half an hour after Donald, and Melinda, to her surprise, formed a very favourable first impression of him. She found him charming, even attractive, relaxed and easy to talk to. There was normal social chit-chat at the dinner table and no one would have suspected that two of the threesome were about to embark on a journey fraught with risk and uncertainty. After dinner, Donald repeated, this time in the presence of Roger Styles, the announcement that he and Roger would have to go out to see someone on 'business'. They would probably not be long, but Melinda was not to worry if they were late. Melinda, unwilling to revive her former argument with her husband in front of their guest, contented herself with asking whether their business—since it was already getting on for nine o'clock—could not equally well be left till the morning. But Donald with regret insisted that there was no other way, and Melinda talked for a few minutes alone with Roger Styles while Donald went out of the house to stoke the furnace (two points that no one made much of at the time). Then Donald and Styles bowed out. There was no farewell kiss and nothing more had been said about their being away for the night and Melinda sat up reading. Near midnight she went to bed, alone.

Melinda's personal summing up of the disappearance of her husband 'delivered', one report said, 'in a low voice in which her American accent was still distinct' was equally inconclusive: 'My husband had no reason to go away,' she said. 'I know no more than any of his friends. I don't believe people who say he was a Communist. What else is there to say?'

Within hours a security officer showed her a photograph of a man that she was able to identify—'Roger Styles'. But the face was Guy Burgess. And when she learnt this, she may have wondered, as so many others might have, how such a mystery-man came to be her husband's colleague.

# 3

# The Boy Burgess

Guy Burgess was a freak, but the reason why he became one is not at once apparent. His father, Malcolm Kingston de Moncy Burgess, was an officer in that most traditional of Services, the Royal Navy, and served in it with distinction. He joined the Service in 1897 as a Naval Cadet on the old Britannia Training Ship moored at Dartmouth. At the outbreak of the Kaiser's war he was a Lieutenant-Commander in command of H.M.S. *Hebe*, a torpedo gun-boat. He served through the war and was promoted in 1916 to the rank of Commander. While in the Middle East he evidently earned the gratitude of the post-war rulers of Egypt for which he was awarded a foreign decoration, the Order of the Nile, which the Admiralty allowed him to wear on public occasions. He died in 1924, the year Guy went to Eton, leaving Guy with a permanent sense of insecurity which his mother's second marriage did nothing to allay.

Burgess intended to follow his father's career and spent only a year at Eton before being accepted for the Royal Naval College at Dartmouth. One of his contemporaries there was Nigel Tangye, a Cadet Captain who afterwards married the actress and film producer Ann Todd. Tangye recalls sitting next to Burgess for 252 meals at Dartmouth and was dismayed to find he knew him no better at the end of that time than at the beginning. Burgess, it appears, was tall for his age, with a fresh complexion of the type that looks polished and clean under all circumstances, an asset that Tangye believed would last him his lifetime. He was already sophisticated, at ease, with a cool detached manner, an intellectually superior being without conceit; an individual among a community of 650 cadets and a person of great charm and some mystery since at the age of fifteen and a half he returned to Eton without any of his fellow cadets getting a hint of how this transfer came about. (Admiralty examiners had discovered a slight defect in his eyesight which meant that he was no longer eligible for operational duties at sea.)

Obviously at this stage he was regarded as a potential asset to Eton because his house master, Mr F. W. Dobbs, went to some trouble on his behalf in asking leave from the Provost and Fellows for Burgess to return to Eton. He stayed there for nearly three more years as an Oppidan, apparently in a state of contentment. He was a better than average oarsman, runner, swimmer and football player, and was awarded his House colours for the Eton Field Game (a hybrid sport half way between rugger and soccer). He reached the sixth form, and his interest in history was stimulated by the headmaster, Dr Robert Birley, regarded, according to the political stance of the observer, as either 'Red Robert' or an honest liberal. Birley, who had great hopes of Burgess, found him well-read and ready to air his opinions on most things from Vermeer to Meredith—lively, amusing and very good-natured. Above all, Birley noticed, Burgess thought for himself. Even after Burgess had 'defected', Mr Dobbs continued to speak well of his former pupil and remained convinced that he was innocent of any ill-feeling or treachery towards his country. Guy's dearest ambition, he believed, was to complete the life of Lord Salisbury that was left unfinished at her death, by Lady Gwendolen Cecil.

According to Burgess, his social conscience was first stimulated by a visiting lecturer, a dockers' Trade Union organizer, who described his own background and told the boys bluntly that they had no conception of what poverty really meant.

While at Eton, Burgess also became familiar with such books as Arthur Morrison's *Tales of Mean Streets*, an account of the social horrors of the East End of London—though admittedly in pre-World War I times. His housemaster also read passages to him from *Across the Bridges* by Alexander Paterson, alerting Burgess, for the first time, as he afterwards told Tom Driberg, to the fact that butter was less often seen at the tables of the poor than jam.

Burgess's only form of protest at Eton appears to have been to turn away from the birchings that he was compelled to witness there (as he had from similar ceremonial chastisements at Dartmouth).

In his last few months at Eton, Burgess won the Gladstone Memorial Scholarship, entitling him to £100 (almost enough to buy a new car in those days) and a copy of Morley's *Life of Gladstone*, signed by a member of the family. He also won an open scholarship to Trinity College, Cambridge, largely, he believed, by virtue of a paper referring to the French Revolution in which he criticized Castlereagh—though at first sight it is hard to see why, since Castlereagh's energies at the time of the French Revolution were devoted almost entirely to the Irish question.

Nevertheless Burgess's scholastic record at Cambridge justified the examiners' verdict. At the end of a year he was awarded a first class in the Mays examination. At the end of his second year in June 1932 he won a first in Part I of the History Tripos. Then he was elected a senior scholar of Trinity, and in his third year, he obtained another first in Part II despite the fact that a breakdown in health prevented him from completing the papers.

He was sought after by the dons—for in those days there was competition between them to see who could discover, train and exhibit the brilliant intellectuals of the future. To them, Burgess seemed treasure-trove. In November 1932 he was elected a member of the Apostles, that exclusive and, in theory, anonymous society of mutual admiration founded in the eighteen twenties for the pursuit, usually over dinner, of the absolute verities, by men of complete integrity who withheld no secrets from each other. The poet Tennyson had been one of the earlier members, and Henry Hallam, the younger brother of Arthur Hallam whose death inspired Tennyson's *In Memoriam*, also belonged. Today, no doubt, the Apostles would be classed as 'elitist' and some members certainly resented the attempts of Burgess, aided at times by his friend Anthony Blunt, to turn members' gatherings into political discussions in which truth was to be looked for east of the Beresina river. But in its day membership of the Apostles was one of the glittering prizes.

Those were golden times for the undergraduates, their custom sought after by obsequious tradesmen, their lunch parties catered for by an appointed college servant. The young men were free to select their own studies, their own pastimes. Choosing was what mattered. And Burgess chose. His interests were not entirely academic. The motor car, its design and its achievements enthralled him, and he attended the Cambridge University motor club races in which his Harrovian friend Victor Rothschild (later as Lord Rothschild the director of the political 'brain tank' established by Prime Minister Harold Wilson) drove a 100-miles-per-hour Mercedes with great aplomb. Burgess was also elected to the socially exclusive Pitt Club, frequented by tweed-cap-wearing philistine aristos intent on winning races at the Cottenham Point-to-Point and on improving their polo handicap. He was even seen out with the beagles—uncharacteristically, since he soon took the advice of his art master Eric Powell, a former leading oarsman who told him: 'If you go on taking exercise now, you'll always have to, as I've had to.' He appeared now and then at the poker table.

He was one of those compulsive 'joiners' who feel that no organization or indeed social assembly can function at its best without their assistance. He was, too, a wit. He had also developed into a confirmed homosexual—a fact much written about in connection with his Foreign Office career.

Today, perhaps, we should not pay so much attention to his case. Homosexuals no longer feel called on to justify, still less to apologize for, their sex-relations. Some people are born left-handed; others have red hair, and a few have double-jointed thumbs, it is argued, and some people just cannot stand oysters. In the thirties at Cambridge, as at Oxford, a number of unmarried dons were enthusiastic homosexuals, and others, though too old themselves to practise, still had happy memories of days gone by.

Yet as the law stood in the thirties, and remained until 1967, homosexual relations between men, even between consenting adults, could lead to prosecution and imprisonment, and those who were known to have participated could therefore be blackmailed—a handicap for a man who intended to enter public service. Guy never troubled to conceal his indifference to women and his preference for boys, with whom he paraded in the streets of Cambridge under the increasingly unconvincing pretext that they were his nephews. He may have thought this made him more or less immune to threats of exposure. Yet it can hardly be imagined that he would fit easily into the social life of diplomats, their wives and families, the majority of whom were heterosexual.

At times he must have seen himself as a member of a persecuted minority, discriminated against because of innate desires from which he neither could nor would free himself. And if this were so, it would surely help to account for one of Guy Burgess's favourite epigrams: 'The important thing is not so much to understand the world as to change it.'

In addition to joining the homosexuals, Guy Burgess entered another under-privileged minority sect, that of the Communists. The Communist Party of Great Britain, founded in 1920, had spent the first ten years of its life endeavouring to indoctrinate the British working man, to infiltrate the Labour Party and to subvert as many key civil servants as possible. None of these ambitions had been fulfilled and it was after this failure in the early thirties that its leaders decided to launch an intellectual assault on the more advanced centres of learning, e.g. Oxford, Cambridge, University College, London and the London School of Economics, with a view to capturing the minds of future leaders.

The conditions were especially favourable. The Wall Street crash of 1929 had touched off the great slump—an impressive demonstration, the Communists considered, of the failure of the capitalist system. Already people were asking whether the crisis was too serious to be remedied by a social-democratic Westminster-type parliament, dedicated to the principle of compromise. The Labour Party had apparently taken to its death bed, for on 24th August 1931 its leader Ramsay MacDonald had left its ranks to form a coalition National Government with the Liberals and Conservatives. In the election that followed the Tories won by a landslide.

At University College, the Gower Socialist Society, outpost of the Communists, was founded in 1931 and held its meetings in a pub because the University refused to give it house room. In the same year the Marxist Society was founded in the London School of Economics and, in 1932, the October Society was established at Oxford and helped to promote the Oxford Union resolution passed in February 1933, according to which 'this House would in no circumstances fight for King and Country'.

But Cambridge proved the best seed-bed. A number of cloth-cap miners, supported by grants from the Workers' Educational Association, were already studying there for university degrees. They brought with them bitter memories of the General Strike of 1926 in the course of which the TUC leaders, eager to maintain the shreds of their authority, caved in to the Baldwin Government, abandoning the interests of the coal miners who were still out on strike.

One of these new students was Harry Dawes who had worked for ten years at the pit face and did not allow the undergraduates with their gentlemanly accents and free-spending habits to forget the fact. At the Union, the main Cambridge Debating Society, Dawes called for the abolition of all landlords and the nationalization of farm land. He was quick to join the Cambridge University Socialist Society, successor to the University Labour Club, defunct in 1931. At debates there he argued that the traditional step-by-step approach to socialism generally accepted within the Labour Party no longer met the requirements of the situation.

To the left of Dawes was another miner, Jim Lees, who belonged to the Independent Labour Party, the ginger group of the British Labour Movement. His pit had been closed for more than six months after the General Strike.

Both Dawes and Lees, already balding and spectacled, had at first a curiosity value (like that of a freak stamp) to undergraduates who had never seen a pitman in their lives—still less talked to one. But both were left behind in the political hurricane stirred up at Cambridge by the Communists.

Maurice Dobb, a young Trinity economics tutor who put forward his anti-capitalism arguments in a genial, almost precious style, can fairly be called the progenitor of the movement at Cambridge. He had begun to recruit left-wing political workers even before the 1926 General Strike, and had founded the League against Imperialism soon afterwards. He wrote books, composed pamphlets and produced articles for the *Sunday Worker*, commending the well disciplined socialism practised in the Soviet Union, and deprecating the British style of democracy which he compared to a marionette show (though it is hard to imagine what could be more disciplined than a marionette).

Dobb's League against Imperialism remained little more than a

Marxist discussion group, but its success evidently encouraged the Communist Party of Great Britain to arrange in June 1931 to send down one of their most talented and brilliant propagandists Clemens Palme Dutt, former Balliol scholar and an experienced worker among students. A handpicked list of converts and potential converts—some were students, some dons—were invited to meet him. J. D. Bernal, then a thirty-year-old crystallographer and already a Marxist, was one, though he preferred to keep himself aloof from student politics. Roy Pascal, a Fellow of Pembroke College, Cambridge, who shared Dobb's house, was another Communist-minded supporter.

That very afternoon a Communist cell consisting of both dons and students was formed.

The students included Jim Lees and Bugsy Wolfe, who had grown up in the rough-house area of Stepney in London's East End dockland, and was now studying biochemistry under Professor J. B. S. Haldane. Both men at that time saw the traditional Labour Party as the biggest obstacle in the path of true socialism. But the recruit who contributed most to the success of the cell was David Haden Guest, a young man who had come up to Cambridge from Oundle in 1929 to read philosophy and mathematical logic. In 1930, however, he transferred to Göttingen University in Germany for a year's sandwich course on his chosen subjects. There he found the Nazis gaining control and Heine's works banned from the library and, on Easter Sunday 1931 while attending a Communist youth demonstration in Brunskick, he was arrested, held in solitary confinement for a fortnight and released only after he had gone on hunger strike. Guest had arrived in Germany a pacifist socialist; he left it a militant Communist.

When Guest returned to Cambridge, appearing in college hall with a hammer and sickle in his buttonhole, he was canonized among the faithful as a minor martyr—the only undergraduate to have fought in the front line on the side of the Communists against their oppressors. He not only joined the Communist Party of Great Britain, but took over the leadership of the cell, and, by the middle of 1932 had succeeded in splitting the Cambridge University Socialist Society into two halves in preparation for a Communist take-over the following year.

Meanwhile Guy Burgess who, it will be remembered, had come up to Cambridge in 1930, before the Communist cell had been founded, had met Jim Lees in the rooms of a history don, George Kitson Clark, and made friends with him. Lees introduced Burgess to Guest, and Guest passed Burgess on to Maurice Cornforth who, having already taken a degree in London, had come to Cambridge to work for his Doctorate of Philosophy. Cornforth had been recruited by Guest and brought to the Party the organizing ability that was to take him later onto the board of Lawrence and Wishart, the Communist publishing house. He married the vivacious sister of another Communist and friend of Burgess, James Klugmann, son of a prosperous Jewish businessman, who had come up to Cambridge a year after Burgess to read modern languages. Klugmann was later to become one of the leading officials in the Central Committee of the British Communist Party.

Burgess in his first year at Cambridge joined the Cambridge anti-war movement but found the pacifist philosophy unsatisfactory. He complained to Klugmann that it was useless to try and abolish war without first dealing with the factors that led to it. Klugmann's answer was 'If that's the way you feel, your place is in the Party'. This conversation, or rather conversion, took place in all probability some time before November 1932 when Burgess avowed his Communist credo to the Apostles.

The following year a newcomer, John Cornford, a young Trinity historian, succeeded Guest as cell-leader. Cornford did not believe that it was necessary to conceal any longer the activities of the party in Cambridge. In fact he favoured publicity obtained by 'agitprop' and 'socialism in action'. He could have found no more willing lieutenant than Burgess for executing his new policy.

On Armistice Day 1933 the Cambridge Communists insisted on laying a wreath on the War Memorial inscribed 'In memory of the victims of an imperialist war which was not of their making'. They claimed that their demonstration would help to prevent similar crimes of imperialism in the future, an attitude which provoked the promoters of the Armistice Day 'Poppy Rag' (a charity foray made by the heartier undergraduates to raise money for ex-servicemen's welfare funds) to violence.

The Communists, fighting for peace, discomfited their rivals according to Burgess, by driving a 1925 Morris-Cowley protected with mattresses tied round it, into the midst of the hearties, scattering them and their collecting boxes.

Burgess organized a strike of waiters at Trinity in protest against the practice of engaging them only during the term time and dismissing them as soon as the vacations, which lasted for a third of the year, began. In 1934 he went with his friends out to Huntingdon to meet the so-called hunger marchers, foot-slogged with them to Cambridge, and then travelled by train to London to meet them again and march with them in solidarity to Hyde Park.

And when Neville Chamberlain, then Chancellor of the Exchequer, as guest of honour at Trinity College Founder's Feast, assured his audience that the unemployed and their families were suffering no real hardship or hunger, it was Burgess who led the booing and encouraged others to follow his example.

No doubt there was in Burgess, as more than one of his friends remarked, a sense of mischief, which helped to render these activities strangely satisfying to him as an ex-Etonian as well as correct in the political sense. But his approach to Communism was intellectual as well as political. As a historian, he was called on to study the political structure and organization of the modern state. He found that Lenin's interpretation of the state and its power base was far more convincing and more complete than that of any university lecturer he had heard.

In the course of his researches, Burgess came to hold views about English history that were unusual and, to some dons, disturbing. Thus the Civil War, in which King Charles lost his head, became not the struggle of the Puritans against the Bishops who stood between them and their God, nor yet that of Parliament against the tyranny of the Crown, but the bourgeois revolution of the middle-classes, in particular the professional and business men, against the powers of the hereditary landowners. Similarly, the Indian Mutiny was no longer an act of treachery but a demonstration of national sentiment.

During his last year and a half at Cambridge Burgess held a research studentship which meant that he taught as well as studied history. One of his pupils was Lord Talbot de Malahide who afterwards said that but for Burgess he would never have been able to pass the entry examination to the Foreign Office. Burgess later told Tom Driberg that 'strange as it may seem' his Lordship's was the only name he could recall from among those he had taught. Yet perhaps this was not so strange after all, because Lord Talbot was not only unique in possessing the title of Hereditary Admiral of Malahide and Adjacent Seas and a motor launch to go with it; he was also the Under-Secretary in charge of Security at the Foreign Office at the time when Burgess and Maclean disappeared.

While Burgess was still at Cambridge he visited the Soviet Union together with an Oxford Communist friend and homosexual, Derek Blaikie. This was not so far as is known a trip specially sponsored by the Communist Party in London or the Soviet Government. The two comrades travelled economy class in a Soviet ship and paid £1 a day all-in to 'Intourist', and the introductions which Blaikie had obtained came in part and indirectly from Nancy, Lady Astor who had visited the USSR three years before with George Bernard Shaw and had returned from there far from enchanted. Some of the Russians Burgess met could hardly believe that a young fellow of his age could be a full member of the British Communist Party.

Burgess did not find a workers' paradise, at any rate by British standards, in the Soviet Union nor, after having just been rebuked for walking on the grass or, according to a less charitable account, for being drunk in the Park of Rest and Culture, was he completely convinced when an Englishman living in Moscow told him it was the freest country in the world. And when he got home the comrades in Cambridge found his report a good deal less enthusiastic than they had expected.

Party workers in Britain also noticed a change in his attitude. He began to argue that it was more important to end British imperialism by encouraging the nationalist movement in India than to sell copies of the *Daily Worker* on the street corners of Cambridge. This was not music in the ears of the faithful but Burgess persisted that he was right.

Later, in his official statement issued in Moscow more than twenty years later he said that he had decided to withdraw from political activities because he thought that he could do more to put Communist ideas into practice by joining 'the public service'. In other words, he could best serve the Communist Party by giving up all public connection with it so that he could attack the public service more effectively from within. At any rate the initiated now believe that Burgess's open disavowment of Communism marks the definitive date of his recruitment as a Soviet agent.

And so Guy Burgess renounced the idea of seeking a Fellowship at a Cambridge college—it was in any case becoming rather less likely that he would be awarded one—and, in the spring of 1935, he left the university for good, ready to offer his services to a not yet grateful and less than academic world.

# 4

# Wartime For Burgess

Many of the newly fledged graduates who came down from Cambridge about the same time as Guy Burgess were heirs to estates or to family directorships, or were inheriting money when they came of age, if not before. Others among his contemporaries had already chosen a profession and gone some way towards qualifying as doctors, engineers or lawyers and were prepared, particularly if they were among interlopers who had arrived at Cambridge from state schools, to work even harder than before.

Burgess did not belong to either of these groups, and having stayed on at Cambridge nearly two years beyond the normal term in order to pursue historical researches, he was now too old to enter the Foreign Office or any other branch of the Civil Service through the normal channels. He suffered from the additional handicap of having a reputation as a loose liver and former Communist—an additional disadvantage at a time when jobs were scarce.

His first efforts to penetrate an organization where he could act as a good Communist failed. The Research Department of the Tory Party to whom he first offered his services did not consider that the material he was likely to produce would justify offering him a full time job, although its Chief, Sir Joseph Ball, himself an old MI5 man, evidently considered Burgess potentially useful to him in matters handled outside the normal establishment channels.

Burgess was equally unsuccessful in his attempts to bore into the woodwork of the Tory Party's Central Office. His reputation had got there ahead of him, and although it was urged, untruthfully, on his behalf that he had now 'dropped all that Communist nonsense' he had indulged in at Cambridge, his appearance, which at times resembled that of a garage mechanic fresh from the workbench, destroyed much of the value of the assurances given by his sponsor.

Nevertheless Burgess persevered in his efforts to find some employment with Tory connections and secured a job as personal assistant with occasional trips abroad thrown in, to a friend of his, Colonel 'Jack' Macnamara, MP for Chelmsford, who was a prominent member of the Anglo-German Fellowship, and in close touch with other way-out right-wingers, who believed, at any rate until Hitler signed his pact with Stalin, that it might still be possible to come to an understanding with the German Fuehrer.

Guy, of course, can hardly have imagined that any such arrangement was feasible, and his convictions were strengthened in March 1935 when Hitler introduced conscription as a preliminary to occupying the Rhineland.

Burgess's association with Colonel Jack and his fellow right-wingers dismayed the Cambridge Marxists who were not informed of Burgess's reasons for severing his links with the Communist Party.

Somehow, nevertheless, Burgess managed to keep in touch with his friend Victor Rothschild, despite the fact that the latter, as a Jew, was passionately opposed to Hitler and Hitlerism, and, as it happened, Victor's mother, Mrs Charles Rothschild provided Burgess with his main source of income while he was job-hunting. For some time she had been dissatisfied with the advice on her investments that she had been receiving from the Rothschild experts at New Street in the City. She felt they were not in sufficiently close touch with political realities, and that this shortcoming had lost her a considerable amount of money.

Guy Burgess, on the other hand, was always willing to expound on the actualities of politics. He told her, for instance, that the railways of a Latin American state were likely to be nationalized and that she should sell her shares in them as quickly as possible. She did so just in time, despite advice to the contrary from her bankers. Mrs Rothschild also remembered that during one of his vacations, Guy had forecast that there was bound to be a rise in armament shares soon and that Rolls Royce shares would be the safest to buy. Victor Rothschild followed this advice and had presented Guy with a cheque for £100 out of the profits. Putting two and two together, Victor's mother now offered to pay Guy a fee of £100 a month to act as her personal adviser on investments. It was probably three times as much money as his friends who had become reporters or advertising copywriters were earning. From the date of his new appointment, Guy succeeded in living two lives. To himself he remained a Communist. As adviser to Mrs Rothschild he acted out the thoughts and emotions of the top-hat-wearing capitalist so beloved by the Labour cartoonists of the day, even going to the length of advising her to sell her investments in Europe and perhaps, except for armament shares, in Britain too—a course which, from patriotic motives, she rejected.

His political friendship with Colonel Jack Macnamara involved him in a fact-finding tour to Nazi Germany in company with the Ven. J. H. Sharp, a member of the Foreign Relations Council of the Church of England, and Mr Tom Wyllie, Private Secretary to the Permanent Under-Secretary at the War Office. At the same time, possibly through the homosexual network (the 'homintern' as Maurice Bowra called it), he made the acquaintance of M. Edouard Pfeiffer, Secretary-General of the French Radical Party and Chef de Cabinet to another Edouard, the French Prime Minister, M. Daladier. According to one of Burgess's more improbable stories, he once called on Pfeiffer and found him about to attend a Cabinet meeting, dressed in frock coat, playing table tennis with a colleague similarly attired, using, instead of a net, and to Burgess's delight, the stark naked body of a young man, who, Pfeiffer explained, was a professional cyclist of strong right-wing views. Burgess recalled that he had been deeply impressed. But that was part of the trouble. His stories were sometimes so impressive that even his closest friends wondered at times whether he had not made them up.

The desire to embellish might perhaps have been one reason why Burgess was unable to keep his first regular job—a month's trial as a sub-editor (the man who cuts and polishes the reporters' copy) on the London *Times* newspaper, though no definite cause for complaint arose.

Having failed with *The Times*, Burgess laid siege to the BBC. He induced Dr G. M. Trevelyan, one of the most readable and perceptive of Cambridge historians, who had already tried, without success, to persuade Pembroke College to award Burgess a Fellowship, to approach Sir Cecil Graves, an eminent official of the Corporation. The plan worked. Burgess started work at the BBC Staff Training College on 1st October 1936 and was soon helping to produce talks on current affairs. The job suited him. He had always been far more at home with the spoken than with the written word. He could choose subjects that appealed to him and invariably endowed them with originality. He aroused the interest of his speakers, inspiring them to clothe their most commonplace sentiments in words that sounded natural yet stylish. He was even prepared to lend them some of his epigrams. And he soon learnt that no amount of flattery is too much for a speaker to absorb.

His talks were all the more stimulating for having a political application. A talk on nutrition would focus on how little the poor had to eat in comparison with the rich, with whom, however, he was only too glad to consort.

In September 1938 Burgess approached Winston Churchill, at that time still a political outcast, and suggested it was time for him to repeat his warnings against Hitler. As a result, Churchill presented Burgess with a copy of *Arms and the Covenant*, a book of his selected speeches, inscribed 'To Guy Burgess from Winston S. Churchill to confirm his admirable sentiments'. This was the month in which Chamberlain signed the 'peace in our time' Munich agreement with the German Fuehrer.

Regular employment at the BBC did not inhibit Burgess who was an inveterate meddler from pursuing sideline activities yielding information which could be of great value both to the Communists and to the British Prime Minister, although only two of the three parties concerned, Burgess and the Communists, knew at the time what was afoot.

In March 1938 at the time Hitler occupied Austria, Burgess flew to Paris to see his friend Pfeiffer and learnt from him the discussions that took place in the French Cabinet about what counteraction France should take. Burgess brought back with him a detailed and dramatic account of the proceedings and the attitude taken by each of the principal Ministers. According to him, the French decision not to intervene by themselves was taken by a majority of only one, and would almost certainly have been different if there had been any assurance of support from the British.

Back in London, Burgess reported what he had learnt to a friend of his, a distinguished novelist, who, Guy may or may not have known, worked for the Secret Service. Not long afterwards, he received from the novelist enough money to cover the expenses of his trip.

Soon after meeting Churchill, Guy was acting as a courier between Daladier and Chamberlain who, in attempting to reach an understanding with Hitler, preferred his own style of negotiation to that of the Foreign Office.

The correspondence between them was regarded as so secret that the letters were signed in the names of subordinates so that the documents could, if necessary, be disowned. The chain of communication, according to Burgess, ran from Pfeiffer to the Prime Minister through Sir Joseph Ball who, with a cover job as Director of Publicity at the Tory Central Office, was uniquely placed to act as Chamberlain's private Intelligence officer. Sir Horace Wilson (who as Chief of the Civil Service was administratively responsible for the Secret Service) was also kept informed. Burgess's friend Pfeiffer did not know, and Chamberlain probably preferred not to be told, that Guy, during his journeys between London and Paris, habitually called at the St Ermin's Hotel where, to use the jargon, the letters were 'intercepted', i.e. opened, read, photographed and resealed before being returned to Burgess for onward transmission. Burgess says that he was shown the contents, but presumably had to rely on his own memory if he wanted to impart his knowledge to any of his Russian friends.

There were five things that particularly interested the Russians at this time:

(1) What moves were the British Government making to come to terms with Hitler?

(2) What encouragement was the British Government giving to Hitler to expand eastwards at Russia's expense?

(3) How strong was the trend towards pacifism in Britain?

(4) How united was the Commonwealth?

(5) To what extent was anti-American feeling growing in Britain?

Meanwhile on one occasion, at least, he was able, according to his lights, to be of service to the cause of peace, by suppressing and not delivering a letter from Daladier urging Chamberlain to cancel an order given by Duff Cooper, then First Lord of the Admiralty, for the mobilization of the British Fleet.

Burgess also claimed to have been the courier who forwarded messages sent by Neville Chamberlain, without the knowledge of the British Foreign Office, to Count Ciano, Mussolini's son-in-law and Foreign Secretary.

Whether the Secret Service paymasters, who stumped up handsomely for the cost of Burgess's jaunts to Paris and elsewhere were aware of this extra gloss is unclear, but in December 1938, a friend of Guy's, Colonel Laurence Grand, offered him a post in Section D (for Destruction) of the Secret Intelligence Service. As war now seemed imminent Section D had been set up to handle subversion and sabotage in enemy-occupied territory. Broadcasting of a kind came under this heading. One of Burgess's tasks was to arrange for pro-British broadcasts to be disseminated through channels and by methods with which the BBC preferred not to be associated.

This was made clear when Burgess asked the BBC to keep him on their staff while he was away on his new job. They refused, and Burgess preferred to resign from the Talks Department even though his new employers could guarantee him no more than six months' work.

His new field offered Burgess a very much larger range of opportunities. Instead of working at Langham Place under close supervision, he had the whole of Europe in his sights.

Guy suggested that his organization should buy time, nominally through a small firm already in existence, the Hendon Travel Bureau, on Radio Luxembourg to broadcast what the BBC felt unable to do in peace time—anti-Hitler propaganda. Guy's former Communist friends were only too pleased to come forward as speakers.

At the start of World War II he also began to plan a network of underground broadcasting services which, he considered, could best be operated through the well-disciplined resistance brigades of the Communist parties or of the more militant trade unions controlled by them.

Above ground he was associated with the Joint Broadcasting Council whose chief aim was to put Britain's case to American listeners and in his search for speakers and official information to guide them, Burgess kept in touch with the Ministry of Information, to which his friend Harold Nicolson eventually became Parliamentary Under-Secretary.

In addition, according to Kim Philby, a Cambridge friend of Guy Burgess and defector-to-be who was already working in the British Secret Service, Burgess suggested that a school for training saboteurs should be set up and, while he was still with the organization, a start was made in training Norwegians, Belgians, Spaniards and others for the work of disruption, also to be carried out under the direction of the Communists. After the fall of France, Guy suggested a scheme by which Britain would supply arms to the Communists there in return for Russia supplying arms to the non-Communist governments of eastern Europe. But while Burgess was even on his way to Moscow to negotiate the conditions which would probably have led to the U.S.S.R. paramountcy in France as well as the Balkans, and had already reached Washington. he was recalled and brought back to London. Another set-back occurred in September 1940 when he appeared at Marlborough Street Magistrates Court on a charge of being under the influence of drink while driving a War Office car. The Defence Solicitor pleaded that Burgess was doing rather confidential work which compelled him to travel to an office thirty miles out of London and that on this occasion he had been working for fourteen hours continuously. The charge was dismissed on payment of costs.

It was surely at this period that Burgess ran the greatest risk of being discovered for what he was—a secret agent. True, some of his closest collaborators were social if not problem drinkers, which gave them a certain built-in toleration of Guy, and many were eccentrics drawn from widely different professions, who were prepared to make allowances, in wartime at least, for the peculiarities of other eccentrics. Also, it was the convention that members of different branches of Intelligence did not talk shop when off duty. Yet there were gossips too among the Intelligence fraternity and today it seems hard to believe that they would not have heard in some roundabout way of Guy's attempt to recruit his friend Goronwy Rees into the Soviet spy network. As Rees tells the story, Guy's opening gambit was to praise with unusual extravagance Rees's review in the *Spectator* of a book dealing with conditions of the unemployed in Britain. In it, Rees argued that the plight of the depressed areas had been inherited from the past and could not be remedied without concerted political action. Guy began by praising the review extravagantly and after a lapse of some days returned to the subject again. He said the review showed that Rees had 'the heart of the matter' in him and, then, in a solemn voice, announced that he had been a Communist agent ever since he came down from Cambridge and had only been pretending, under orders, to be interested in Conservatives and the Nazis. He asked Rees to undertake work with him and to carry out his tasks that would be allotted him with unconditional and unquestioning obedience. Was anyone else in the know, inquired Rees, disregarding Burgess's veto on asking questions. 'A few,' said Burgess, and provided the name of a highly respected mutual friend, exacting at the same time a promise that Rees would never mention the subject to the friend, as the kind of work they were doing made it essential to maintain secrecy as far as possible about who was involved. Later that evening Burgess spoke of how difficult he had found it to break away from his Communist friends at Cambridge to lead a life of subterfuge and concealment. No more was said about Rees's political future, and the two men remained friends to the extent at least that Guy was later godfather to one of Rees's two sons.

Rees, however, was puzzled. He speculated on the question of whether, after all, Guy might have an object in life, or whether he was showing himself as a hero-leader of a revolutionary conspiracy. He wondered why Guy had revealed the name of a fellow conspirator since, by doing so, he showed himself to be either indiscreet in revealing the truth and therefore unreliable, or untruthful and therefore equally unreliable, and Rees asked himself what object Burgess could have in trying to establish his bona fides by naming someone whose allegiance could in no way be directly verified.

It was puzzling, too, how Burgess at the International Writers' Conference in Paris in 1937 both supported the orthodox Communist line against all-comers and yet found time to cultivate the almost incredibly right-wing Pfeiffer for the latest information on the French political situation.

In any case, Rees took no chances. He it was who consulted Rosamund Lehmann, the novelist, about Burgess's approach and, though he was bluffing, told Burgess later that he had made a written record of Burgess's disclosures and deposited it for safe keeping with his lawyer. Burgess exploded, but he must have realized that it was a precaution that anyone might have taken to avoid being press-ganged against his will into the Communist spy ring.

On one occasion when Rees was showing some scepticism about Burgess's alleged exploits, Guy said that his method of passing secret information on to the Russians was to meet one of them at regular intervals in an East End café; and, though this explanation did not entirely settle the matter for Rees, it was in fact borne out to some extent when, after Burgess's disappearance, the authorities came to question his friends.

A married couple, remembering their meetings with Burgess, recalled that one Sunday morning a fair time back he had rung up and suggested that the three of them went down to lunch at a Chinese restaurant in dockland, one of several well-known ones that it was then considered smart to visit. Burgess said that he had a personal letter to deliver in that area. When the three of them arrived at the restaurant, Burgess left them for a moment, crossed the road and poked a letter through a slit in the closed door of a shop selling seamen's clothing. Believing it not unlikely that Guy was in mid-affair with some deck-hand, the couple thought no more about the incident. But when they told the story to MI5 investigators, the security men brightened visibly and insisted on driving back to the restaurant where they asked the couple to point to the door through which Burgess had put the letter. It was one used in times gone by as an accommodation drop by Soviet agents.

And Burgess, thoughtful as ever, had provided himself with an excellent cover story for being in the area in case the surroundings were being watched at the time by unfriendly sleuths.

Meanwhile, the reappearance of Churchill, for whom Guy Burgess had evinced such a warm regard at the time of Munich, as Prime Minister did not improve Guy's prospects. For partly as a result of the lack of liaison between the British Secret Service and the individuals most likely to provide information, namely the left-wing resistance movements, Churchill had become dissatisfied with his Intelligence machine. Towards the end of 1940 a shake-up took place in which heads fell.

One of them was Burgess's. But at least he was once more, officially at least, a character who could be openly employed by the BBC.

He returned to them and later he produced the highly successful 'Week in Westminster' programme which gave MPs of all complexions the chance of saying on the radio without interruption what they wished they had said in the House. It also allowed Burgess to meet almost everyone he wished—with a fair chance of persuading them to be rather less unsympathetic to the cause of Socialism than they might otherwise have been. The future Lord Hailsham was one. Harold Nicolson with strong connections to the Foreign Office was another. Burgess also 'discovered' Mr John Strachey, Old Etonian extreme left-winger, who had written in his work *The Coming Struggle for Power*: 'If men hesitate before the task of achieving a new civilization; if they draw back because no new order of society can be born without violent conflict, they will not achieve an epoch of peaceful stability.' Strachey's broadcasts about the RAF helped to advance him to the post of Under-Secretary of State for Air, but as late as 1956 he retained the view that there is a fundamental incompatibility between the last stage of capitalism and social democracy as practised by the British Labour Party.

Hector McNeil, who was then a news editor at the BBC, was another of Burgess's contacts. McNeil, who came to London from a Glasgow newspaper, grew up in Greenock on the Clyde and claimed that until the age of seventeen he had been fed exclusively on potatoes and herrings. He was a burly, fair-haired extrovert. Like Burgess, he had a specially close relationship with his mother. Being something of an intellectual snob, he soon responded to Burgess's academic professionalism and was not averse at times to accompanying Guy on drinking sprees. His genuine Scottish accent helped him later to become an effective broadcaster.

But the fact that Burgess had become once more politically employable did not mean that his private life had become any less outrageous. He remained a compulsive homosexual and his craving to be loved still unappeased, made persistent and persuasive advances as a matter of course to any 'delicious boy' or even contemporary that he thought he might be able to seduce. It was a question of 'mothers lock up your sons' when Burgess was looking round for a new 'sex companion'. Even after thirty he retained a certain boyish attractiveness, though as Rebecca West was to point out later, it was the attractiveness of a certain kind of boy (though not an effeminate one). His success rate in affairs of the double bed was probably increased by his completely frank attitude about his sexual preferences (except on the occasion when he was accused of importuning a young man by passing a note from one compartment of a public lavatory to the next—a charge which he refuted by claiming that his neighbour had passed him a note which he had very properly rejected; after an examination of the handwriting, he was cleared). His liaisons were of a purely physical nature and unclouded by any form of romanticism, and in this way he was able to liberate his partners from guilt complexes with which they might otherwise have found themselves encumbered. His affairs appeared to be transitory and impermanent, but he managed in many cases to retain the goodwill of his former lovers and when he could no longer bring himself to liberate their inhibitions in person, he endeavoured to find suitable substitutes for them.

Whether Guy, who was a compulsive meddler, merely wished to direct the lives of his former sex partners, or whether he had a more serious purpose, is not clear. But Goronwy Rees who, despite being heterosexual and non Communist-minded ever since the Hitler–Stalin pact, remained a friend of Burgess, could not fail to notice that Guy, whom few would have thought of as a man with a filing system, had carefully docketed and kept a series of love letters he had received from a homosexually-minded young don.

One might ask at this point how it was that a determined homosexual like Guy managed to retain any friends in normal society. One explanation was that he also had normal interests, of which motoring was only one. He adored burlesque variety and when in London regularly attended the Monday night performance at the Chelsea Palace Theatre. He was intelligent, alert and witty. He was an accomplished mimic and his imitations of Churchill—as later of Khrushev's bibulous encounter with President Tito—were memorable. Another reason, as John Lehmann and others noticed, was that he remained a permanent undergraduate with an undergraduate sense of humour. He was always prepared to pull the pin out of the social grenade, to light the blue paper of his home-produced thunderflashes placed beneath the seats of the mighty and invite bystanders to stay and observe the effect. Mischief was usually afoot when he was around, and Kim Philby, the super spy, recalled the delight with which Burgess chortling and dimpling his way through the official minefields of Whitehall found delight in passing on reports according to which parachutes between eighty and zero in number had been seen dropping in the area round Brickondenbury Hall, Hertfordshire, where Guy happened to be working at the time. Not even the Duty Officer at the War Office was able to persuade him to be more precise, to add anything more to what he had been told, or to pass judgement on the reliability of the sources of his information. Guy's figures turned out to be accurate in the strict sense of the term. The number of parachutes which had descended was one; it carried a land-mine and had wrapped itself harmlessly round a tree.

Then in addition there was the fact that Guy was a card. There was no need for him to be a raconteur in his own right. His life-style was a story in itself. Already in earlier days his flat at 28 Chester Square, near Victoria Station, was notorious for the drunken, striptease (strictly male) parties he held there. His 'Union Jack' colourscheme there—white walls, red carpet and blue curtains and counterpane—contrasted with the squalor—broken glasses, overturned ashtrays, tables scarred with cigarette burns, unwashed plates, books and papers scattered on the floor. Guy liked to put it about that he favoured the same breakfast dishes that Lord Palmerston had enjoyed: two lamb chops and a glass of port. But in fact he both ate and drank without much discretion. Kippers, bacon, onions and smoked eel came alike to his maw, but as a special delicacy he favoured dried fish, which he hung outside his window on a string so that he could pull it into the room when he so desired and cut off a piece. As for drink, Burgess, who could relieve tensions in others, was victim to various kinds of strain himself. For years he suffered from insomnia and relied on alcohol for relief. He favoured John Jameson whiskey but apart from that cared little for what kind of liquor he poured down his throat. And as for port, he quaffed it not from the kind of wineglass that Lord Palmerston might have cherished but from a special large measure bumper which became known at the Reform Club as a double Burgess.

Burgess seldom kept his flats for long: the landlords found him an expensively destructive, and noisy, tenant, and in any case his rooms in Chester Square had been too near the roof to be comfortable once Hitler began his blitz on London.

Burgess therefore transferred his patronage to a basement flat at No. 5 Bentinck Street under the offices of a highly respectable medical journal *The Practitioner*. In earlier days the flat had been taken by Burgess's old motoring friend, Victor Rothschild, now engaged on counter-sabotage work with Teresa Mayor, a cousin of Malcolm Muggeridge's wife, as his assistant. (He afterwards married her.) But now the premises were used for irregular periods (and purposes) not only by Burgess but by other more prominent members of the Security Services.

Malcolm Muggeridge was among those who went to 5 Bentinck Street and met Burgess along with John Strachey, J. D. Bernal and Anthony Blunt.

'Sheltering so distinguished a company—Cabinet Minister-to-be, honoured guru of the extreme left-to-be, Connoisseur Extraordinary-to-be, and other notabilities, all in a sense grouped round Burgess; Etonian mudlark and sick toast of a sick society ...'. he wrote later in his autobiography.

He noted that rubber bones had been provided for guests to bite on if the blitz strain became too intense.

Burgess continued to mudlark in Bentinck Street on and off until he returned to the BBC. But his second spell, like the first, was a temporary affair and he resigned on 4th June 1944. For miraculously it seemed he had been given the chance to join the organization he had always fancied above all others—the Foreign Office.

# 5

# Peacetime For Burgess

Burgess was not called on to pass the usual stiff examination for entry to the Foreign Office. He first applied for and was accepted as a 'temporary' employee. Then, two years later, he 'took the opportunity open to temporary employees to present himself for establishment', and appeared before a Civil Service Commission Board. He was accepted as a member of the permanent staff.

It was the era of the so-called Eden Reforms which were to transmogrify the traditions of the Diplomatic Service. Hitherto there had been two classes of official—the diplomats who served abroad, and the Civil Service administrators in the Foreign Office who stayed at home. Now the two classes were to merge together with the Consular Service and specialists such as Commercial Attachés. Information Officers and the like, who had not previously been regarded as career diplomats. Henceforward, transfers from one branch of the new Foreign Service to another were to be made easier, and promotion more flexible and less closely tied to seniority. There was also to be a 'broader system of entry', and better pay to ensure that men of ability were not deterred from entering the Foreign Service by the fact that they had no private income of their own. The Eden Reforms became law in 1943 and, although they were not to enter into force until after the war, the Foreign Office prudently made preparations to adapt its structure to the wind of change. In 1944 a brand new Personnel Department was set up to deal with staff matters, which had previously been handled by an Assistant Private Secretary to the Secretary of State, with the help of an official called the Chief Clerk who concerned himself especially with pay and finance. It was obviously a sound move, since the Eden Reforms would entail a large number of new postings for the liberated countries of Europe and the Far East.

Here, then, was one reason why Burgess slipped through the net.

Understandably, since Burgess had presumably been vetted by the Security Services before being employed on Intelligence work, it might have seemed superfluous and even unreasonable to repeat the process again when he became a diplomat.

Burgess's first official post was in the Foreign Office News Department, that is the Department that interprets Foreign Office policy and actions—not always the same—to the Diplomatic Correspondents of British newspapers and broadcasting services, and to foreign correspondents in London. It was a job that might have been created specially for Guy. It gave him a chance to keep abreast of day-to-day events in the Foreign Office and provided him at the same time with unlimited opportunities for pontification and argument, both inside and outside the office.

One such extra-mural opportunity occurred in February 1945 when, as Harold Nicolson records in his diary, he dined with Burgess. It was the time when efforts were being made to establish a 'strong, free, independent and democratic Poland' as had been agreed at the Yalta Conference that month between Roosevelt, Churchill and Stalin. Stalin insisted that the Communist-run Polish Provisional Government set up in Lublin should be the nucleus around which any Polish Government of National Unity should be formed. But, since the country was under Russian occupation, neither Britain nor the United States were allowed to send observers there. Stalin had, however, allowed a Commission consisting of his own Foreign Minister, Vyacheslav Molotov, and the British and United States Ambassadors in Moscow to be set up with a view to seeing fair play, and during dinner Burgess tried to convince Nicolson that the Commission would be able to play an effective role in reaching an acceptable solution.

As it turned out, the Commission carried no weight at all, for Molotov and Stalin continued to argue that only the Lublin Government was prepared to accept all the terms of the Yalta agreement—which included the secession of a large chunk of territory to the Soviet Union. Consequently only those in agreement with the Lublin administration could participate in the government of Poland.

While talking to Nicolson, Burgess buttressed his views by taking from his pocket the Foreign Office telegrams exchanged between London and Moscow and showed them to Nicolson who, although an MP and a Governor of the BBC, was now a back-bencher with no official position in the Government. Seen in retrospect, this was, therefore, a technical breach of the Official Secrets Act and one which, again technically, compromised the unwary and innocent Nicolson. But one cannot help reflecting that the information in the telegrams might have been useful to other friends of Guy Burgess. Furthermore, by showing them to Nicolson, Burgess had given himself an excellent cover story if some busy-body noticed that these documents, so valuable to the Russians in their efforts to turn Poland into a 'socialist' state, had been removed even temporarily from the Foreign Office.

Later that year, while Burgess was still a member of the Foreign

Office News Department, Harold Nicolson, as the author of *Diplomacy*, a standard work on the subject, was invited to give a lecture to some young men who had passed into the Foreign Service through its new examination procedure. Nicolson reflected with amusement that the lecture was given on premises in Carlton House Terrace that had formerly housed the Ribbentrop Embassy.

During his address to the likely lads, Nicolson selected reliability as the most important of all the qualities needed by a member of the Foreign Service, adding that reliability included 'truthfulness, precision, loyalty, modesty, and a sense of proportion', all of which, be it said, Nicolson himself had shown as a diplomat in his younger days.

One of his audience asked what reply one should give to a foreign diplomat who asked whether some important but confidential fact was true.

Nicolson's advice was: 'If you don't know, then you should say: "I have no idea at all", but if you do know, you should reply "You ought not to have asked me that question".' Another young hopeful then asked what should one do if a foreign official says he will tell one something interesting provided it is not passed on. Nicolson's recommended reply: 'If what you are about to tell me is merely a piece of gossip of secondary importance, I promise not to repeat it. But if it is of vital importance, I am bound to inform my Ambassador, so you had better not tell me.'

Presumably the question of what to do if one sees another member of the Foreign Service showing telegrams to an MP over the dinner table at the Reform Club, or Brooke's or the Garrick (clubs at which Nicolson and Burgess were accustomed to meet) was not touched on.

Neither can it be supposed that Burgess, at work in the News Department, would have been so foolish as to tell the Diplomatic Correspondents who came to him for information 'You ought not to have asked me that question', for newsmen, though not endowed with the sensitivity of diplomats, habitually resent being told what questions they should or should not ask. But the end-result was often the same. Osbert Lancaster—no admirer—said of Burgess: 'Among his many qualities was an ability developed to a degree I have never encountered elsewhere to answer at length any and every question except the one put to him.'

Heinz Alexander, long-term correspondent of the German magazine *Der Spiegel* and, later, President of the Foreign Press Association in London, recalls Burgess as having been 'bright and breezy', and a helpful member of the News Department. 'He interpreted the Foreign Office rules more freely than the other spokesmen but without, however, going beyond them,' Alexander says.

One particular opportunity for Burgess to be 'helpful' occurred in March 1946 on the occasion of Winston Churchill's speech in Fulton, Missouri, in which the old warrior, now in opposition again, drew attention, not for the first time, to the 'Iron Curtain' that had fallen between the West and the East. (He had already used the phrase in May 1945 in a message to President Truman deploring Stalin's failure to respect the Yalta decisions on Poland.)

Burgess was on duty in the News Department when quotes from the speech began to filter in, and some correspondents asked, naturally enough, whether Churchill's views were in line with, or contrary to, Foreign Office policy. Burgess, according to his own story, went up to Bevin's office to ask what he should say, and was told that Bevin had not seen the full text of the speech as delivered, which was true, but that he disapproved of what he had seen in reports so far. Burgess was also told, not to pass on to the correspondents, the news that Bevin had not only been shown, but had approved of, the advance text of what Churchill proposed to say. In Parliament, Prime Minister Attlee afterwards resolutely declined to condemn a speech made by a private individual, however exalted.

Burgess saw the Fulton speech and the reaction of the British Government to it as the start of the Cold War and it has been represented that the conflict of interest which now existed between the two countries to which, in different ways, Burgess was now committed, added to the strain to which he was subjected, and consequently increased his consumption of liquor.

Osbert Lancaster, however, who worked alongside Burgess in the News Department during an earlier period, long before Fulton, believed that by then Burgess's constitution was already wrecked beyond repair. Lancaster—and he was not alone in this—did not take kindly to Guy's proletarian costume (nails, when not dirty, bitten to the quick, with the three-quarters-finished cigarette smouldering behind the palm of the hand).

At the time when Burgess joined the News Department, it was quartered, together with the wartime information service of other Government departments, and the voluntary news-censorship establishment, within the University of London buildings in Bloomsbury. It was therefore necessary for the Foreign Office spokesman, Sir Charles Peake, and members of his staff, if they wished to acquire any news-fodder for the correspondents, to make the journey from Bloomsbury to Downing Street—a good mile and a half—as early as Foreign Office etiquette would permit. But Sir Osbert was disturbed to find that, on the occasions when he accompanied Burgess on these voyages of discovery, his fellow-passenger would insist during opening hours on halting the car two or three times *en route* in order to gulp down rapid slugs of whiskey as a chaser for an impressive number of Benzedrine tablets which he forced down by the handful.

Another cause for complaint arose from the fact that each member of the News Department, which at that time included a number of stalwart independents such as Dick Scott, later Paris Correspondent for *The Guardian* and the Hon. Arthur 'Boofey' Gore, the future Earl of Arran, were required twice a week to remain on late night duty. Burgess, however, was already considered to be too unreliable to be left on his own. One of his colleagues, therefore, was compelled to do an additional and completely undeserved late turn, each holding, figuratively speaking, Burgess's hand.

There were moments of gladness, too, as for instance when Burgess, according to his own story, succeeded in imprisoning Gore in a mail-bag and keeping him there throughout one of the Foreign Office briefings.

One day during a briefing, the Foreign Office spokesman of the day, Sir William Ridsdale, then colloquially known as 'Rids' noticed among members of his staff a certain want of attention to the matter in hand. Guy Burgess was showing them an object which was evidently of absorbing interest. 'What have you got there?' Rids asked. 'I'm showing them a photograph of my latest boy-friend,' replied Burgess. 'Well, put it away at once,' enjoined Rids. The briefing then continued.

John Price, who after a distinguished career in the Foreign Office became Merseyside's 'ambassador' in London, was also among those serving in the News Department at the same time as Burgess. He recalls Burgess as a non-conformist who habitually entered the Foreign Office not through the normal Downing Street portal but through the Park entrance which had its own lift and was in theory reserved for Counsellors (who might wish to exercise a certain discretion about the times of their arrival and departures from their desks.)

Price, like Burgess, was a newcomer to the Diplomatic Service and believed that he could advance his prospects by studying the policy papers prepared by regional experts before he had joined the Service. The most convenient time for doing so was on Saturday afternoons (by which time the Sunday papers had completed the bulk of their inquiries at the News Department). Often enough Price would find himself in company with Guy Burgess who showed himself unusually willing to take the Saturday duty turn—when, incidentally, he was allowed the keys to Rids' cupboard in which the more confidential memoranda were normally locked.

Price detected no signs of homosexual 'gaiety' in Burgess and the closest they came to camaraderie was one Saturday evening when Burgess tapped Price on the shoulder and said impressively: 'Come with me; I'm going to introduce you to the "Guvnor".' But the

'Guvnor' turned out to be the landlord of the Red Lion, the nearest pub to the Foreign Office.

Nor was there anything remarkable about Burgess's views as expressed either to correspondents or in discussions with Foreign Office staff. He played the role of a social democrat opposed to Communism—a stance also adopted by Hector McNeil (whose international reputation rested on speeches made from 1947 onwards, and provided in part by Burgess, attacking the Soviet Union as a disturber of the peace and a menace to the independence of small nations). Indeed Price remembers Burgess as the man who provided the News Department with their most convincing arguments against Communism, although the references to past history with which Guy supported his views were often inaccurate.

Even now Price, looking back, wonders whether Burgess in his heart of hearts had any real political convictions, or whether he was not at first motivated by an immense love of intrigue.

Then in 1945 Burgess profited by another stroke of luck. Burgess's old chum Hector McNeil, who had been serving his time as Parliamentary Private Secretary to the disarmament king, Philip Noel Baker, was appointed Parliamentary Under-Secretary at the Foreign Office. After only three weeks in his new job as Parliamentary Under-Secretary, McNeil had to defend in the House of Commons the Government's policy on Poland. He did so to great effect, and it would be hardly surprising if he had not turned to Burgess as well as to officials for advice, both on the arguments to be used and the manner in which they were to be presented.

Having won his spurs, McNeil was promoted the following year to be Minister of State at the Foreign Office and a member of the Privy Council. Two months later Burgess was appointed as his personal Assistant Secretary. And so it came about that Burgess, the newcomer, who had yet to prove his worth in the field (he was still a 'temporary' civil servant) of conventional diplomacy, became elevated not merely to the corridors of power but to the desk-side of a man who, from time to time, was to represent the Foreign Secretary and to act as Britain's mouthpiece at the newly established United Nations Organisation. Burgess assisted unwillingly at the birth of the Brussels Treaty which preceded the foundation of NATO and was also present at the creation of the Marshall Aid plan which, though it helped to restore the European economy, did so, according to all good Communists, by turning its participants into satellites of the United States.

Goronwy Rees, in his *Chapter of Accidents*, a prime source for those interested in the psychology of Burgess, recalls two incidents illustrating Guy's general attitude at this time towards his work. Calling on Burgess in the Foreign Office one day, he was present when a bell sounded, indicating a summons to McNeil's office next door. 'You go, Fred,' pleaded Guy to his senior colleague, 'I went last time.' A discussion then ensued as to whose responsibility it was to answer the bell and what on earth the Minister could be wanting. But, although the deliberations between Fred and Guy lasted for a considerable time, the summons was not repeated. Whatever it was, it could not have been important, Guy concluded, in which case it was most inconsiderate of McNeil to have rung in the first place.

Rees noted that the 'in-tray' was full, as also were the ash-trays—and the desks were covered with an indescribable confusion of papers. But there was less evidence of output.

Rees also recalls Burgess chortling because he kept in the Foreign Office—though why is not at first clear—a copy of Kinsey's *Study of the Behaviour of the Human Male*—at that time a fashionable work in great demand. Burgess offered to show it to Rees and led his visitor into an area of the Foreign Office where even Guy seemed to lack his usual self-assurance. Cautiously Burgess put his head round the corner of the door of a prestigious office. Then he turned back to Rees. 'It's all right,' he said. 'He's not there.'

It was the vast office of the Foreign Secretary himself. Burgess moved swiftly to a safe—a disused one, according to the story he later told—and extracted the book. Rees was duly impressed and somewhat appalled. But is it fanciful to suppose that we are once again witnessing one of Burgess's elaborate cover plants? Here was an excuse—all the more plausible because it chimed in with Burgess's reputation as a joker—for being in the Foreign Secretary's office at any time when it was empty. And what better way of removing—or returning—confidential documents belonging to the Foreign Secretary's office than between the covers of a book that no typist or messenger or even perhaps right-minded senior diplomat would ask to inspect.

As Hector McNeil's Personal Secretary, Guy shared a room with Fred Warner, afterwards Britain's Ambassador to Tokyo, in whom the Security Services clearly never found the slightest traces of disloyalty. Yet, for Burgess, Fred was a particularly congenial colleague. True, he had renounced the markedly left-wing views which (like Donald Maclean) he had formerly held, but perhaps Burgess made a point of not talking politics, or continued his pose as a social democrat—or simply assumed his accustomed role as court jester. The other quality which no doubt endeared Fred to Burgess was his *joie de vivre*. A highly extrovert, broad-shouldered six-footer of the Jack Hulbert type, a *bon viveur* as well as an intelligent diplomat and at that time a foot-loose bachelor, Fred had no objection at all to joining Burgess on his extra-mural night patrols in the Soho area or to discussing next day in the office the merits of the various night clubs and bars which they had visited.

While still at the Foreign Office in London, Burgess took over a flat, which had been previously let to another Foreign Office colleague, at No. 3 Clifford Chambers, 10 New Bond Street. Its select position ('right opposite Asprey's, old boy') and its nearness to the borders of Guy's beloved Soho made it especially convenient for a man-about-town with special tastes.

Clifford Chambers, as shown by the inscribed stone high above the pavement, had been constructed in 1877. It possessed agreeable bay windows with views towards the west, but its amenities were not then what they are today, and the 'kitchen' and bathroom were undivided. As was his wont, Guy favoured a preposterous red, white and blue colour scheme, an enormous double bed, with a carved wood bedhead. The sitting-room featured a marble mantelpiece and was decorated with a number of mascots, including the straw-stuffed figure of a Regency buck. There was also a frigate in a bottle, a nineteenth-century American-made harmonium which he frequently played, and a large number of expensive political volumes and treatises, some of which accorded with his own views. Prominent on the bookshelf was *Portrait of America* by Diego Rivera, the artist whose 1933 mural 'Man at the Crossroads', commissioned for the Rockefeller Center in New York featured a recognizable Lenin as the progressive leader of the people. (After much controversy, the work was eventually chipped away from the wall and reassembled in the Palace of Fine Arts, Mexico City.)

As part of his life-style, Burgess shared his flat with Jack Hewit, an ex-ballet dancer who had toured as part of the chorus in *No, No, Nanette*, and was now the office supervisor in an engineering firm. Hewit had formed part of the Burgess *entourage* since 1937 and had carried out minor Intelligence work of a more or less harmless nature for Guy. He had even been admitted for a time to the Bentinck Street 'club' and knew, for example, that Burgess's friend, Sir Anthony Blunt, Keeper of the King's Pictures, had been engaged in Intelligence work during the war.

At night, Burgess continued to lead a characteristic existence, favouring such spots as the Gargoyle, off Dean Street, Soho, kept by the Hon. David Tennant, and much frequented by progressive pleasure seekers and their intellectual girl-friends. But he also patronized other more tinselly haunts as, for example, The Nest and the Bag o' Nails, with his custom.

But sometimes it was fun to stay at home. The solicitors through whom the flat had been let to Burgess began to get complaints from other tenants of all-night parties, of fights and screams coming from

Flat 3. Burgess excused himself by explaining that his job at the Foreign Office involved a great deal of entertaining.

For a while there was an improvement, but one Sunday morning in the Spring of 1949 the family in the flat above Burgess's were woken by their little girl who, they said, was in tears and trembling with fear. They could hear an almost indescribable din coming from the flat below. Then an ambulance drew up and Burgess, with his head and arm in bandages, was taken away to hospital on a stretcher. The hospital reported that he had a fractured skull, a broken jaw and arm injuries. Burgess's story was that he had slipped down the steps of his club on Saturday night. This could have been the stone steps leading from the door of the Reform Club to the street. According to Philby, it was the Gargoyle Club, which also has a long staircase leading into the street—a much longer one. Someone else mentioned a restaurant in Chelsea. But Jack Hewit afterwards said that the accident happened in Clifford Chambers, where the fifty-eight steps were at that time of uncarpeted stone. After coming out of hospital, Burgess went on holiday with his mother to County Wicklow in Ireland. But while piloting a car down Dublin's Grafton Street, he was involved in what was described as a 'collision' and charged with driving while drunk. His defence was that he had had an accident in England, and had until recently been in hospital. The magistrate, a Mr O'Flynn, decided in his wisdom, according to the account in the *Evening Standard*, that Burgess was 'a man of brilliance who appeared to be overwrought'.

This was also the year in which Guy took a holiday in Gibraltar and Tangier during which he visited the local representatives of MI6 and subsequently discussed their qualifications and abilities in public bars—a liberty which may have raised his value considerably with his Soviet friends.

But his conduct on holiday was also to decrease his value to his employers at home for not long after he returned, 'a common informer' (could it have been one of 'our men in Tangier'?) laid a deposition to the effect that Burgess had been spending foreign currency in the bars of Tangier in excess of his travel allowance and had acquired foreign currency in a black market exchange deal. Although the particular sum involved was less than £100, it was considered substantial enough for the matter to be investigated and Burgess was summoned to appear before a Civil Service Disciplinary Board.

His defence, when confronted with the evidence, was vintage Burgess of the kind which would have made one of his more probable-improbable after-dinner stories. He told the Board that it was true that he tended to live in greater luxury than was to be expected from his earnings and this was true in Tangier as much

as at home. The money, however, came from his mother. She had
had the good sense, he said, to choose men friends of indulgence
and resource and was glad to expend some of the benefits on her
son. 'In fact,' said Burgess in a tone of mocking banter, as he prepared to take his leave of the Board Room, 'you could say in your
report that I was living on my mother's immoral earnings.'

The Board, when their eyebrows had returned to horn-rim level,
however, were understandably disinclined to make this the main
feature of their findings and no prosecution appears to have followed.

Inside the Foreign Office, however, things had not been going
entirely to Guy's liking. There was, first of all, the undoubted fact
that, if he was going to pursue a career in the Diplomatic Service,
he could not remain indefinitely as personal assistant to a man who
would almost certainly be removed in time from the Foreign Office
to some other Government post. Burgess's first reaction was to
suggest that, since he was now doing senior work he should be
re-classified without further ado and removed from 'B' branch in
which he was then working to 'A' branch. Hector McNeil supported
the proposal. But senior officials opposed it, pointing out that it was
not in the interests of the Service for a man who had never worked
in one of the regional sections of the Foreign Office or served in an
Embassy abroad to be promoted over the heads of other more
experienced diplomats.

So Burgess was faced with the choice: either he could stay with
McNeil and lose chances of advancement later or he could join the
diplomatic mainstream at once and prove his worth on his own merit
first at home and then abroad. Regretfully, he said farewell to his
protector, and was posted to the Department of the Foreign Office
dealing with Far Eastern affairs.

Diplomats in the Foreign Office at that time hinted that McNeil
was not averse to Burgess's removal from his office. He had received
at least one warning—from Osbert Lancaster—that Burgess was not
to be relied on. But his answer was that he had never known Burgess
to be drunk before six in the evening. Later he said that he could
never have believed Burgess capable of leading a double life because
he was obviously incapable of successfully organizing a single one.

The 1st November 1948, the day on which Burgess joined the Far
East section of the Foreign Office, was a crucial one in the affairs of
that region. For the city of Mukden, one of the last to be defended
with determination by Chiang-Kai-Shek's forces, had just been overrun by Mao Tse Tung's Communist troops, sealing the future of a
nation housing nearly a quarter of the world's population.

It was a revolutionary success after Burgess's heart but he found
among his colleagues, most of whom were, like himself, Old
Etonians, a sense of realism about China agreeably in line with his

own thinking. The victory of the Communists had been foreseen and predicted by the Ambassador of the time, Sir Ralph Stevenson, and his views had been accepted by Peter Scarlett, Head of the Far Eastern Department as well as by the Under-Secretary immediately above him, Sir Esler Denning. They advised Ernest Bevin to take an early opportunity of recognizing the new Communist government, which he did. Burgess's main value to the department seems to have been the unwavering support he gave to his own views.

Yet neither these welcome portents nor the presence of congenial fellow-spirits in the Department contrived to reconcile Guy to the fetters of office life. Accustomed as he was to Apostle-style discussion in depth, he found it hard to compress his thoughts into the short, crisp minutes that save other people's time. His work was patchy, and his mode of living told against him. His colleagues were not amused when it was discovered that Guy had read and left behind an important Foreign Office telegram. He had been studying it on the lavatory seat. One fellow diplomat recalls how Guy would arrive late, having taken a taxi in order to save the short walk from his flat or possibly even the shorter walk to the Foreign Office from the Reform Club in Pall Mall where he would have called on the way to cash a cheque. Sometimes—for Burgess's sense of insecurity had turned him into an inveterate exhibitionist—he would breakfast unshaven at the Ritz Hotel. Having shown his face round the door of his room at the Foreign Office, he would depart to the canteen, taking with him a bottle of his favourite whiskey. And to mask the resulting fumes of alcohol, he chewed garlic, a practice which led to an official minute forbidding him to do so in the building.

Guy's stint in the Far Eastern Department came to an end in the late summer of 1950 when he was posted as Second Secretary to the British Embassy in Washington. It has often been asked why a man as unreliable as Burgess should have been sent to represent Britain in a mission as important as Washington. Some have even blamed Hector McNeil for the appointment. But McNeil had already left the Foreign Office six months earlier when he became Secretary of State for Scotland with a seat in the Cabinet. So the decision was made without any pressure from him. The Foreign Office staff men who pondered over Burgess's future may have had two considerations in mind. The first was that Burgess's expertise on the Far East could be useful in rebutting accusations in Washington that Britain's Labour Government, by abandoning Chiang-Kai-Shek, had 'gone soft' on Communism. A second consideration may have been that Burgess could be given a more limited and strictly junior role and be more easily disciplined in a large Embassy where he would have no direct access to the Ambassador himself. And although he was known to have no liking for the America of the day, it was hoped that his views would change once he lived in the country.

Burgess afterwards declared that he had warned all concerned of his left-wing views and of his fears that he might be forbidden to air them in Washington. He was urged by (Sir) George Middleton, Head of Personnel in the Foreign Office, to be discreet.

The same advice came to him from Hector McNeil who was present at Guy's farewell party at his flat, a function attended also by fellow-Communists, spy-hunters, male prostitutes and other eccentric personalities, including two women whose friendship Guy had managed to retain.

As he left the party, Hector was heard telling his host: 'For God's sake, Guy, remember three things when you get to the States. Don't be too aggressively left-wing. Don't get involved in race relations; and above all, make sure that there aren't any homosexual incidents which might cause trouble.' According to another guest who happened to be leaving at the same time, Guy replied: 'I understand Hector: what you mean is that I mustn't make a pass at Paul Robeson.'

(The point about this story, I have always felt, is not that Burgess was still sober enough to make an apt response, or that even the anecdote was not manufactured by Burgess himself, but that it indicates that Guy's reputation as a homosexual was by now well known to Hector McNeil, as well as within the Foreign Office.)

It was under these circumstances that Guy set out on his final mission as a diplomat.

# 6

# A Fling To Be Flung

Burgess's reputation had, indeed, arrived in Washington ahead of him. Sir Robert Mackenzie, the Foreign Office's Regional Security Officer for North and Central America, had received an impressively long memorandum from ex-Group Captain Carey Foster, Head of the Foreign Office Security Branch, delineating Burgess's habits and tastes, and speculating that there might be worse incidents yet to come. 'What does he mean "worse"?' Mackenzie muttered to Philby. 'Goats?'

Mackenzie was somewhat relieved, however, when Philby volunteered that he knew Burgess well, that Burgess would be staying with him, and that he, Philby, would be keeping an eye on him.

There has been much speculation as to why Philby agreed to receive Burgess as a house-guest, for Burgess's presence, to say the least, meant heavy drinking, broken glasses, liquor stains and burnt coverlets. And it could have done Philby no good at all with the British Secret Service, for whom Philby was supposed to be working, to have living with him a man who was so notoriously indiscreet with documents and confidential information. Equally, from the Russian point of view, it was undesirable to have two of their agents sleeping under the same roof. For if one was detected, the other would almost certainly be unmasked too.

Philby's explanation was that if either of them were being seriously investigated by MI6, then the connection between them, which had existed ever since university days, would have already come to light. The sleuths, for instance, would have unearthed the fact that Burgess had collected money for Philby and his Communist friends as far back as 1934, that Kim had recommended him as a prospect for recruitment into the Soviet Secret Service, that he had carried funds to Kim during the Spanish Civil War and that he had already stayed in Philby's house once before, on a 'professional visit', according to Philby, in 1948. It may therefore have been something of a double-or-quits bluff which made Philby agree to Burgess's request for house-room. Ht had nothing to lose that was not already at risk.

But then what made Burgess, who had always valued his individual independence so much, impose himself on Philby? Was it laziness? Or the yearning for congenial company? Was it to save money? (We know from more than one source that Burgess was unusually hard up at this time—possibly because he was hardly worth as much to the Russians as a junior with doubtful prospects in the Far Eastern Department of the Foreign Office, as he had been when Personal Assistant to a Minister of State.) Or did the Russians order Burgess to stay with his compatriot simply because Philby understood Burgess so much better than any other local 'control' man the Russians had at that time in the United States?

My own view is that whatever Burgess's activities in the United States might or might not be, they would require lengthy discussion with Philby, that this could most easily be carried out in the privacy of 4100 Nebraska Avenue, where the Philbys lived, and that the logic of the situation must have been as apparent to the Russians and Burgess as it was to Philby.

But although this cosy arrangement brought some relief, as Philby suggests, to Sir Robert Mackenzie, the rest of the security staff within the Embassy were considerably less happy.

Part of their disquiet arose from the difficulties of maintaining any security at all in an Embassy with a staff of nearly a thousand with officers scattered in seven or eight down-town missions remote from the main Chancery. During the war, the task of beating off enemy spies had been tackled by British Security Co-ordination, the body which ran most of Britain's secret activities in the Americas. But its members had shown little interest in the kind of humdrum precautions with which an Embassy is supposed to guard its peacetime secrets.

In its early post-war years, the Embassy had no security zones in which confidential papers were to be lodged every evening. No records were kept of how many copies had been made of confidential memoranda, nor to whom they had been issued. Staff took documents out of the office and into their homes at will, proclaiming the fact by carrying them about in cases marked with the royal insignia, and many of the security guards who were supposed to protect the premises, and cypher machines, were locally hired ex-chauffeurs or waiters—glorified doormen, untrained to cope with emergencies of the wiles of counter-agents.

Squadron-Leader Tommy Thompson, a former Chief Instructor and Co-founder of the RAF Police and Security School, who was responsible for Embassy security, found difficulty in convincing the average Foreign Office man of the need for a watertight system of control. Diplomats, for the most part, resent having to carry and show passes, thus accounting, like suspected persons, for their comings and goings to the doormen. Furthermore it has been the practice in British missions to place the Security Officer under the control of a non-security official whose acquaintanceship with security is usually a temporary, reluctant affair and marginal to his main career.

Burgess, doubtless wishing to build up as quickly as possible his cover reputation for being casual with documents (while at the same time considering himself something of an expert in security matters), showed his usual reluctance to conform. He 'cut' the security briefing usually given to new arrivals at the Embassy, and was soon in trouble for leaving classified documents 'unprotected' in his office. His written excuse, 'it was an oversight', was shown to his immediate superior and filed.

A few weeks later he sinned again by not returning confidential papers to the Registry at night. Burgess was told to make his report, this time not to his immediate superior, but higher up to his chief. Conveniently the form on which Guy was to record his misdeed went missing and was never found. But Tommy Thompson made *his* report and found the Head of Chancery very doubtful about Burgess's value to the Embassy.

Burgess, it must be admitted, had similar thoughts about the value of the Embassy to him. When posted to Washington, he evidently thought that his task would be to reconcile the State Department and the American people to the British Government views on the Far East.

But once there, he said he found his own colleagues were not so convinced of the British case that they could resist the tides of American public opinion flowing in the opposite direction. (Twenty years were to pass before a reconciliation took place between the United States and Communist China.) He was asked by the Ambassador to write a memorandum summarizing the British attitude on Formosa and later told Tom Driberg that he was astonished that at this date, that should be necessary. It did not apparently occur to him that the Ambassador must have already received a number of communications from London bearing on Formosa and might be anxious to see how closely Guy would follow them and whether his written presentation of the issue was likely to be acceptable to the State Department, or could stand up to the battering it would receive from Chiang-Kai-Shek's 'China Lobby' in the U.S. Congress.

Burgess was also given the job of sorting and answering hundreds of letters which a U.S. broadcaster suggested should be sent to the British Embassy in protest at Britain's Far East policy, a tedious task and unrewarding as well since, according to Burgess, he was, soon afterwards, taken off Far Eastern work. At one point he poured out his troubles to his old friend Hector McNeil, but must have realized that Hector, once away from the Foreign Office, could be of little help.

He was put on to preparing general reports on the situation in America but was chagrined to learn that the Ambassador had refused to send to London his dispatch which analysed the U.S. political situation and concluded that it was a danger to peace.

But it was Guy's conduct outside the office that led the Ambassador, Oliver Franks, to ask for his recall to London, which led the Foreign Office in turn to ask for his resignation.

Not long before Burgess had been posted to Washington, Marcus Cheke, who was then Vice-Marshal of the Diplomatic Corps in London, had prepared a guidance on foreign usages, ceremony and other matters as an aid to a member of the Foreign Service on his first appointment to a post abroad. The work must certainly have passed through Burgess's hands. There was the dickens of a row when the contents were leaked later to the Press in Washington. The mythical name chosen for the country to which the equally mythical young diplomat, Mr John Bull, was being sent was Mauretania, a state which did not then exist.

It would have been hard to write another book so full of precepts consistently disregarded while in Washington by Guy Burgess. One of its earlier paragraphs of advice, for instance, enjoins Mr Bull, if faced, in any small matter, by two alternative courses of action—the one easy, but appearing somewhat over-familiar, and the other more respectful, but appearing somewhat pompous or old-fashioned— let him choose the latter rather than the former. This preference to the over-respectful rather than the over-familiar was, according to Cheke, the first Golden Rule. It was seldom if ever Burgess's rule.

Turning from manners to dress, Cheke quoted Lord Chesterfield who deprecated both fops and slouches; 'But of the two, I would rather have a young fellow too much than too little dressed; the excess on that side will soon wear off with a little age and reflection; but if he is negligent at twenty, he will be a sloven at forty, and stink at fifty years old.'

Burgess had metaphorically already reached his fiftieth birthday.

On Washington, Cheke wrote: 'But if protocol presents few problems, there are more general standards of behaviour which Mr and Mrs Bull will ignore at their peril. To be shy is a defect; to look bored is a fault; but to appear superior is the eighth deadly sin.'

It was in this respect that Burgess was most remiss during social encounters. In December 1950, Joe Alsop, the distinguished political columnist, who wrote extensively about United States policy in the Far East, gave a dinner party for Michael Berry, who was in effect the proprietor of the London *Daily Telegraph*, and his wife, Lady Pamela. It was, for once, a formal affair with the men in dinner jackets and the women in evening dress. Burgess, who had been at Eton with Berry, turned up uninvited—the only man in street clothes. He also became involved in a heated argument with Alsop in front of a less than captive audience. And Alsop eventually threw him out of the house. Burgess declares that by this time he had already decided to leave the Foreign Office and that Berry, hearing this, offered him a job on the *Telegraph*. Berry denies that there was any such offer, and indeed it is difficult to imagine that either side could have concluded any mutually satisfactory contract.

But Burgess realized by now that he had already committed one indiscretion too many by complaining to Kenneth Younger, Hector McNeil's successor as Minister of State, who was in New York for the United Nations Assembly, about the competence of his colleagues in the Embassy, asking Younger to take up the matter with the Ambassador.

The exact circumstances in which Burgess came to leave Washington are, however, particularly intriguing.

In the Spring of 1951 Burgess, who drove a ten-year-old twelve-clinder convertible Lincoln sports, was booked for exceeding the speed limit three times in a single day. On one of these occasions, acording to his own account, he was driving himself at more than a hundred miles an hour. But later he admitted that at least one of the speeding offences was committed when a friend, whose name he professed not to know and whom he had picked up on the road as one way of getting to know people, was in the driving seat. The friend turned out later to be a known sex pervert with a police record, but no driving licence.

In many ways this was unfortunate for Burgess, for it happened that Governor John Battle of the State of Virginia, in which the offences were committed, was by no means an anglophile. And there had already been an outcry after an American citizen had been killed in a road accident by a foreign diplomat (not British) who had pleaded diplomatic immunity in order to avoid prosecution.

After waiting two days, Burgess told the Embassy Security Officer of his crime, and about the same time, the security man confronted him with yet another instance of confidential papers being left about unprotected.

It seemed almost as if he was daring the Ambassador to have him recalled so that he could reach London as quickly as possible.

Meanwhile Philby's own position was now in danger. Carey Foster, while on a visit to Washington, had told him how undesirable it was for him to have Burgess as a guest. And the U.S. secret servicemen with whom Philby was supposed to liaise were looking askance at his association with Burgess. Guy had already broken up a party which Philby had given for his American opposite number, and guests had stormed out after Burgess had drawn an insulting caricature of one of the women.

But there was another reason from Philby's point of view why Burgess's departure could not be delayed for too long. He had to protect the man with whom his name will always be associated— Donald Maclean—whose life and times we shall now consider.

# 7

# Maclean & Son

The key to the personality of Donald Maclean is to be found in the character of his parents, Sir Donald and Lady Maclean.

Sir Donald was an eminent politician. A former Grammar-school boy, he had qualified as a solicitor in Cardiff, and had entered Parliament in 1906 at the time of the great Liberal revival. He became Deputy Speaker of the House of Commons five years later, and, after the 1918 General Election, leader of the Independent Liberals. He was deeply interested in welfare work, in the advancement of old-age pensions and the cause of temperance; he was a teetotaller himself and had no hesitation in recommending his views both in public and private. He appeared serenely untroubled by any doubts about this philosophy of life. He had long been a Privy Councillor and finally accepted the post of President of the Board of Education in the Ramsay MacDonald–Stanley Baldwin Coalition Government of 1931.

When he died of heart failure in June 1932 the King sent a telegram of sympathy to Lady Maclean. So did Ramsay MacDonald, Neville Chamberlain, Herbert Samuel and Sir John Simon, who were all at the time in Lausanne, negotiating reparations and war debts to be paid by Germany. Sir John Simon spoke of him as 'gallant and sweet-tempered'.

It was a formidable task for any son to live up to such a reputation. One wonders at times whether Donald really thought it possible or even desirable. His feelings of inadequacy may even have been tinged with disapproval. By the time his father died, he must have read in the newspapers and heard from his more progressive contemporaries much criticism of his father's political friend, Sir Herbert Samuel, whose mediation had led to the defeat of the miners in the General Strike, if not of his father for associating with Ramsay MacDonald, 'the betrayer of the Labour Party'.

His mother, the daughter of a Surrey JP, idolized first her husband—thus adding to Donald's feelings of inadequacy—and then her sons, making it even more difficult for Donald to find his sex-balance amid the swirling currents of the thirties.

Life in the Maclean home at 6 Southwick Place, Hyde Park, was

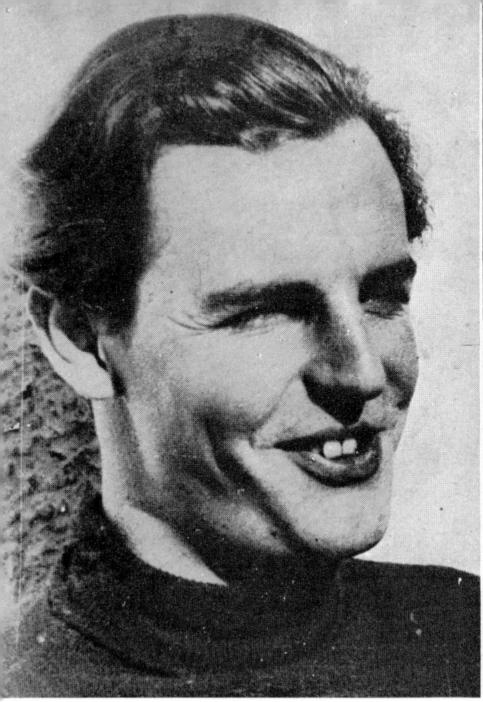

(*Above*) Donald Maclean as a young man, and (*below*) at the British Embassy in Washington, 1947 (*left to right*) Sir Nicholas Henderson, Sir John Balfour, Sir Denis Allen and Donald Maclean

Donald and Melinda in Cairo,
1949

Donald and Melinda with their
two young sons

not calculated to relax any inhibitions that young Donald may have harboured, for although Sir Donald had been brought up in Wales, his outlook was more akin to that of John Knox, the Scottish Presbyterian, whose tract 'Blast of the Trumpet against the Monstrous Regiment of Women' had so offended Queen Elizabeth I. Family prayers were held every day and lasted for a quarter of an hour. There were regular visits to the nearby Scottish Presbyterian Church, in George Street, Marylebone. Maclean senior was much occupied with public affairs in and outside Parliament, which engrossed his time and prevented father and son from seeing much of each other. Furthermore, there was a difference of nearly half a century in their ages.

It was natural, therefore, that there grew up between Donald junior and his mother Gwendolen a special relationship of a nature which almost certainly impeded Donald's emotional development and raised obstacles to a normal sex life.

It may also have led Donald to grasp to himself the discipline and credo of the Communist Party as a substitute for the relationship he lacked with his father.

Over the years Sir Donald had devoted more and more of his time to public affairs and less and less to the legal career which would have made him a wealthy man, and he could not have afforded, even if he had wished, to send Donald, who was only one of three boys, to a leading public school such as Eton. He chose instead Gresham's School, Holt, Norfolk—Motto: 'All Worship be to God'—which, although founded in 1555, had a reputation for being 'progressive'. The school had its own open-air theatre in the school wood where, each summer, the boys acted one of Shakespeare's plays. There was a Debating Society and other societies devoted to Architecture, Botany, Photography and the like. The school had its own orchestra and workshop, and Officer Training Corps. The climate was said to be 'bracing', and the boys were encouraged to play Rugby, Hockey and 'Fives', as well as tennis and cricket in the summer. But in spite of these aids, Donald grew up to be what he remained for some years afterwards—soft-featured and flabby.

He profited at Holt, however, from the fact that modern languages were taught there by the direct method, in which pupils were encouraged to think directly in the language that they were learning instead of translating their thoughts first from English, and this helped him to win a scholarship in modern languages at Trinity Hall, Cambridge.

He arrived at the university in October 1931, eighteen years old, to find himself engulfed in the same kind of political and intellectual ferment as his contemporary Guy Burgess. He was probably more emotionally moved than Burgess by the hopeless miseries of the jobless and less tolerant than Burgess of the trivialities of the thirties, of the trashy novels which people read and glorified, of the club-tie snobbery and aristo-worship which existed at Cambridge, of the vulgarities of the stage and screen.

But he saw the problem in political as well as social terms. Poverty and unemployment, he came to believe, could not be explained away as the fault of those who suffered from it, nor yet as a temporary phenomenon, but was the inevitable consequence of the capitalist system, and therefore, a political issue. He joined the Cambridge University Socialist Society which was formed in 1931 in protest against the coalition formed by Labour's Ramsay MacDonald with the Tories, and had soon achieved a reputation as a writer and speaker. In particular, he demanded the right to use college and university lecture rooms for all political meetings.

But to many of the young idealists of the day, it seemed that mere reform of the existing system would not be enough. Only the Soviet Union, they felt, had got its sense of values right. In the late twenties, after the departure of Leon Trotsky, the theme of world revolution had been dropped in Moscow in favour of 'planned scientific and social engineering'. This, then, was what the world needed. The planning which would avoid great depressions. Here, then, was the promised land of the thirties.

Donald Maclean's first plan was to emigrate to the Soviet Union (as he did some twenty years later). He could help to advance the cause of socialism there, by teaching English to Russians so that they in turn could communicate more effectively with British workers. And since there seemed every prospect of the capitalist system collapsing in the near future, there might be, though Maclean did not say so, the chance of his playing an important role when the Communists came to power in Britain as they inevitably would.

Britain, as John Strachey had written, would become an independent republic in a Soviet Union which would embrace first Europe and then the world.

Among his fellow undergraduates at Cambridge were three whose names would later become known far and wide to the security authorities. One was Alan Nunn May who considered he was furthering the cause of peace in 1945 by betraying U.S. nuclear secrets to the Russians, and another the spy-incarnate Kim Philby. A third Communist, David Klugmann had been at Gresham's School with Maclean.

They would have helped to convince Donald that here was the road to the perfect society in which social justice prevailed, a community in which the citizen worked according to his ability and received according to his needs.

Arthur Koestler, later to become thoroughly disillusioned, has described how he felt when he first became a convinced Communist: 'To say that one had "seen the light" is a poor description of the mental rapture which only the convert knows. The whole universe falls into pattern like the stray pieces of a jig-saw puzzle assembled by magic at one stroke.'

Over the years, the Communist philosophers had provided answers to deal with all contingencies. Naturally they did not recognize the ties of class, family or nation—the latter having already been weakened by the internationalism of the League of Nations. The Communist war against capitalism knew no frontiers (for the lot of the poor was to be improved everywhere) nor, in the front line of the Communist fighters for peace was there room for individual opinions, doubts about the leadership or anything but unquestioning obedience. It must be accepted that if Communism was to be the dictatorship of the proletariat, then there could be no basis for ideas in disaccord with it. The opponents of Communism, in short, were merely trying to rationalize their own social position, which must inevitably be in conflict with Communist principles. And there was no obligation to keep faith with capitalists.

Friends of Donald have sometimes wondered why it was that Donald Maclean, with his undoubted talents, did not perceive the true meaning of Communism—its contempt for individual liberty and freedom of thought—while other contemporaries, Lehmann, Auden (another Gresham's old-boy), Spender, and a friend closer still to him, Philip Toynbee, all of whom flirted, if nothing more, with the Communist philosophy, did so.

I think there were several reasons for this. The first was that though Maclean possessed a great facility with words which allowed him to sum up and reply to a written memorandum in the shortest possible space of time, yet his capacity for original independent constructive thinking was severely limited. He was content to work with the material placed before him by others without questioning the assumptions on which the material was based.

A second reason must have been that, in 1933, long before any doubts could have been raised in his mind by such things as Stalin's pact with Hitler, the Communist atrocities in Spain or even the later internal purges in the Soviet Union, he had started out on a road from which there could be no turning back.

His Soviet friends had represented to him that he would be much more useful to the cause of socialism if he abandoned the idea of teaching the Russians English and went ahead with plans to enter the Foreign Office—influencing the system from within.

Naturally he could follow this course only by publicly renouncing his Communist links and by concealing both from the Foreign

Office and his family that he not only still retained his left-wing principles but was about to put them into practice by becoming a foreign agent. Logically, the Communists have always maintained that, since no revolution can succeed unless the preparations for it are kept secret, therefore clandestine work and the false pretences that accompany it are no sin but merely a duty, and it seems likely that Donald accepted this reasoning as conclusive.

At any rate, investigators who have studied Maclean's career now believe that they can fix the date of his recruitment as a potential spy with some certainty. It was when he first told his mother that he had put 'that Communist business' behind him, and intended to try for the Diplomatic Service when he came down from Cambridge. And so the die was cast.

His family, now considerably less well-off since the death of his father, scraped together the money not only to see him through his last years at Cambridge but also to pay the fees at Turquet's in Museum Street, then the most successful crammer for the exacting requirements of the Foreign Office language examination. On 11th October 1935 Donald was accepted as Third Secretary in the Foreign Office in London where he remained for the next three years.

He was now trapped. During his early days at the Foreign Office he may have done little more than discuss official thinking on matters of Foreign Office policy with his Soviet contacts, but the very fact that such meetings had to be arranged and held in secrecy fatally compromised him. Disgrace, ostracism and permanent unemployment faced him if his activities outside the Foreign Office became known. But at this stage Maclean might still have found it possible to rationalize his betrayal by refusing payment for it. He appears to have convinced himself that he was engaged on selfless work for the benefit of mankind and not for personal gain. For he has clung to this belief with great persistence throughout the convulsive twists and turns of Soviet policy over the years. There was no other choice.

Once established in his new career, Donald moved out of the family home and took a flat in Chelsea, a district which still retained traces of the artists' studio-village it had once been. Rents there were moderate, for the chain stores and the disco-clothes boutiques had not yet displaced the family shops of Kings Road. The tyrannies of the flight-path overhead were, of course, as yet undreamt of.

In short, it was a suitable area in which a Third Secretary of modest means could live without being too remote from Whitehall. In Chelsea, too, in his new role as a young diplomat, Maclean could link up with his sociable and intelligent friends, including, for example, Robin Campbell, who sat with Donald, unsuccessfully, for the Foreign Office examination, and who was to become eventually Director of Art at the Arts Council of Great Britain, and Cyril Connolly, novelist, editor of *Horizon* magazine and later eminent book-critic of the *Sunday Times*. Connolly knew Maclean well from 1935 onwards and recalled in his work *The Missing Diplomats* another serious problem facing Maclean at this time. 'Meeting him, one was conscious of both amiability and weakness. He did not seem a political animal but resembled the clever helpless youth in a Huxley novel, an outsize Cherubino intent on amorous experience, but too shy and clumsy to succeed.'

Donald in fact had no luck with the girls he would like to have attracted, even though he studied carefully the methods of his long-time friend, Mark Culme-Seymour, a handsome charmer and habitual party-goer, who was assured and experienced in chatting-up and cultivating the attractive and fun-loving nymphs, abundant, even in those days, in London.

To Connolly, Maclean's bolster-like figure was covered with puppy fat which would one day disappear. To others, less charitable, his curvaceous contours and girlish mouth could have suggested a figure in 'drag' fancy dress—perhaps even a female impersonator.

It must have been a serious handicap for a young diplomat, potentially a superior person, to find that he could not enjoy the same success as common fellows had with desirable girls. And already there were signs that he was seeking to numb his recurrent feelings of guilt and sense of social inadequacy by drinking more than was good for him.

His colleagues in the Foreign Office, however, evidently knew nothing of his mini-rake's progress and even after four years had passed, a famous British Ambassador was incredulous when Cyril Connolly claimed that he knew Maclean. Connolly, he evidently thought, was not at all the kind of friend that Maclean, the golden boy of the future, would be likely to cultivate.

For Donald Maclean was already on his way up. In September 1938, six days before Hitler and Neville Chamberlain signed the Munich agreement binding their two countries 'never to go to war against each other', Maclean had been posted to Paris to serve in the Embassy presided over soon after by Sir Ronald Hugh Campbell, father of Donald's friend and contemporary Robin.

And at this time, perhaps, more than at any other, Donald must have felt, with Hitler and Mussolini on the war path in Abyssinia and Hitler goose-stepping in the Rhineland, Spain, Austria and finally Czechoslovakia, that he had made the right decision in throwing in his lot with the only nation that as far as could be seen was prepared to stand up against the dictators.

# 8

# Melinda And The Fall Of France

It was still the age of elegance when Maclean reached the Embassy in Paris on his first posting abroad, and the elaborate courtesies and traditional formalities of that time he would have been expected to observe: the despatch of a letter which he had to send to the British Ambassador revealing the pleasure with which he received the news of his appointment to his staff, the formal request he was expected to make to be allowed to pay his respects to the Ambassador, the importance of calling the Ambassador's wife Her Excellency, although she was not strictly speaking entitled to be so called, the need to remain on duty and within call at any reception given by the Ambassador, to stand up when the Ambassador entered the room, the obligation to shake hands in public with his British Embassy colleagues, even if he had already met them at some other reception earlier that day, and to have his visiting cards printed correctly with the inscription: Mr Donald Maclean, Third Secretary of His Britannic Majesty's Embassy.

All this may still have had the appeal of novelty to a Third Secretary anxious to make his way in the diplomatic service, and it is not improbable that Donald, as a new face, and as someone who could automatically without question be placed at the lower end of the dinner table, was asked out and about fairly often.

But even if Donald did not already regard the etiquette of diplomacy as an irrelevant and irksome tyranny, he realized that the centre of literary and artistic life in Paris lay on the left bank of the river in the Quartier Latin. No one would suggest that a young British diplomat abroad should cut himself off from, say, the Press or the University, for much news of a political character is to be learnt in these circles. But Donald was not seeking the secrets of the Third Republic in the Deux Magots, the Coupole, the Brasserie Lipp and other Left Bank rendezvous he patronized.

He sought writers, painters, sculptors, *avant-garde* political journalists and free-thinking students, poor perhaps, but unencumbered with the social and moral taboo with which he himself had been brought up. Here lay the secrets of Paris, of perpetual carnival, of joy unconfined, of delights and adventures not to be found at Southwick Place, Cambridge or even London.

Maclean had been in Paris less than a year—a year during which Czechoslovakia had been dismembered, Albania had been invaded by Mussolini, and the security of Poland threatened by Hitler. On 23rd August 1939 Stalin, allegedly believing that it would be impossible to conclude an effective alliance with Britain and France against Hitler, signed a pact of non-aggression with Hitler. Ten days later World War II had begun.

It was a conflict that many left-wingers had forecast, but the circumstances that led up to it were unacceptable to their consciences. For they had imagined that Stalin, and the Communist party which he represented would be in the van of the fight against Fascist Germany. Instead, Stalin had become Hitler's camp follower. Hardline Communists either echoed Stalin's views that he was compelled by *force majeure* to make a pact with Hitler or propagated the more subtle line that the war was no longer anti-fascist but had become a struggle between capitalists. Maclean apparently agreed. But in any case it was now too late for him to withdraw from the path he had chosen. To resign from the Foreign Office would have been perilous enough in peace time. Now, in war time, there was the added risk that if his Soviet contacts were exposed, he would face the death sentence.

But these unpleasant thoughts may have been far from his mind one December night when the snow already lay thick on the ground in Paris. Theatres were full during the phoney war period as long as the German army remained quiescent but there was little official entertaining among the diplomatic community in Paris and Maclean had more of his evenings free than he would have done in peace time. Having finished work for the day, Maclean had joined forces with his old friend Mark Culme-Seymour, at that time working in Paris, for an evening on the town. For some time they had been frequenting the Café de Flore on the Boulevard St Germain, a small, cosy bar with tables packed closely together. Donald had begun to know the regulars by sight. One of them was a piquant, pale-faced, dark-haired, neatly dressed American girl who often carried under her arm a copy of the *New Statesman* or the works of the seer of existentialism, Jean Paul Sartre, and was occasionally seen smoking a cigar—the current sign of feminist liberation. She was said to have met both Sartre and Picasso.

Mark Culme-Seymour, followed by Maclean thrust a way through the smoke-filled room, towards the table at which the American girl was sitting with her friends, one of whom already knew Donald. And so Donald met Melinda Marling, the girl he was to haunt and be haunted by for the rest of his life. She was dark, delicate-skinned, lightly built and feminine and shapely.

Melinda was twenty-three, four years younger than Donald, but emancipated and in some ways, though not academically, far more experienced than the gauche Maclean. Her family life had not been easy. Her mother's mother, also named Melinda, had run away from her husband at a time when a divorce in the family was regarded as an extremely serious matter. Melinda's mother had eloped at the age of twenty with Francis Marling, advertising manager of the Pure Oil Company, and had three children by him—Melinda, the eldest, Catherine, two years younger, and then Harriet, two years younger than Catherine. But in 1928 this marriage, too, broke up and was followed in 1930 by a divorce. Mrs Marling then married a Mr Hal Dunbar, a wealthy oil man from Oklahoma. Consequently Melinda had not had too placid a time. At thirteen she had been sent with her sisters overseas to school at Vevey, near Lausanne in Switzerland. For a time their mother rented a villa there and they spent their holidays in the south of France. Then mother Melinda returned to the States for her divorce. After that the children were brought home again and Melinda, aged fifteen, was sent to the fashionable Spence School in New York for the next three years. At eighteen she could have gone to college, as her sisters did, but being far from academic, she preferred not to. When she left school she took a secretarial course and there was much talk of her getting a job; but most of her efforts got no further than buying a simple black frock which she considered might suggest to a prospective employer that she could be a serious-minded and reliable recruit. She did in fact work for a few months in the book section of Macy's, the big New York department store. But in fact she preferred reading not books but movie magazines and other more specialized publications of the *Romantic Confessions* type.

In 1936 at twenty, after inheriting a little money, she went with her mother's and stepfather's consent to live away from home in the American Women's Association Hotel, where her two sisters eventually joined her.

At twenty-two, restless as ever, Melinda went to Paris on the pretext of perfecting her French and taking a course in French Literature and Artistic Appreciation at the Sorbonne—following the American-in-Paris tradition of Henry James, George Gershwin, Ernest Hemingway, F. Scott Fitzgerald and many another. At first she lived with a French family in the rather fashionable sector near the Etoile. But, once she had enrolled at the Sorbonne, she moved to the Left Bank, and took a room at the Hotel Montana, eating her meals with other students in nearby cafés. In the summer of 1939 she was joined by Harriet who was also to spend a year at the Sorbonne with a group of students, and the two of them actually toured France together in September at the time World War II broke out. Harriet was summoned home but Melinda insisted on staying on. She had found a new interest: Donald Maclean.

The two of them seemed to have a hypnotic fascination for each other. To Melinda, Donald was all she could never be: an intellectual from another world, a 'vedy-vedy' Englishman, tall and blue-eyed with an amiable manner, someone who could introduce her to a life of diplomatic parties and dinners, the innocent, the near-virgin into whom she could inject the serum of sophistication which would make him the virile lover she met so often in the pages of *True Romance*. It was the kind of thrill she had never experienced before; here was a prize above all others.

To Donald, as others equipped with receptive antennae, Melinda radiated sex. She was 'contemporary', familiar with current student jargon and, edgy and nervous but once her reserves had been penetrated, ready to be coquettish. Her voice was soft but agreeably husky and almost without accent. Donald felt at last that he had found someone attractive enough to overcome all his inhibitions but willing, at the same time, to be dominated by him intellectually. Here was the perfect woman for him: his wife to be.

The hopes of both partners were, of course, to be disappointed. Melinda was not, as Donald might have thought, unintelligent. But she was guided by impulse, emotion and the opinions of others to an extent which made her relatively impervious to logical arguments. She had found it profitable during her life to appear frail and defenceless when she needed help but had learnt also that in the end everyone has to make up their own mind. Little of this would have been evident to Donald when he first met her. Another fact of which he might have been ignorant was the strong relationship which Melinda still had with her mother, a factor which added to the difficulties of Donald's relationship with his future wife.

Philip Toynbee whom Donald had first met at a deb-dance in 1936 was now in Paris on honeymoon and the Toynbees, Maclean and Melinda spent evenings together, though Philip and Melinda found they had little in common.

Melinda, in the nine months she had known Donald, might also have suspected that he might have feet of clay. Certainly he already had spells of unrestricted toping, the forerunners of the alcoholic storms of the future, and Melinda at one time advised him to stay at home when he felt the urge coming on so that at least he would not have difficulty in getting safely to bed.

As far as her mother could tell, there was no question up until the beginning of May 1940 of Melinda marrying Donald. But soon after the middle of that month when the German Twelfth Army broke through the French lines either side of Sedan, most of France was declared a war zone and all American citizens were ordered out of it. It was at this point that Donald proposed to Melinda. Here was a dilemma. Melinda had moods of desperate homesickness. At first she refused Donald's proposal and he offered, nevertheless, to do all he could to get her to an Atlantic port and so back to the United States alone. But he pointed out that if she left him now, she might never see him again. It would be goodbye to the romance of a lifetime. Her American friends had all left Paris. Notably casual, Melinda hesitated. She asked for time to think it over. But there was no time. The moment had now passed when she could have got home alone.

Wives and 'lady members' of the British Embassy staff had already been sent home by boat on 16th May, and for five days bonfires were lit in the Embassy gardens to burn the secrets of twenty-five years. French newspapers, heavily censored, had shrunk to a mere two pages, and Alexander Werth, one of the British correspondents in Paris, was sending his dispatches to the Manchester *Guardian* via Malta. On 28th May Major-General Spears found the Ritz Hotel almost deserted when he lunched there with the British Military Attaché, General Lord Malise Graham.

Travel was getting more difficult every day. The 1st June was the last day when Britons could travel in France without a permit.

A limit had been put on the amount of baggage to be taken on trains and the premium for insuring goods sent by road from Paris to Bordeaux had risen to 20 centimes per thousand francs.

Maclean's marriage plans had already been officially approved by 8th June when 'Roddie' Barclay, later our Ambassador in Brussels and Maclean's colleague both in Paris and Washington, gave a bachelor dinner party for Maclean at his flat. Maclean was on his best behaviour and the meal—a sober affair, with Embassy guests only—had, as Barclay recalls it, to be cut short so that the guests could return to the Embassy to deal with telegrams. Barclay had met Melinda only a few days before and found her rather a dull little thing, and not particularly attractive. He wondered what Maclean could see in her.

Meanwhile, the very appearance of Paris was changing. There were sandbags round the famous statue of Henry IV as well as round the Pont Neuf. French workers were forbidden to leave Paris but on 9th June officials of the French Ministry of Information as well as of the Ministry of Supply and Air Ministry left their desks. Only a skeleton staff remained at the Quai d'Orsay, the French Foreign Office, and they went the following morning without giving notice of the fact.

Donald and the Embassy staff were about to leave the capital and Melinda, unless married, would be left behind. As the wife of a diplomat she could, however, save herself. If she married Donald at once, she would be able, as an Embassy wife, not only to leave Paris but also to travel to her home—that is to the United States. A fine start to the marriage but a practical solution to her own personal difficulties.

The British Embassy did indeed leave the capital on 10th June in three parties, the advance group containing some of the youngest members of the staff first, then the remainder of the Chancery Staff, and finally the Ambassador, Sir Ronald H. Campbell, Oliver Harvey, the Minister, and the Military Attaché. It was on the very day of this evacuation that Donald Maclean got married.

It has been suggested from a letter which Melinda wrote to her mother early in June that she may have had another convincing reason for marrying Donald without further delay: namely that she was pregnant. She told her mother that she was planning to go straight from Paris to Bordeaux to try to get a boat home and would soon be seeing her. She added that her greatest desire was to have a baby while she was home and that she could not bear to have it away from her mother. But the birth of her first child, which was still-born, did not take place until the following April. So it seems more likely that she was merely in love with the idea of being a mother—or at most fancied that she might already be pregnant, which, nevertheless, would certainly have provided a compelling argument for an expeditious marriage.

The wedding took place at half past two in the afternoon at the Mairie of the Seventh Arrondissement, 116 Rue de Grenelle, and the details given in the Register make interesting reading.

Donald gave his address as 11 Rue de Bellechasse, a street within a few minutes walk of the Quai d'Orsay, of the Register Office and, incidentally, the Soviet Embassy. Melinda Marling is described as having no profession and as living at the Rue St-Benoist 28 [*sic*], in the St Germain des Prés area, having moved there from the Rue de la Chaise, almost round the corner from Donald's lodging. Melinda's father, Francis Marling, is described in the register as a publicity agent. One of the two witnesses was John Mallet, an official of the Embassy, the other Virginia Anderson 'an industrial representative'.

In 1940, as now, banns of the marriage had to be published ten consecutive days before the wedding, and foreigners were required to be domiciled in the *arrondissement* where the marriage was to be celebrated for at least one month before the publication of the banns—making a total of nearly six weeks. In other words, the arrangements would normally have had to be set in hand in the very early days of May. But apart from the evidence of her letters, it seems very unlikely that Melinda finally made up her mind to marry Donald until the Germans were almost within sight of Paris, and Donald may have used his official position at the Embassy to speed up the formalities at the Mairie.

The regulations requiring that the two foreigners should have lived for at least a month in the district where the marriage was to take place are also reflected in the two addresses given for Melinda. Thus at the time of her marriage she was not living in the seventh *arrondissement* but in Rue St-Benoit (wrongly spelt Benoist in the marriage certificate) in the sixth district, but had previously been residing in the Rue de la Chaise, which was in the seventh district.

Donald had been told to make his own arrangements for leaving Paris and seeing to the safety of his wife, and he was able to get hold of a car, doubtless with diplomatic number plates at the front. It must have been difficult. There were, of course, long queues at the petrol pumps, and Alexander Werth remembers the case of one petrol pump attendant who refused to serve any more customers because his arm had become too sore from working the pump. General Beaufré said of the exodus: 'It was at once tragic and comic, a sort of sad funfair on the move, made up of disbanded soldiers, girls, frightened families, rich cars piled high with miscellaneous baggage, perambulators filled with pots and pans, pushed by two old people.'

The French Government, led by Paul Reynaud, was to reassemble at Tours and the British Embassy had been allotted accommodation at the Château Champchevrier, about fifteen miles north-west of that city. It was a gigantic sixteenth-century moated castle in which Louis XIII was said once to have slept during a hunting expedition. Its rooms were decorated with fine tapestries and elegant furniture, and there were two baths. Unfortunately, however, there was no running water of any kind—not even cold water. Roderick Barclay relates in his account of the crisis that he slept in the library of the château—to be near the only telephone in the building. The Ambassador and his staff arrived at the château the following morning 11th June about 4 a.m. Some of his staff had to be billeted in the castle stable-block, others in the village. The Foreign Ministry, with which the Ambassador had to keep in touch, had been sent to another château more than twelve miles away. The French High Command was at Briare, near Orleans, the Ambassadors of Canada and South Africa (then still within the Commonwealth) elsewhere in the countryside, while the Supreme War Council had its headquarters at the Prefecture in the city of Tours. In these circumstances the Ambassador could well have done with the help of one of his junior secretaries and it must have been vexing to some that Donald

Maclean had chosen apparently to give priority to his private affairs over the needs of the Embassy.

On 13th June, the day on which the French Prime Minister, Paul Reynaud, prompted by his mistress Madame de Portes, had asked Winston Churchill to release France from her undertaking not to make a separate peace with the Germans, the French Government decided to move from Tours to Bordeaux and sent a message to the British Ambassador to warn him that the German tanks were now advancing so rapidly that it was essential to get across to the south bank of the Loire before 10 a.m. if they wanted to cross at all.

Early on 14th June the British party of ten cars, headed by the Ambassador in his Rolls Royce, including a second Rolls Royce lent by Lord Derby, took the road south via Poitiers and the Charente to their rendezvous on the far side of the River Garonne, arriving there about 9 p.m. Two portable radio transmitter receivers which they had had the foresight to procure from the Air Ministry in London formed their main contact with the outside world.

There, Barclay learnt from the British Consulate that only the Ambassador and a few key members of his staff could be put up in Bordeaux itself in the Hôtel Montre. The others would have to sleep at the Château Filhot in the Sauternes countryside, about two miles south of Château d'Yquem and nearly thirty miles south-east of Bordeaux. The French Ministry of Foreign Affairs was set up in a school. The Belgian Government was installed in a cargo-carrying merchant ship on which cabinet meetings were called by a steward ringing a bell. Messages to London had, for safety, to be sent in duplicate—one copy via New York and the other via the nearest British warship to the Admiralty. Much of the day was taken up with ciphering and deciphering urgent messages about the fate of the French Government and the possibility of saving the French Fleet.

It was in these circumstances that Maclean and Melinda arrived at Bordeaux, and a precious bedroom in the hotel had to be given up to them while Barclay shared another room which also became the Chancery Office, with two other colleagues, Anthony Nutting and Henry Hankey. As soon as possible Maclean and Melinda were sent off to Château Filhot to be evacuated with other Embassy staff not considered to be essential. It was nearly a week since the wedding, and Melinda with a sense of unreality, had been hoping for a conventional honeymoon. Instead, according to her account, they left Paris immediately after the wedding and spent their first married night in a field near Chartres. The weather was perfect. They had thought of travelling on to Biarritz near the Spanish border, which indeed did become one of the last jumping-off places for refugees, and did spend two days in a village not far from

Biarritz—thus overshooting the Ambassador and his staff by nearly a hundred miles. Then, still according to Melinda, they hurried back to Bordeaux and boarded a British destroyer which sailed on the afternoon of 23rd June (two days after Hitler had accepted the French surrender at Compiègne).

But the actual course of events was not quite like Melinda's account. In fact, one of the fullest reports of the Maclean departure is to be found in the report of the Air Attaché of the British Embassy of the Evacuation of RAF and other Personnel from Bordeaux.

From this it is clear that the orders to move from Château Filhot were received at 11.30 a.m. on the morning of 17th June—six days earlier than the date given by Melinda, (or possibly her mother), to Geoffrey Hoare. Neither Maclean's name nor Melinda's appears among those present at Château Filhot when the evacuation orders came. Most of those on the list of Embassy personnel could clearly have been spared. They included the Ambassador's valet, the Ambassador's chauffeur, Mr Page, his wife Mrs Page and their daughter Miss Page, together with Emile, another Embassy driver. In addition, there were contingents from the Military Attaché's Branch, the Air Attaché's Branch, the Passport Control Office, the Postal Censorship Department, the Telephone Operators and the Mechanized Transport Company.

The convoy from Château Filhot was under orders to be on the quay of the port of Bordeaux at 2 p.m. and set off through the rain with an hour to go, carrying emergency rations. At that time the River Garonne was still mined and therefore closed to merchant ships. The passengers, therefore, embarked on to HMS *Berkeley*, a destroyer, and were transferred off shore to the SS *Nariva*, a twenty-year-old cargo vessel belonging to the Royal Mail Lines, returning from carrying coal to South America. Apart from her bunker space, she possessed three decks and a shelter deck.

The Air Attaché's report was evidently prepared under stress (the name Filhot being spelt wrongly: 'Philot', and it is possible that some of those present in the château at 11.30 a.m. were not included in the list prepared at that time, or that the Macleans arrived between then and the time when the convoy left at 1 p.m.).

Alternatively, other passengers to be taken on the SS *Nariva* arrived at the dock independently or in other convoys. At any rate, the passenger list of the SS *Nariva* with the names of Mr and Mrs Maclean on it—at the head of those from the Embassy—is considerably larger. It included Royal Air Force personnel, members of the Canadian and South African Legations, members of the British Expeditionary Force, the Ministry of Information, the Mechanized Transport Corps, some nuns, some unattached citizens and members of what was called 'the French Party' led by the Press Counsellor of the British Embassy, Mr Noble Hall. Mme Tabouis, the political journalist in whose breast lay many a French Cabinet secret, was one of them.

For the Macleans it could have been no pleasure cruise. The transfer from the *Berkeley* to the *Nariva* took place to an accompaniment of German bombs falling into the sea nearby. The passengers were divided into sections, each under section leaders. The stores and rations brought on board were requisitioned and handed into a central store.

Cabins, as far as available, were allotted to the women passengers. Melinda shared the cook's cabin with three other women while Donald slept on the floor outside. Meals were arranged in relays of twenty in the saloon and ten in the after-mess. Each passenger received a meal ticket to be surrendered when rations were dished out. An anti-submarine watch made up of two officers and four other ranks was kept, and an anti-aircraft guard of six rifles was also mounted. During the night of 18th June an SOS was received from the ship astern saying that she had been torpedoed and was sinking.

As the food supplies dwindled the rations the passengers received became more and more skimpy. It was no longer worth sitting down to meals and whatever could be spared was handed to the passengers walking in a continuous file through the saloon. On the last day of the voyage, only tea could be served.

At first the *Nariva* made for Falmouth, but when the ship was nearing port, orders were received to go on to Milford Haven, where she arrived on the evening of 20th June. Next morning the passengers, including the Macleans, were landed and sent on to London.

Only then was Melinda able to send a telegram to her mother announcing that she was now Mrs Donald Maclean.

# 9

# Homer Comes To Washington

There could hardly have been a greater contrast to Paris before the fall of France than the atmosphere in London afterwards. Britain seemed quite alone and abandoned. Indeed spurned, for Marshal Petain had rejected Winston Churchill's offer of British citizenship for all Frenchmen and French citizenship for all Britons, with the comment that it would be fusion with a corpse. The country faced invasion, and the daylight raiders had scarcely been beaten off during the summer Battle of Britain when the swarms of German bombers droned back night after night to mount the Blitz on London. On 15th October at the time of the full moon, a force of nearly 500 aircraft dropped 386 tons of high explosives on London and 70,000 fire bombs. This was not the life Melinda had expected when she left the United States for Europe, and it could never be her war, just as, in a different sense, it could never be Donald's.

Nor could London be a substitute for Paris. For Melinda, Paris had been the eternal city of pleasure, peopled with students with their lives before them, artists seeking beauty, absorbed in the pursuit of happiness. London, on the other hand, was a place of work, a city at war, an impersonal metropolis in which the citizens were part of a regimented civilian army, unable to travel freely about the country, subservient to Air Raid Wardens, and, because of the censorship, ignorant of what was really happening. Also, there were fewer admirers for Mrs Maclean, a young married woman, than there had been for the unattached Melinda Marling.

Donald, too, was finding that his work at the Foreign Office left him with very little time for his wife. His desertion of the Paris Embassy in its hour of need had not apparently prejudiced his career, for in October 1940 he was promoted from the rank of Third Secretary to be a Second Secretary. Greater responsibilities meant longer hours. In the early thirties, young gentlemen joining the Service had hardly needed to start work until eleven in the morning. There was no work on Saturdays and two months holiday a year. Lunch was a movable feast, and scones, biscuits and fruit cakes were served at tea. Ten years later, the picture was a different one.

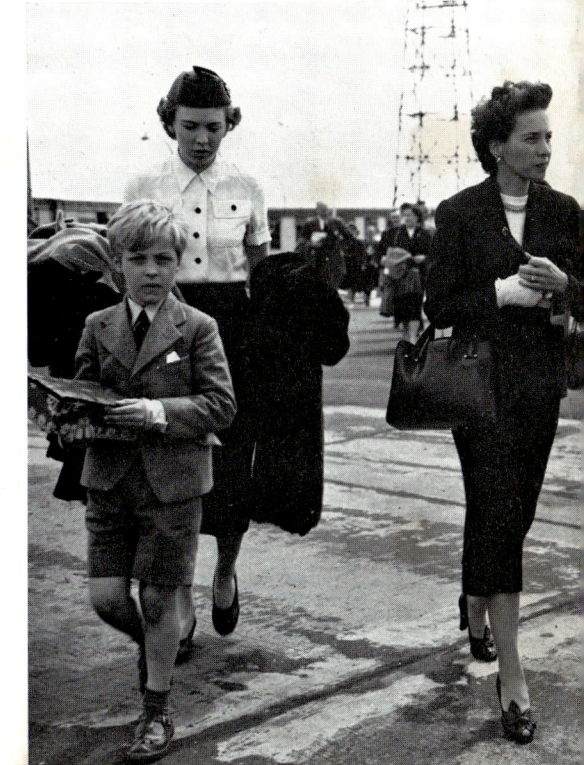

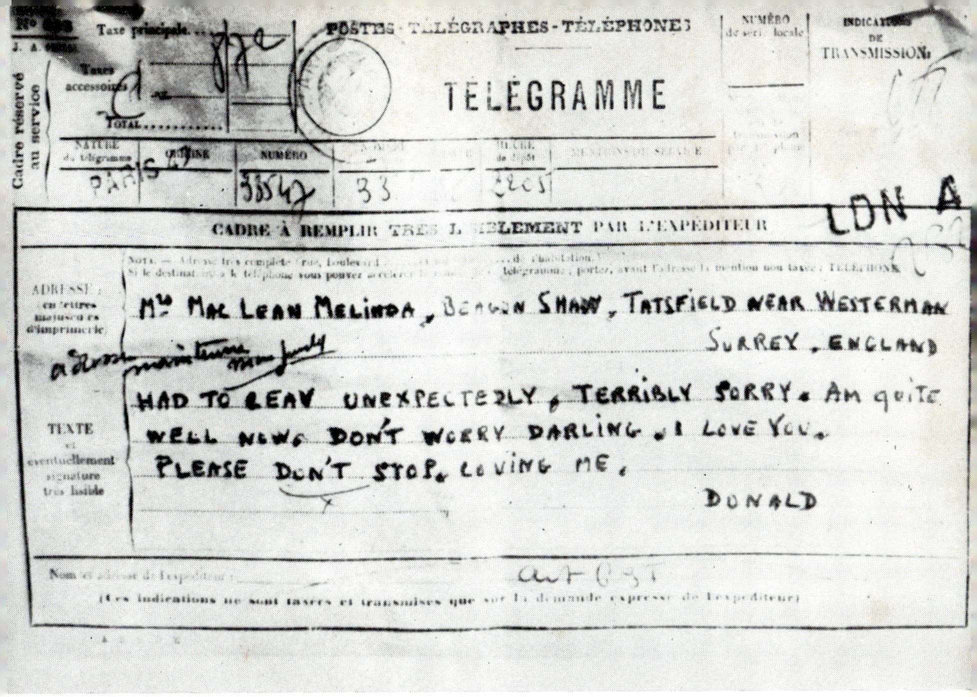
POSTES-TÉLÉGRAPHES-TÉLÉPHONES

TÉLÉGRAMME

Taxe principale

Taxes accessoires

TOTAL

Cadre réservé au service

NUMÉRO de série locale

INDICATIONS DE TRANSMISSION

NATURE du télégramme | ORIGINE | NUMÉRO | HEURE de dépôt | MENTIONS DE SERVICE

PARIS 27 | 33542 | 33 | 22 05

LDN A

CADRE À REMPLIR TRÈS LISIBLEMENT PAR L'EXPÉDITEUR

ADRESSE:

Mme MAC LEAN MELINDA, BEACON SHAW, TATSFIELD NEAR WESTERMAN SURREY, ENGLAND

TEXTE et éventuellement signature très lisible

HAD TO LEAV UNEXPECTEDLY, TERRIBLY SORRY. AM QUITE WELL NOW. DON'T WORRY DARLING. I LOVE YOU. PLEASE DON'T STOP LOVING ME.

DONALD

Nom et adresse de l'expéditeur:

(Ces indications ne sont taxées et transmises que sur la demande expresse de l'expéditeur)

The telegram sent to Melinda shortly after Donald's defection, 1951

Melinda leaves Britain for good, Northolt Airport, June, 1952

(*Above*) Guy Burgess, and (*below*) relaxing by the Black Sea, 1956

Work began an hour or two earlier and often finished late into the evening.

Nor was Melinda's domestic life turning out well. The hastily improvised marriage celebrated at a time when the Germans were almost at the gates of Paris may have seemed romantic enough at the time to Melinda, but Lady Maclean, who had been brought up in the 'bride wears a white veil' school, could not have relished the idea of a wedding unsanctified by the church or even the Embassy Chaplain, the Rev. Eustace Wade. And no wedding presents, no iced wedding cake, no champagne reception—only the *fait accompli* and tolerance rather than acclamation from the Foreign Office.

There was—perhaps there had always been—an unusually close relationship between Donald and his mother—an almost unhealthy one which Melinda eventually concluded helped to account for Donald's shortcomings as a husband and for the latent homosexuality which became more and more apparent as time went on. Furthermore, and apart from this, Melinda received a strong impression that Lady Maclean did not consider her a suitable match for her son.

In these circumstances, when Melinda became pregnant some weeks later, she decided to hold to her original plan and have the baby at home in the United States. Towards the end of November she sailed the Atlantic in a convoy, and was reunited with her mother and sisters in New York. She went on to stay on the family farm, Merriebrook, at South Egremont, not far from New York City. It was there that the baby was born in April, dead.

The question then arose as to what she should do next. Her mother and sisters would have been happy to keep her with them rather than let her face the uncertainties of another transatlantic crossing, followed by the black-out and the blitz. On the other hand, Melinda had a pronounced streak of obstinacy and, even though she may have become somewhat disillusioned with Donald, yet this was her marriage, the choice that she made on her own without, for once, the advice of her mother, as precious to her as a badge of her independence as the cigars she once flaunted in public. She seems to have felt the urge to be a mother and to be seen to be one. In May she flew back via Bermuda and Lisbon to Donald in London.

Together they 'took it' with the other Londoners and were bombed out of two different flats. When women were called up for war work, Melinda, remembering her time in Macy's, took a job with the Times Book Shop in Wigmore Street. Gradually the tides of war began to turn in favour of the Allies. In 1941 Hitler invaded the Soviet Union (making the struggle against Germany no longer a

F

capitalist-imperialist war but, once more, an anti-fascist crusade.) In the same year, Japan attacked the United States Fleet in Pearl Harbour, bringing America into the war. In 1942 the British Forces in North Africa won their first memorable victory at El Alamein while the German Army became encircled outside Stalingrad. The following year Sicily and Italy were invaded and plans to land on the Normandy beaches were, as the jargon went, finalized.

In 1944 with the D-Day landings in Normandy only a few weeks away, there was good news for the Macleans too. Donald was posted to the Washington Embassy. This surely was closer to the life Melinda had dreamed of. There was a place in the establishment—with an entertainment allowance. She would be able to show off her prize to her family and receive their congratulations at having married someone so obviously destined for promotion. And once again she was pregnant. She would be a mother too—able to show to the world the proof of her husband's devotion.

But strange to relate, the second honeymoon, which could perhaps have solidified the marriage, failed to materialize. One reason for this was that, once they reached the promised land, Donald did not encourage Melinda to leave New York, where her mother, Mrs Dunbar, was living, and come to Washington. Possibly he was anxious to settle into his new job without the added complication of looking after a pregnant wife, who could hardly be expected to fulfil the exacting social obligations of being entertained, let alone do any entertaining. In any case, accommodation in war-bloated Washington was extremely scarce and the call-up had drained Washington of servants suitable for the house of a diplomat.

Privately, Donald was telling close friends that he thought sex a greatly over-rated pastime. For her part, Mrs Dunbar must have been particularly anxious to ensure by personal supervision that Melinda's second pregnancy was successful and that she did not lose the baby. One result was that Melinda was anchored in New York with no husband to talk to or house to run. She began to revert once more to the kind of life she had enjoyed so greatly before her marriage—visiting cocktail bars and the lounges of smart hotels with her sister Harriet. She was looking once more for the kind of romances she had already met with in *True Confession* magazines but which in real life proved so elusive.

A second result was that Mrs Dunbar soon became aware that her daughter, despite her marriage, remained, as she would have put it, unfulfilled. Mrs Dunbar did not approve either of Donald's manner or his bow ties. She regarded him as supercilious and ineffective—as indeed some of his own countrymen did. Her own marriage to Hal Dunbar was about to break up, but she remained an incurable romantic herself and held strong convictions that her daughters should not be deprived of the physical satisfaction she felt was their due. She also felt and hinted in the family circle, in Donald's presence, that Melinda was a passionate but unsatisfied wife.

Unfortunately she made the fatal mistake of many doting mothers in overplaying her hand, and the more strongly she criticized Donald, the more determined Melinda became to cling to her marriage and demonstrate to her mother that she could run her own affairs and her own life. Like many daughters from broken homes, she seemed pathetically anxious that her own should not become one. And so, just before Christmas, some twelve weeks after the birth of Melinda's first child, Fergus by Caesarean operation, she left New York to join Donald in Washington.

Once again, however, the war raised obstacles to a normal existence. The United States had got into the war at a rather late stage but the Americans with their vast resources and genius for improvisation had caught up fast and their war effort was now on a vast scale. The Government had succeeded in mobilizing the whole country in one way or another and the whole country seemed to have arrived in Washington to discuss projects of every kind involving shipping, landing craft, manpower, materials, food supplies, finance, propaganda, economic warfare and, in fact, almost any topic it was possible to agree on.

Also the British alliance with the United States made special demands on the Embassy staff. Winston Churchill and President Roosevelt had built up a special relationship between the two countries. Lend-lease—the arrangement by which the United States loaned equipment to Britain and other allies for the duration of the emergency had come into effect early in 1941. Even before that, the Americans had built war planes to our orders, bought them from the U.K. but allowed Britain to continue using them. The U.S. War Department placed orders for munitions it did not need so that when finished they could be turned over to the British. A fleet of U.S. destroyers which had been taken out of service but not broken up were renovated and lent to the U.K. Strategic planning of the war and for concluding a peace settlement were discussed without reserve. There was contact at almost every level.

Amid the blizzards of paper work that these operations engendered, Donald Maclean thrived. A man who could fillet a memo and draft a reply in record time was invaluable. In December 1944 he was promoted to be an acting First Secretary, and acting Head of Chancery. All the hopes of his mother, who came to stay with him towards the end of 1946, were being fulfilled. But Lady Maclean's life style was as different from Mrs Dunbar's as brogue shoes are from high-heels. And Lady Maclean must have reflected primly, as yet another Bourbon hit the rocks, that her son had made a success of his career in spite of having married this frivolous little American.

Then, after a visit to London in the spring of 1947, there came a new promotion for Donald—he was appointed as Secretary to the British Delegation on the Combined Policy Committee, which determined the nuclear policies of the United States, the United Kingdom and Canada. It had been set up under the Quebec Agreement of 1943 signed between Churchill and Roosevelt, a compact so secret that even Congress knew nothing about it. It bound the signatories to disclose their atomic research programmes. In July 1946, some months before Maclean took up his new appointment, Congress had passed the MacMahon Act banning such exchanges. But its provisions did not cover such matters as the raw materials used for atomic projects or patents, details of which had inevitably to be published for the protection of the device or process concerned. Nor was there a ban on discussion between countries on what information, as time went by, it would be safe to publicize.

Thus Maclean knew, for example, how much uranium ore would be available to the three Governments, how much they would need for their individual atomic energy programmes and in what areas they were still collaborating on joint projects.

He must have known the source of the allied supplies of uranium, also the prices paid, and where the next purchases would be made: information invaluable to the Russians who, at a time when uranium was thought to be scarce, could step in ahead of the West. The figures of requirement would also give the Russians an idea of how many atom bombs the West was in a position to make. Maclean was also privy to the plans to extract uranium from South African gold about ten years before the details of the process were made public.

Atomic energy would not, of course, have been the only subject of interest to the Soviets with which Maclean would have familiarized himself. There was the Marshall Plan, first suggested in June 1947 for giving American economic aid to the war areas of Europe (its scope not originally confined to the Western Allies). The Soviets would want to know how much aid the U.S. was contemplating and how it would be received. There was also the fact that three months after the signature of the Brussels Defence Treaty of March 1948, Canada and the United States decided to send observers to the policy meetings of the five powers concerned. What were the observers told by the British?

There was the attitude of the British and United States Governments towards the newly formed United Nations, and also towards the expansion of the Soviet empire—a development which led

Mr Paul-Henri Spaak, at that time the Belgian Prime Minister and Minister for Foreign Affairs, to tell the General Assembly of the United Nations in 1948: 'There is but one great power that emerged from the war having conquered other territories, and that power is the U.S.S.R.'

In April 1948 Canada suggested that the Brussels Defence Pact should be superseded by a single mutual defence organization in which Canada would be ready to play her part. In June 1948 the resolution sponsored by Senator Vandenberg enabled the United States to take a similar stance. It was the prelude to the North Atlantic Treaty, signed, despite Russia's insistence that this would be regarded as a hostile act, the following April. Did Maclean tell the Soviet Union that Britain might back down if Stalin thumped the table hard enough?

If Maclean managed to keep the Russians abreast of these developments in addition to his work on the Combined Policy Committee and the Chancery in Washington, it was certainly a remarkable performance. In private, Donald drank at times as he always had, and found that alcohol induced gloom and self-reproach rather than laughter and good companionship as it did to his mother-in-law, for example. But he also gardened and played tennis twice a week—a pastime which commended him to the Ambassador Lord Halifax who, despite having only one arm, had a disconcertingly long reach and contrived to play a passable game. His colleagues working in the Embassy at the time included Paul Gore-Booth, who afterwards filled the post of Permanent Under-Secretary—the most senior appointment in the whole of the Service—Nicholas Henderson, a close friend of Maclean then and afterwards, who eventually became U.K. Ambassador first in Bonn and then in Paris, and at least three other percipient diplomats who achieved ambassadorial rank. None of them suspected him for a moment of leading a double life. Peter Masefield, who later became Chief Executive of British European Airways, was then Civil Aviation Attaché in Washington, said later: 'At that time I am sure they were an ordinary, pleasant, loyal English couple. Something must have happened later.' On the British side, there was no one to watch him once he left the office. To most of those at the Embassy, Maclean was the soulless bureaucrat, the perfect civil servant, cold and humourless. He did little entertaining and Melinda, for all her cosmopolitan upbringing, remained the shy little hostess still at sea in the political maelstrom around her. At times they stayed on the fringe of parties holding hands—either because Melinda had, despite her shyness, a streak of exhibitionism or because she needed to stop Donald from drinking. Diplomats came to accept the fact that the most serious discussion in the cultural field to be expected from

Melinda was on the sex-philosophy of De Maupassant or Stendhal.

A second child was on the way and still she had not achieved the perfect marriage. She had never found it easy to take an interest in her husband's work, but there were many attractions for her outside the Embassy circle. There were weekends on the farm at Merriebrook, canoeing trips in Connecticut, an expedition to colonial Williamsburg, ski-ing in Vermont, and in January 1947 a trip to Key West, Florida. Sometimes in the afternoons she would meet a friend for drinks at the Statler Hotel in Washington, looking for companionship in the same way as she once used to at the Café Flore. And even if she found no one to talk to, it was fun to be admired, if only from a nearby table. She sought the company of others wherever she might be, at the swimming-pool, the country club or even at a picture gallery.

Often she would find an excuse to run up to New York for a dentist's appointment. She would meet Harriet and sit at ease with her in the Palm Court of the Plaza Hotel, or the old Lafayette. The settlement made after her divorce from Hal Dunbar had left Melinda's mother very comfortably off with an apartment on fashionable East 69th Street where Melinda often stayed on for the night.

Then, in the midst of all this activity, came the news that Donald was to be posted from Washington to Cairo—as Counsellor— promotion for Donald but a loss to the Soviets of a first-class source in a top capital.

Neither he nor Melinda relished the move which would cut Melinda off once more from her mother and sisters, and Donald from Big Power politics. But this time 'the exigencies of the Service', as the official phrase has it, had to come first. Melinda and the children were packed off to New York on a farewell visit to her mother while Donald moved into a flat with the Embassy's First Secretary for Information, Nigel Gaydon, whose wife was then visiting her family in England. Once more, Maclean had an extra pretext for taking his 'work', i.e. briefcases stuffed with fascinating documents to somewhere not a thousand miles from the Soviet Consulate-General in New York. Not even his flatmate suspected for a moment that he was harbouring a super-spy.

# 10

# Crisis in Cairo

For the Macleans, Cairo in 1948, unlike London or Washington, really was 'abroad', and Melinda, despite being cut off from her mother and sisters, sparkled like champagne in its hot-house atmosphere. The Egyptian capital which, in the early forties had been threatened by Rommel's armies, had since blossomed out first as a leave-centre and then as a coveted leisure resort for the war-weary. Food, clothes, petrol and drink: all were off the ration.

Britain's stock stood high and the prestige which Montgomery and the British Army had earned for itself in routing first the Italians and then the Germans still lingered. Few Egyptians realized that the British Empire, with its imperial lifeline through the Suez Canal to India and the Far East, would soon dissolve. The wealthy Copts, hospitable by nature, entertained on a lavish scale, and treasured their European connections. The Arabs considered it a privilege to display in public their connection, if any, with the world of diplomacy and the British Embassy in particular. King Farouk, the last of his line, set them an example in prodigal expenditure.

Moreover in Cairo the Macleans faced none of the problems of house-hunting they had encountered in London and Washington. They were allotted an attractive house on Gezireh Island, one of the most spacious and attractive districts of the city. The street, the Sharia Ibn Zanki, in which the house lay, was remote from the heat, noise and squalor of commercial Cairo, and was lined with date palms and flowering trees and shrubs—mauve jacarandas, scarlet oleanders, purple bougainvillaea and the like.

Its rooms had been decorated and furnished by the Office of Works in London, with fine oriental rugs and luxurious curtains, and one of the features of the drawing-room was a mother-of-pearl table set out as a chess-board peopled with ivory chessmen. Four Sudanese servants and a butler, used to coping with a succession of luncheon parties, dinner parties, cocktail parties, went with the house. There was also a nanny and a gardener.

There had been times in Washington when Melinda, as wife of the acting Counsellor, had had to stand in as hostess for the wife of the Minister or even the Ambassador. As a young woman of twenty-seven, she had found it an ordeal to act as leading lady before the censorious eyes of wives who were much older than herself. She was thought to be shy and nervous. In Cairo, however, the Embassy was smaller and cosier; and there were fewer Americans to envy—and perhaps disparage—their countrywoman's social qualifications.

Melinda, if suitably primed, could always call up a soda-stream of small talk and social patter, and no accomplishment could have been more useful to her in the brittle, superficial and often insincere atmosphere of Cairo. She could talk with first-hand knowledge of Paris which was then, perhaps even more than now, the spiritual home of Middle East cosmopolitans. She had dress sense, and a good figure. She liked appearing in public whether it was at Groppi's, the cake and coffee rendezvous of the morning after the party, Shepheard's Hotel, for drinks before lunch, or the Auberge des Pyramides, a few miles out of Cairo, a popular meeting place for swimming, dining and dancing.

She gained much prestige when the Duke of Edinburgh visited Cairo and fancied the idea of a 'young people's party'. Melinda gave a dinner party for twelve of Cairo's young élite, and invited others in for an after-dinner reception and drawing-room games.

On quiet evenings the Macleans would make their way through the fence at the end of their garden into that of the Geoffrey Hoares for family Bridge. Geoffrey was up to international standard and his chief entertainment was to anticipate the more obvious mistakes which the other three would make.

Donald meanwhile was also acquiring new prestige. His Ambassador was Ronald Ian Campbell, known as 'little Ronnie' to distinguish him from the Ronald Hugh Campbell that Donald had known in Paris. And 'little Ronnie' shared 'big Ronnie's' good opinion of Maclean's abilities.

Donald began to cultivate the society of students at Cairo's university. He had a friendly personality which gave him access to circles barred to other foreign diplomats. It should certainly have been the duty of someone, though not necessarily of the Head of Chancery, to take note of the out-of-college activities of the students —rather as the Soviet recruiters had in pre-war Cambridge. In Egypt, however, the students had more influence than the undergraduates of Cambridge on the political life of their country, and an objective study of their thinking and political outlook could have been of considerable value to the British Embassy. They were, for instance, the most likely 'lead-in' to the underground terrorist organization, the Muslim Brotherhood, which, shortly after the Macleans arrived in Cairo, sent a student disguised in police uniform to assassinate the Prime Minister, Nokrashy Pasha, in his office one morning at 10 a.m. Donald may have warned his colleagues about the strength of the feeling among Egyptians at the continued 'occupation' by the British troops of a part of their country which had, in theory, become independent a quarter of a century earlier. He could perhaps even have got to hear of the existence of the group of junior Egyptian army officers formed under Mahommed Neguib in 1947 with the dual aim of expelling both the British and King Farouk from Egypt. He was probably one of the few Westerners who could have foretold 'Black Saturday' in January 1952 when Shepheard's Hotel, the British Overseas Airways offices and banks were burnt to the ground and at least three Britons killed. It is possible that Donald's reports—if any—on his meetings with students, were objective and unbiased.

At the time the Macleans were stationed in Cairo, a struggle to capture the minds of the students was being fought. The King, his ministers and the religious Muslim leaders were, of course, strongly opposed to any form of Communism, and the Egyptian police eventually expelled the Russian director of an import-export agency who had been working for Soviet Intelligence. Maclean had occasionally gone to receptions given by the firm. On the other hand, the Russians were on safe ground when they attacked the United States as the sponsors of the newly created state of Israel.

But the issue that gripped him most strongly was the difference in the standard of living between the pashas in Cairo and the peasants in the countryside. Britain, he felt, should take the lead in persuading King Farouk and his ministers to introduce reforms aimed at distributing the national wealth more evenly.

Unfortunately he did not expound these views only in confidential papers circulated in the Embassy. He publicly deplored both the failings of Farouk's ministers and the policies of his own Government towards Egypt, thus breaking two fundamental rules which forbid a diplomat to criticize in public either his own Government or the Government to which he is accredited. One evening he was asked to leave the Royal Automobile Club in Cairo—a favourite haunt of Farouk's—because of remarks he had made about the King.

It was a pointless exercise because, as long as his army remained loyal, King Farouk was perfectly well able to look after himself, without advice from Maclean or even the British Ambassador. To nationalist politicians of Egypt, the King took the line that he could not be more independent because his hands were tied by the British. And to the British he took the line that he could do no more than his best to control the anti-British demonstrations which were becoming more and more frequent.

Farouk possessed an extremely good internal police force with a

network of informers working in some cases in the homes of diplomats, and it was not long before the Egyptian police got to hear of
the English diplomat who attended potentially subversive meetings
of students and had been heard to make derogatory statements
about the Egyptian Government.

For Maclean it was Washington all over again. The really heavy
drinking which led to Maclean's recall from Cairo does not seem
to have started until the beginning of 1950 when he had been
in his post for more than a year, and the first serious incident
involved only Donald himself. He had been to two cocktail parties
in a single evening, as a result of which he cast off the inhibitions of
a diplomat. Later that evening he was found by the police lying
dead drunk on a bench near a grotto in the Ezbekiyeh public
gardens. At first, even when he showed them his identity papers,
they refused to believe he was a member of the British Embassy
staff. Somehow, the incident was hushed up. There were other less
publicized incidents at home and Maclean did so much damage
to the walls, woodwork and light fittings that the owner lodged a
complaint with the Embassy. When people asked Melinda to a
party she began to say: 'I'd love to come but please don't ask
Donald.'

Then came the famous Maclean expedition up the Nile. It had
been Melinda's suggestion that Harriet, who had come out to stay
with them that spring, would enjoy a surprise dinner party with
friends, the Tyrell-Martins, who lived at Helouan, fifteen miles
upstream from Cairo, Mrs Tyrell-Martin known to her friends as
'Babsy-Wabsy' was an English ex-deb and one of Cairo's prominent
party-goers. Two feluccas—small barge-like vessels rigged with the
traditional Arab three-cornered lateen sail—were hired for the
party of eight. The evening was badly chosen, for it was moonless,
and without charm, and only one felucca turned up instead of two,
halving the accommodation at a stroke.

The plan had been for Melinda as the organizer to provide drinks
to be taken during the voyage, while the Tyrell-Martins at Helouan
would provide dinner, to be served some time between eight and
nine. But there were two other obstacles to success. The wind
seemed to have dropped, while at the same time the Nile was beginning to flood—that is, some of the melted snow from the mountains
near the source was already beginning to increase the strength of
the current against which the boat, with its double load of passengers,
had to contend.

The result was that the journey, instead of taking two or three
hours, took nearly eight, and as Melinda had brought no food
there was nothing else to do but drink. It was so dark that the
party had to land once on the way in the hope of finding out just
where they were. An American who was in the party stumbled over

the jetty and fell to the ground, cracking his skull. As the evening drew on, Donald the diplomat was replaced by a roaring drunkard. All his anger turned on Melinda for not having organized things better. He seized her by the throat and made as if to strangle her. He lurched around the deck, his speech so slurred that no one could understand him. His friends had never seen him in this wild, berserk mood before.

When the party finally arrived at Helouan, the chief boatman, suspecting that there would be little chance of assembling his passengers again for an orderly return to Cairo, asked to be paid—double fare because he had taken twice as many people as originally bargained for. Donald threatened to throw him into the Nile. A nightwatchman guarding the Tyrell-Martin's house appeared, and, since the country was still under martial law as a result of the war with Israel, he carried a loaded rifle. Moreover, he turned out to be a relative of the boatman. Matters began to look serious—especially when Donald snatched the watchman's rifle, whirled it round his head and threatened to bash in his skull. Lees Mayall, another First Secretary at the British Embassy, who was standing near, was the only man tall enough to have a chance of grappling with Donald. He came up behind Maclean and tried to hold his arms. But Donald, the more heavily built of the two, lurched backwards, pinning Mayall against the edge of the bank and breaking his leg.

Maclean sobered up then and went off to the house for help. But the owner, having heard the screams of his would-be guests and the hoarse shouts of the watchman, was in no mood to become involved. It was some time before he agreed to admit Maclean and friends, and then only after he had locked up the supplies of liquor for which Maclean was already asking. In the end Maclean was issued with a single bottle of gin which he took to Mayall as a kind of peace offering and anaesthetic. Mayall obviously could not be moved so Maclean stayed with him until a taxi could reach Helouan. It was dawn before they got back to Cairo, where Mayall was packed off to hospital.

Not long afterwards, Donald Maclean's old friend Philip Toynbee turned up in Cairo. He had, of course, been a long-term non-conformist. When Melinda had met him in Paris ten years earlier she considered even then that he had a bad influence on her husband. While still at his prep school, Toynbee had written home: 'Dear Mummy and Daddy, Such a lovely thing has happened. An anti-Toynbee society has been started.' He ran away from his public school (Rugby) to join up with Esmond Romilly who at fifteen had run away from Wellington to found a centre of schoolboy rebellion in London. At Christ Church, Oxford, to which he won a History Scholarship, he learnt the art of emptying a whisky bottle against the clock, and joined the Communists, only to part company with them after the Stalin pact with Hitler. Now, still suffering from the emotional hangover of a divorce, he had arrived in Cairo as correspondent for the *Observer*. The two companions settled down to hit the bottle or, rather, bottles, for they mixed duty-free whisky with Egyptian *zebib*, a drink distilled from white grapes and flavoured with aniseed. Sometime during Toynbee's visit, Melinda and Harriet decided they would like to visit and stay at a desert oasis which was then being turned into an attraction for the richer tourist. It was probably then that Maclean, according to research carried out by Miss Margaret Pope, a British journalist who worked for the Egyptian paper *Al Misri*, once more got away on his own and sought solace in the docks of Alexandria, where the police locked him up in a compound specially reserved for drunken mariners. For two days—presumably during a weekend—he stayed in the jail, too overcome to give an account of himself, while the police pursued their inquiries along the waterfront, thinking that he might be a seaman missing from some ship.

The resources of the Embassy Press Department were again devoted to keeping Donald's indiscretion under wraps and out of the anti-British Egyptian newspapers, at least until Maclean had left Cairo—an event which occurred not long after Melinda and Harriet got back from their excursion.

On Monday 8th May Melinda, Donald, Harriet and Philip Toynbee had all been invited to a cocktail party, to be followed by a late evening party. Melinda went with the others to the cocktail party but was feeling in poor form and decided to spend the rest of the evening at home. Philip Toynbee also felt like an early night and went home with Melinda. But Donald went on with Harriet to the second party. As Donald began to get more and more drunk, Harriet decided that she, too, would come home. Donald stayed out until nearly three o'clock and when he tiptoed upstairs, it was to persuade Philip Toynbee to get up and join him in a round of visits to night clubs and bars. When the last of these had closed, Donald bethought him of an Embassy colleague at whose flat they might be able to continue drinking. They banged on the door until they were allowed in—and given a bottle of whisky. They were still in the flat, drunker than ever, when their host went off to work. Later during the day, they again ran short of liquor and Donald had another inspiration. He remembered a few days earlier meeting a girl who worked as a librarian in the American Embassy and had a flat in the same building. They ran upstairs, pushed past the servant who opened the door, and Donald then proceeded to wreck the flat, deriving extra satisfaction from the fact that it belonged to a woman (he hated all women—even Melinda —when he was drunk) and to an American woman. Maclean opened her cupboards and pushed her clothes down the lavatory pan. He smashed a table and Philip Toynbee remembered with astonishment that when Donald lifted a marble-framed mirror and dashed it into the bath, it was the bath that broke. Content at last, they went downstairs again to their previous host's flat to sleep off the effects of their spree. For their own safety they were locked in.

It was there, after discreet inquiries at the Embassy, that Melinda found Donald in the early evening, and with Harriet's help got him into the car and drove him home. Later, Harriet, with the help of a servant, got Toynbee into a car and took him home, too.

Now, at last, there was no question of being able to hush things up. The American Embassy, Donald's *bête noir*, was involved, and so was the British Embassy, for Donald's unexplained absence from work occurred on a Tuesday. The American Ambassador called on 'little Ronnie' and threatened that if Campbell did not report the incident to the Foreign Office, he would do so himself. There was only one thing to do. Melinda went to see Campbell and told him that Donald was suffering from a nervous breakdown and must be given sick leave to go to London and see his own doctor at once. Donald conceivably could have provided a second excuse for his breakdown, but it was one that Melinda could hardly offer. She was being pursued by an Egyptian prince who wished to have an affair with her, thus adding to the strain on Donald.

And so on the following Thursday, 11th May 1950, Donald was seen off by Melinda, Harriet and the British Minister, as he took the plane home to London. To Geoffrey Hoare, who happened to be flying to London on the same plane, Maclean seemed perfectly normal. He told Hoare that he was returning to London on private business for a few days. It was the last time the two men saw each other.

At this point, just after Maclean's breakdown, it seems legitimate to ask why, in view of the many incidents that preceded it, he was not sent home a good deal earlier.

There was, of course, an unusual sense of protective comradeship among colleagues in the Diplomatic Service, fuelled not to any great extent by a sense of public-school élitism (of which there is far less than is suspected by ex-pupils of comprehensive schools). Nevertheless a Foreign Office man posted abroad sees himself as a member of a closely knit team dedicated to promoting the interests of his country. These interests cannot be served unless the team presents a united front both to the nationals of the host country and to other foreign diplomats stationed there. In these circumstances, to listen to gossip from outsiders about a colleague in one's own Embassy weakens not only his position but one's own diplomatic impregnability. When anything goes wrong, it is best to hush it up.

Loyalties between diplomats in the same Embassy are strengthened by the fact that they spend so much more time together outside office hours than they would if they belonged to a purely commercial organization in which an office party is held perhaps once a year. Friendships grow up between the wives and children of Embassy families—particularly in posts where living conditions are difficult or where the British, for one reason or another, are locally unpopular.

Also, as a matter of self-interest, British diplomats must remain on friendly terms with each other. They never know that at some time in the future they will not be posted to an Embassy in the back of beyond where good relations between them are part of a survival kit.

Among Donald's colleagues, there was a natural reluctance to believe that such an able Head of Chancery had become an alcoholic. To Lees Mayall, for example, the Helouan incident was an isolated escapade for which a man did not deserve to have his career ruined. Donald was, during at least part of his time in Cairo, a cyclic drinker, that is, a drinker whose bouts are set off by psychic disturbances in between which there are recuperative calms. Those who had known Maclean longer realized that Donald could on occasion be two completely different men. There was, as Philip Toynbee first suggested, 'Sir Donald', the diplomat, wise, amiable, sober, dutiful and responsible, with a mildly cynical wit, an agreeable and cultivated conversationalist with a lively mind. And there was the fiery wild boar, the emblem on the Gordon's Export gin bottle, whose conduct in a drawing-room would probably have been no worse than Donald's when on a whisky-and-*zebib* diet. The idea that Donald was really two people with a single body occurred to Philip one morning in Cairo when, after a hard night's drinking, he helped Maclean to dress and go to work. Maclean was in a low state, retching and vomiting in between groans, and Toynbee thought it best to go with him in a taxi to the office. He need not however have worried, for when they neared the Embassy gates and came within sight of the guard who was about to salute, Maclean's personality switched. His features composed themselves into those of 'Sir Donald', the reincarnation of his father, the real Sir Donald.

The dual personality conception evidently appealed to Donald as a piece of rationalization and he talked without reserve to friends of the days when Gordon the beast reappeared and put the civilized 'Sir Donald' to flight.

Thus tradition, loyalty, self-interest and self-deception combined to shield Donald from criticism within the Embassy. And there were other reasons why the Ambassador was unaware for a considerable time of Gordon's existence. The chief of these was that there was no normal way in which the staff could communicate with the

Ambassador without their note going through Donald as Head of Chancery. Another factor was that the Ambassador did his work in the Residence, a building separated from the Chancery. There was no popping of the Ambassadorial head round the door of Donald's office on a day when he had a hangover. A third complicating factor during the hotter months of the year, or when the King moved out of Cairo to his palace beside the sea, was that the Ambassador moved, too—to a kind of sub-embassy in Alexandria, leaving Maclean, as often as not, as a backstop in Cairo.

The role of the Ambassador was crucial. He had formed a high opinion of Maclean's work and had reported favourably on it to London. How could he be expected to react when it turned out that Maclean, sent out to him as the white hope of the Foreign Office had, while under his command, turned into a drunkard? Surely the explanation must be, as Mrs Maclean suggested, that Maclean's collapse was due to overwork, in Cairo or more likely, Sir Ronald doubtless hoped, under his previous Ambassador in Washington.

The Ambassador's views on the subject may also have been prejudiced by the fact that he had already received and disregarded an earlier warning on the subject of Maclean's drinking habits. The warning had come from the Embassy Chief Security Officer, Major A. W. Sansom, who had already been engaged in a running battle with Maclean over Embassy security. Sansom, as he afterwards wrote in his autobiographical book *I Spied Spies*, was informed when he arrived in Cairo that his main duty would be to see that secret documents were not left lying around. The staff, he was told, had all been vetted for security, so that he would not have to worry about their loyalty, though of course if he saw anyone acting suspiciously he would have to look into the matter, however distasteful this might be. But Sansom, who had been trained to regard all staff on all occasions to be potentially disloyal, without waiting for them to be seen acting suspiciously, and whose training did not incline him to look on security work as being 'distasteful', was duly amazed by this introductory briefing.

It must be added, however, that security men never had an easy time in the Foreign Office and a posting to the Security Branch was regarded as a hindrance rather than a help to promotion.

Donald, according to Sansom, showed a particular interest in security arrangements almost as soon as he arrived at the Cairo Embassy (his Soviet contacts would want to know about that) but refused to respect the precautions which Sansom suggested. Maclean habitually left the Embassy with a briefcase stuffed with secret documents, and refused to countenance Sansom's suggestion that from time to time girl secretaries leaving the office should be searched to see that they were not taking out confidential documents. Maclean described the proposal as outrageous and, indeed, there was a general feeling within the Foreign Office that work could proceed only on a basis of trust and the knowledge that security is something looked after by policemen (although commercial firms today are advised to incorporate the right to search in their employees' contracts of engagement).

As time went on, Sansom got reports that Maclean not only drank too much but became violent when he did so. Maclean was also known to drink in the office. It was apparently a matter of gossip among Egyptian servants. Sansom says that he spoke to both Maclean and Mrs Maclean about these reports and learnt from Melinda that things had been just as bad in Washington. Melinda said that in Washington 'everyone' knew that Donald smashed the place up when he got drunk. Sansom wondered what he should do next. It would be useless to send a report to the Ambassador which would inevitably have to go through Donald as Head of Chancery. He therefore wrote to G. A. Carey Foster, then the Head of the Foreign Office Security Branch, who, in due course, passed the report on to Maclean's superiors at the Foreign Office.

They took it sufficiently seriously to send to Cairo a sealed hand written note 'for the eyes of the Ambassador only' so that no secretaries or cypher clerks (or Maclean) would handle it at either end. The note spoke of the reports that had reached London and asked Sir Ronald Campbell for his comments and suggested that he, too, should reply by handwritten sealed note.

The result was explosive. The Ambassador delivered an indignant protest at being questioned about his staff on the basis of reports from a third party (he could well have guessed, if he did not already know, that the third party was his own Security Officer). He had never in his experience in the Diplomatic Service heard of such a request being made to an Ambassador about his Head of Chancery. But since he had been asked for his views, he could say that Maclean was the most outstanding man in that position that he had met with during his service with the Foreign Office.

In these circumstances, it would have been understandable if the Ambassador, when preparing his report on the events leading up to Maclean's final request for sick leave, should have clung to the suggestion that, while his staff might have been overworked, they were not over-indulging, and it would not have been surprising if he had been rigorous in excluding from his report any lurid details which could possibly have been considered irrelevant to the occasion.

This, then, was the state of play in the middle of May 1950 when Donald Maclean arrived home and took up residence there with his mother.

# 11

# Maclean Takes The Cure

Maclean was received by the Foreign Office with surprising bland-
ness when he returned to London after his breakdown in Cairo. He
had lunch the day after he arrived with George Middleton, whom
he had known and played tennis with at the Embassy in Washington
and who was now Head of Personnel at the Foreign Office. According to Maclean in a letter dated 12th May to 'Lin' (Melinda), quoted
by Geoffrey Hoare, he 'told him (George Middleton) the score' and
found him 'very understanding' and 'extremely decent'.

Middleton arranged for Maclean to see a doctor, Henry Wilson,
who was employed as a consultant by the Foreign Office when, as
Maclean euphemistically put it 'their employee's psyches miss a
beat'. Wilson, then aged fifty-four, practised at 142 Harley Street
and was indeed one of the leading authorities in his field. He
specialized in 'psychiatric emergencies' which could mean treating
patients suffering from obsessions, hallucinations, sexual disorders
or even suicidal tendencies. He was also consulted by neurologists
and specialists in nervous diseases. He should have been the very
person to put 'Gordon' the pig to flight. Wilson was known within
his profession as a cheerful, kindly character, outspoken and
occasionally even explosive when colleagues questioned the importance and responsibilities of the psychiatrists' calling—as some
still did in those days.

As a Quaker, he should have appealed to Maclean, and he was
said to have a liberal outlook both in religion and politics. He was
also a water-colour painter of some distinction and had a house in
Donald's own university city, Cambridge.

At the time of Maclean's first letter to Melinda, he had not yet
seen Dr Wilson. But, he wrote: 'I have still have my lid off and I
am prepared, therefore to ask for help; if he (Dr Wilson) says I need
more exercise, I shall go round the corner to Erna (from Harley to
Wimpole—not far). I see no point in resisting George (Middleton's)
offer to start me on this path anyhow; but also if it looks like being
what I need, I should get an analysis for nothing; but I promise to
be expensive and go to Erna or elsewhere if it doesn't look good.'

Clearly, then, Melinda had already pressed Donald not to spare
expense but go to another psychologist, a woman who practised in
Wimpole Street, whom both she and Donald already knew. (Mrs

Dunbar was a great believer in the value of psychotherapy as a cure for 'inhibitions' and other obstacles to self-fulfilment, and at one time had both Melinda and Harriet analysed.)

So it was with some reservations that Maclean went two days later to see Dr Wilson. His misgivings increased when he learnt that Dr Wilson would like him to go into a clinic for an indefinite period for tests of all kinds. Then he resisted. He said that at the moment he could not face going into a clinic mainly because of fear but also because he doubted that there could be any sense in it.

With hindsight, one wonders what could Donald have been afraid of. Were his fears completely irrational? Did he think he would be hypnotized by MI5 men while in the clinic—or subjected to the truth drug or some other form of third degree? Did his Soviet contacts have fears that he might break down and confess once he was in the clinic, softened up by kindness of the sort that had made Fuchs tell all? Or did he feel that the tests would show what he must have known already, namely that he had already reached the lower slopes of the 'downhill-only' piste of alcoholism?

Anyway he was not immured in a clinic and was treated by psychoanalysis, which is what he said he came home for.

But who was the woman psychiatrist who analysed him? Donald talked about her quite freely as 'Dr Rosie'. Previous accounts have described her as an Austrian and a follower of Freud. In fact she was neither. Dr Erna Rosenbaum was born in Germany and studied medicine at Freiburg and Munich; after having qualified, she worked on the medical staff of a number of hospitals before moving to Zurich to be trained as a psychotherapist under the famous Carl Jung. She was not merely his pupil but was accepted into a kind of 'inner circle' which had grown up round him. She practised for some years in Berlin, and, according to a close relative, accepted some patients from the British Embassy there. She came to Britain in the late thirties and built up a successful practice in London with consulting rooms first at 14 Upper Wimpole Street, and later at 49 Wimpole Street.

Her friends in the Jung Society knew her as a hospitable, cultivated woman of considerable charm and intelligence. She married Dr R. Redfern, also a psychoanalyst, some years before she treated Maclean.

In short, there was no medical reason why Dr Wilson if not the Foreign Office should not have approved of Maclean's visits to her.

From all accounts Dr Rosie was widely known for her matter-of-fact, down-to-earth, no-nonsense views on the problems of psychoanalysis which she expressed in a strong German accent. She most decidedly rejected the more speculative and sometimes fanciful theories which fashionable writers of the time attributed to Freud or Adler. Exactly what she said to Maclean we do not know, but he found the sessions something of an ordeal and there were times when he hung about outside the door of her consulting-rooms like a schoolboy before an awkward interview with the headmaster.

As far as a layman can understand these matters, Jung's principles which Dr Rosenbaum would have followed in her analysis of Maclean showed a considerable advance over the earlier techniques of Freud.

Freud, for example, had concentrated on tracing back psychiatric problems to maladjustments, particularly in the sexual sphere, during early childhood. For example, he suggested that one cause of homosexualism in men might be that a man, when young, felt guilty about being sexually attracted by his mother and therefore turned away, for safety, towards his own sex.

To Jung, however, it was not enough to discover the cause of the patient's mental blockage. He was more interested in the direction in which the patient wanted to move. The whole personality of the patient had to be harmonized and integrated by reassessing not only his inherited male and female characteristics and primitive instincts, but also the persona ('personality') he had acquired through feeling obliged to conform to the demands and expectations of society. All the unconscious forces in the mind of the patient had, in Jung's view, to be reconciled and directed towards the development of a single, well-balanced self, in which all psychic conflicts had not merely been analysed but resolved.

This is a lot to ask of any psychoanalyst whose patient, as in Maclean's case, has acquired a persona not in order to respond to the demands of society but in order to reject not only the demands but the society that made them.

Secondly, there was the problem of Donald's homosexual leanings. It is now generally accepted that there is no fail-safe way of converting a male homosexual into a heterosexual. But early diagnosis leading to the eradication of the maternal guilt complex offers the best chance. But 'overt feminine mannerisms' which Donald certainly had in his youth, and lack of heterosexual experience, from which Donald certainly suffered at the time of his marriage, are additional obstacles to success. In practice, about one in three of those who wish to change are able to do so—if they are under the age of thirty-five. Donald was now thirty-seven.

Maclean's alcoholism added to the difficulties of the case. Originally he had drunk to drown periodical feelings of guilt. But now, the desire for alcohol had taken over in its own right. The main symptoms of persistent drinking were there—the aggressive behaviour, indefinable fears, the persistent remorse, the unreasonable resentments, the early-morning drinks. Thus what was once the side effect of a psychological problem had now become a medical one as well. Neither was readily curable.

But Donald must have hoped for the best. Back in May, the night after he reached home he had written to Melinda:

I am so grateful to you my sweet for taking all you had to put up with without hating me. I am still rather lost, but cling to the idea that you do want me to be cured and come back. I am weary of making promises of being a better husband, since the past ones have all been broken; but perhaps if some technician will strengthen my gasket and enlarge my heart I could make a promise that would stick. Anyhow you have been very sweet to me and I will try to give you something in return. I was overwhelmed with sadness at leaving the boys; I suppose it affects one particularly because they expect one to be there and have no means of understanding why one goes away; it is, however, I suppose, bathetic rather than pathetic as long as they are happy; I know you will keep them so. I hate having left you with all the responsibility for the house, family, car, servants, and long to hear that you are managing all right. Please say a special word of thanks to Harry (Harriet) for me if this reaches you in time. She was so kind when she had much reason not to be and I shall try never to forget her sweetness any more than I shall forget yours.

I saw the Italian film about the bicycle thief today. It was very good, but too sad for you my chickabid!

I will try to keep you posted. I think very much of you my darling, miss you badly and love you. Don't feel sad about me as I will come back a better person and we can be happy together again I am sure.

D.

From this letter it seems that Donald believed he might be returning to Cairo. He had told Geoffrey Hoare—though perhaps this was merely for public consumption—that he was going to London for a few days and may have said something of the same kind to Melinda. It would certainly have strengthened his aversion to entering a clinic for an indefinite period. On 7th June he wrote to tell Melinda that he had now had physical tests including an encephalogram at the Maida Vale Hospital and that the results were negative. He does not seem to have realized yet, or, if he did, did not tell Melinda that the Foreign Office had decided to give him six months' sick leave, by which time his place at the Embassy in Cairo would presumably have been filled.

Even if he had known that he would be out of circulation for six months, he may have hoped to keep the news from reaching Cairo. That way there would be less permanent damage to his career.

As it was, Melinda and the family were kept in suspense. They were not taking home leave this summer and a holiday house by the sea near Alexandria had already been booked. They were due to move into it on 1st July. If Donald were going to come back in, say, six weeks, even if he were still on sick leave, the holiday plans could stand, If not, they would have to resign themselves to sticking out the heat of Cairo. The problem was solved when Mrs Dunbar arrived in Cairo on 1st June.

By now the story of Donald's escapade had got into the Egyptian papers and it was most unlikely that he would be brought back to Cairo. So the holiday in Alexandria was cancelled and Mrs Dunbar took the family to Spain instead. Before leaving she had to settle some remarkably heavy liquor bills, for Donald, either from laziness or caution, had drawn only a small portion of his alcohol supplies through diplomatic duty-free channels. It was probably the period when Melinda's marriage to Donald came nearest to breaking point.

Meanwhile, Donald continued his visits to Dr Rosie without, so far as his friends could tell, material benefit to his condition. As Cyril Connolly wrote in his book *The Missing Diplomats*:

> His appearance was frightening: he had lost his serenity, his hands would tremble, his face was usually a livid yellow and he looked as if he had spent the night sitting up in a tunnel. One evening a man leaving a night-club got into an empty taxi and found him asleep on the rug. When awakened he became very angry and said he had hired it for the evening as his bedroom. ....
> Though he remained detached and amiable as ever, it was clear to us that he was miserable and in a very bad way. In conversation a kind of shutter would fall as if he had returned to some basic and incommunicable anxiety.

One evening in the Gargoyle he lurched over to a table at which Goronwy Rees was sitting and declared in a threatening manner: 'I know all about you. You used to be one of us. But you ratted.' Then he collapsed on the floor breathing heavily. He was in no position to join Melinda and Mrs Dunbar in Spain.

But it was Maclean's sex-life that most worried his friends. It is of course impossible to know exactly what advice he was getting from Dr Rosie or whether he was co-operating with her. But he behaved as though he had received instructions to cast away all feelings of guilt about his homosexual desires—and learn to live with himself without shame. He conceived a passion, about which he talked freely to friends, for a negro porter at the Moonglow Nightclub in Percy Street, and though his advances were repulsed, he was left with the feeling that he could no longer bear the thought of living with Melinda. His feelings of guilt seemed stronger than ever. He began to suffer from delusions.

In September he wrote Melinda a letter of almost total despair. He deplored his behaviour as a husband and a father and admitted that he would understand if Melinda never returned to him. Indeed, it might be better for her own welfare and the children if she never saw him again.

And so Melinda, who might have expected to see Donald in

Spain or at least receive better news of him, realized that here was a new emergency. She left the children in Paris and flew to London. There she sought advice in all quarters: from Donald's friends, his family, and his psychiatrist. Their collective opinion was that Donald would be a lost man if she did not return to him. A second breakdown of the kind that he had suffered in Cairo would finish his career for good. And if that happened, what was to become of the children? Obviously he drank more when Melinda was away, and, equally, his sex-life became more abnormal.

Dr Rosie seems to have convinced Melinda that, although her analysis of Donald was not complete, the marriage might yet be saved if Donald could face his problems more frankly and discuss them with his wife, and this in turn would help to cut down his drinking (though Donald, who probably knew his state of health a good deal better than either Dr Rosie or Dr Wilson, had his doubts). After spending a fortnight together in London, Donald and Melinda decided to try again. Donald would ask the Foreign Office if he could be given a post at home which did not entail giving or going to diplomatic parties. They would live in the country, near enough to London for Donald to be able to commute, but not so near that he would have time for a drink before catching his train.

So Melinda brought the children over from Paris and the family established themselves at a country club not far from Sevenoaks, while they looked round the neighbourhood for a house.

Unfortunately they had still not found anywhere suitable by the beginning of November 1950 when Donald's period of sick leave ended, but just before Christmas they were able to move into Beacon Shaw, an unfashionable-looking stucco and tile-hung house fifteen minutes walk from the village of Tatsfield, near the Surrey–Kent border. It stood at the end of a curved drive behind its own little beech wood where bluebells flowered in the spring, and had a view beyond the garden over open fields to the south. It also had eleven bedrooms, if you counted the attics. Meals had to be cooked on a solid-fuel stove and water pumped by hand. Hot water was provided by a solid-fuel boiler in the cellar. The price was £6,500, £2,000 of which was provided by Melinda. But somehow the Macleans managed to give a house-warming party.

And so Maclean resumed work. Students of the affair have wondered how it was that the reports of both psychiatrists who had treated Maclean were considered by the Foreign Office to be sufficiently encouraging for them to take him back at the end of his sick leave, when he was clearly far from well.

But he had been checked and passed as fit at the beginning of June. Since then he had enjoyed six months freedom from the strain of office work and it could have been urged that far from being unfit for work, Maclean might be in danger of becoming so if he continued much longer in idleness. In any case, Dr Wilson's name had been suggested to the Foreign Office by the Treasury,—the ultimate authority within the Civil Service on staff matters. He was not a Foreign Service expert but an outside consultant who might advise but could not command.

But the clinching argument was a simpler one. In October, Melinda went to the Foreign Office with the news that she was pregnant. This was evidence that anyone could accept without special knowledge of the realms of the unconscious. It was unchallengeable proof that the Maclean marriage which had been on the rocks after Maclean had his breakdown in Cairo had now been rescued. A new start, a fresh child in the family, and no entertainment allowance would surely complete the cure and save the career of a promising diplomat.

And so Donald settled down to the life of a commuter. The family became—and still are—popular among the villagers of Tatsfield, where the theory is widely held that Donald was blackmailed into spying because he had been a queer.

Sylvia Shrubb who looked after the Maclean children was convinced that Donald thought the world of Melinda and the family. The two boys went to local schools and their names, it was understood, had been entered for British public schools. Frank Watson who drove Maclean home each evening from Woldingham remembers Donald as 'very likeable'. 'He never pushed to the front at the barrier at Woldingham,' Mr Watson remembers, 'and when we drove over a rabbit one evening, he worried about it. (But I didn't, I went back afterwards and took it home for dinner.)'

There has also been criticism of the decision to appoint Maclean on his return to the Foreign Office to a key job as Head of the American Department. But if he was to be accepted back into the Service at all, he had to be offered an appointment appropriate to his rank and experience. The American Department job was the only suitable post open at that time.

Also, at this moment, only the tight-lipped security officers suspected that Maclean—or some other senior officer in the Foreign Office—was betraying the secrets of his country. To the average Foreign Office man, the idea would have been fantastic—incredible. It would be almost easier to imagine the Steward of the Jockey Club doping racehorses.

But the political climate of the world was changing. Who would have thought, for instance, in August 1939 that Stalin would make an alliance with Hitler or in October 1939 that the Soviet Union would ever fight on the side of the West against Hitler? In the early 1940s the Soviet Union became 'our gallant ally' and had remained in that position for nearly five years. Now, however, a reassessment of that, too, was taking place.

# 12

# A Change In The Weather

Mistrust of the Soviet Union's motives and intentions continued to grow in the West as a result of the Polish disaster. The Communists were already strongly entrenched in Yugoslavia; in December 1944 they sprang to arms in Greece in a determined effort to seize control of the Government. A civil war had to be fought before the country was saved.

The Russians surged across Austria in the closing stages of World War II and declared—using the same tactics they had employed in Poland—that they were setting up a Provisional Austrian Government in their zone of occupation. They refused at first to admit any Western missions to Vienna; those that arrived were confined to city limits or, as happened to the British Mission early in June 1945, ordered to leave Vienna.

A Soviet drive to overrun Denmark had been narrowly averted when Montgomery pushed forward to Lübeck, but Berlin had already been surrounded by Soviet forces towards the end of April 1945 and Stalin was doing his utmost to exclude Western contingents due to be stationed there. He said the city streets had been mined and were still unsafe.

The meaning of these developments soon became clear to those journalists, politicians and the troops of Western Allies who watched the Russians systematically despoiling the territories they had conquered. During the war, the Russians had been our comrades in arms, and it might have seemed unreasonable to withhold from them information which would help them to fight more effectively against a common enemy. Now, times had changed; the Russians were being uncultivated and non-co-operative, and a menace to the economic recovery, if not the peace of Europe.

Russia held up the signing of peace treaties with Italy, Finland, Bulgaria, Hungary and Rumania for nearly two years. Unsuccessful conferences on the future of Germany and Austria took place in March 1947 in Moscow, and London, November 1947. Communist governments were set up not only in Poland, Rumania, Bulgaria and Hungary but also in Czechoslovakia, where Jan Masaryk, the Foreign Minister who had always claimed that his country would be able to maintain her independence despite her alliance with the Soviet Union, was found dead on the pavement beneath the window of his home in Prague.

And whereas the Western Allies had begun to demobilize their armies and within a year their world strength had shrunk from about five million men to less than a million, the size of Soviet Union forces remained practically unchanged.

Americans, some of whom may have looked on Europe's fears as exaggerated or even hysterical, took heed when they realized that the Russians were not prepared to help re-establish a self-supporting Germany unless it formed part of the Communist empire. Also, it was clear that this empire, established largely by military force, would continue to grow unless Europe possessed its own means of defence.

But the ink had hardly dried on the defence treaty signed by Belgium, France, Luxembourg, the Netherlands and Great Britain in 1948 when the Russians attempted to blockade and starve out western Berlin. The siege lasted for 323 days and was raised only with the help of an Anglo-American airlift of food and fuel to the beleaguered city.

For a short time after the end of World War II American self-confidence had been sustained because the U.S. alone possessed the atom bomb which had been used with such spectacular success in the closing stages of the war against Japan.

But this complacency was soon abruptly disturbed. In September 1945, Igor Gouzenko, a young cable clerk at the Soviet Embassy in Ottawa, risked his life and broke away to tell the Canadian authorities that their Soviet ally had been spying on them.

To people in Britain the chief result of Gouzenko's revelations was the arrest in March 1946 of Dr Alan Nunn May, then a lecturer in Physics at King's College, London, and previously at Cambridge with Burgess and Maclean. Despite his previous Communist leanings, Nunn May had been employed since 1942 on top secret nuclear research, particularly in the production and use of refined uranium at the Canadian Government's plant at Chalk River. Under the code name Alek, he had been passing information to Lieutenant Angelov, Assistant Military Attaché at the Soviet Embassy, known to him as 'Baxter', both about the methods used to refine uranium and the properties of the refined material.

However, Nunn May was only one of a very large Soviet spy ring whose members were inquiring not only into nuclear weapon research in Canada but also into such things as radar, anti-submarine devices and the internal structure of the Canadian Army. It was not long before the alarm felt in Canada spread over the border into the United States.

The Americans had done what they could over the years to protect their own atomic research secrets. (President Truman himself was not told the facts of the atom bomb project until April 1945 although the first controlled self-sustained chain reaction explosion had been carried out in America by Dr Enrico Fermi three years earlier.)

There had, however, been collaboration with the British. In the early stages of the war scientists in the U.K. had been working on the problems of producing nuclear explosives, and enough progress had been made by August 1941 to justify setting up a section of specialists to work under government supervision. To disguise its real purpose the section was given the code name 'The Directorate of Tube Alloys'.

Since the United States had also been conducting research in the same field, President Roosevelt agreed in October 1941 that the two countries should conduct their researches jointly. A year later it was possible to consider setting up large scale production plants and it was at this point that the Americans took the first steps to protect their security. Late in 1942 the President decided that only information that the recipient was capable of utilizing should be passed to him. This decision was followed in August 1943 by the Quebec agreement already mentioned which established that the future programme would be agreed by a joint body on which Britain, the United States and Canada were represented and that it would be the responsibility of this body to allocate the raw materials, the plants to which it should be directed, the methods of research and the facilities to be offered to British scientists in Canada and the U.S. Research and development discoveries were to be shared between workers in the same field, but no information was to be passed on without the consent of the party that had provided it. A similar and more formal agreement to be renounced only with the consent of both parties was concluded in September 1944. It obliged the two sides to exchange military and commercial information needed for the defeat of Japan, but the U.S. Senate Foreign Relations Committee knew nothing of it and it was never ratified by the Senate; and the MacMahon Act of July 1946, which set up the U.S. Atomic Energy Commission, and the Blair House Agreement of 1947 specifically ruled out military items from the list of what could be passed on. Thus some, at least, of the loopholes were closed.

Then came the question of whether the United States should proceed further and manufacture the very much more powerful hydrogen bomb. Here, security was less complete.

Originally the raw material for the American atom bomb had been under the control of U.S. Army engineers and its generals, who naturally enough saw nuclear energy in terms of an explosive, the formula for which should be kept a close military secret. But once the war was over, politicians, genuinely disturbed that they had been kept in ignorance of the original A-bomb project and anxious to get their fingers on the levers of power, played on the public fears that the trigger-happy generals might be in favour of threatening a preventive war against the Soviet Union. They succeeded in taking control out of the hands of the military, and the Atomic Energy Commission established in 1946 had a leavening of civilians, some of whom were rather less security-minded.

At the same time civilians outside the Commission also expressed doubts as to whether the United States should proceed further and manufacture the hydrogen bomb. The question was still under active discussion during the autumn of 1949 and no decision had been taken when two events of major importance occurred.

One was the discovery from atmospheric tests that the Soviet Union had carried out its first nuclear test explosion. Previously it had been thought that it would take the Russians at least until 1952 to perfect their own bomb; indeed, there had been some doubts as to whether there was really any need for America to monitor the atmosphere with a view to detecting nuclear explosions. From then on the monitoring of the atmosphere was intensified, although the Russians were not officially told about this for nearly ten years afterwards.

The second shock which led the United States to press ahead with the hydrogen bomb was the certainty after more than four years that a British scientist, Dr Klaus Fuchs, had as far back as June 1945 already told the Russians about the original American bomb, its size, what it contained, how it was built and how it was detonated. On 2nd June 1945 Fuchs had driven his battered Chevrolet car to the Castillo Bridge at Santa Fé and handed over a sheaf of typewritten notes about the crucial test in the production of the original atom bomb which was to be carried out soon afterwards on 16th July at Alamogordo. Fuchs had been working with the Americans at Los Alamos where the bomb had been assembled; he knew it was about to be taken to pieces, re-assembled, hoisted to the top of a steel tower and detonated. At the same time, independently, David Greenglass, a U.S. Army technician, had supplied the Russians with drawings of how it was proposed to detonate the explosion.

Fuchs was finally trapped when someone remembered a British intercept of a coded Soviet message which mentioned that a Russian spy had a sister at an American university. Of the scientists who could have described the atom bomb, only Fuchs had a sister who had studied at a college in the States. Fuchs, in turn, identified Harry Gold, to whom he had given the particulars of the bomb, and Gold in turn led the investigators to Julius and Ethel Rosenberg, afterwards executed in the electric chair. Fuchs was arrested in February 1950—just about the time of Maclean's breakdown in Cairo, a coincidence which has led to some speculation that Maclean was in mortal terror that Fuchs would compromise him.

One of the least satisfactory aspects of the case was that it had taken nearly four years for the sleuths to discover Fuchs's treachery after a British security officer in Washington helped to eliminate other suspects, and the public began to ask what had happened to American security services. Disquiet had been building up ever since the Japanese surprised the U.S. Fleet in Pearl Harbour and sank four battleships, two of them at their moorings, at the apparent failure of the U.S. intelligence services. Yet no public discussion of the U.S. espionage or counter-espionage services could take place without disclosing that the U.S. had in fact broken the Japanese code system, a fact which had to be concealed until after the Japanese surrender.

In fact, however, the U.S. security services were gradually being reshaped and modernized. Roosevelt had considered the reorganization shortly before his death, and, early in 1946, President Truman set up a Central Intelligence Group, which, after the National Security Act of 1947, became the CIA or Central Intelligence Agency. Its Director was named in the Act as Chief Intelligence Adviser to the President and the CIA was to report to the National Security Council, the body which advised the President and is chaired by him. It was, of course, distinct from the Federal Bureau of Investigation whose main task, more akin to that of Scotland Yard's Special Branch, was to frustrate attempts by U.S. citizens and others to subvert or disrupt the internal security of the State. The aim at this time was to assemble a permanent staff of intelligence experts who would collect and assess 'white' research —that is information obtained in a legitimate manner. Within the CIA were two bodies, the Office of National Estimates which worked on published statistics, and the U.S. Intelligence Board, which correlated these statistics with such other information as it was able to obtain.

But in addition to a defensive role and the collection of 'white' research, the Act empowered the CIA to collect 'covert' as well as open intelligence and to intervene covertly in the affairs of other nations when directed to do so. Thus the CIA was an all-embracing organization in which conflicts of interests between its different branches were certain to arise.

In charge of the CIA during its early days from 1950 to 1953 was General Bedell Smith who had been Eisenhower's Chief of Staff in World War II in the European theatre from June to

December 1945, and U.S. Ambassador in Moscow from 1946 to 1949 during some of the tenser phases of the Cold War.

It was an appointment reassuring to the U.S. Service Chiefs who had feared that their influence was being eroded by 'politicians'. It was also natural that Bedell Smith should be interested primarily in protective security—that is in protecting America's secrets from the Russians. Understandably, after what had happened, he was not even prepared to take the British on trust.

Indeed, all officers in charge of protective security prefer to rely only on their own countrymen for the work—men whose records can be checked exhaustively before they are engaged. But the men whose job is to secure covert intelligence see things differently. Their work cannot be carried out if they have to rely only on men of probity. They need the help of agents who, from motives of greed, spite, vanity, pride, adventurism, 'patriotism' or a love affair, are willing to betray their country. In some cases they are prepared to work with double agents, that is, men who are betraying information to both sides, in the belief that they can feed more false information to the enemy through a double agent than he can feed to them—or alternatively they hope to win over the agent so that he or she will work exclusively for them in the future.

In its efforts to prosecute and convict a spy, a government may be forced to reveal information about the workings of its own security services to an extent that inflicts far more damage than the original spy. Thus, according to the undercover men, when security forces discover an enemy agent, it is often better in the true interests of security *not* to prosecute him, but instead to turn him into a double agent.

In their view the best way of maintaining security is to discover as much as possible about the enemy intelligence services, which cannot be accomplished by staying at home, or by operating only in territories where they can act with the support of the police.

Bedell Smith's deputy, Alan Dulles, one of those whose thoughts ran along these lines, during World War II had already worked with great success in Switzerland in charge of the Office of Strategic Services, at that time the main body responsible for espionage, counter-espionage, underground resistance movements, guerilla campaigns and the like in German-occupied Europe. And he was by no means averse to the more active forms of intelligence-getting such as using U2 spy planes, tunnelling into the East Berlin telephone exchange or breaking codes by feeding false messages to known enemy agents in the hope that they would give away their codes when transmitting them.

But inevitably he had to devote some of his attention to protective security at home, particularly in connection with Soviet atom espionage. One reason for this was the certainty that the leakage of information on the atom bomb from Los Alamos, later traced to Fuchs, was not the only one to take place in 1945. There had been other serious leakages at the same time through the British Embassy in Washington. The Soviet Consulate General in New York had made the mistake of using a low-grade cypher which told Western intelligence monitors that a spy code-named 'Homer' was delivering documents of a top level character from the British Embassy in Washington to a Soviet contact. Kim Philby, the spy who, all along, had been a double agent, says that he was briefed in London, shortly before he went to Washington to take up his appointment as Head of the British Secret Intelligence Services in September 1949, and told that joint investigations by the U.S. and British Secret Services had led to a strong suspicion that there had also been a leakage through the British Embassy in Washington four years earlier. (He could equally well have heard this from the Russians, who in turn had been informed by Judith Coplon, a young woman who worked in the U.S. Department of Justice building.)

Philby claims, no doubt with some truth, that he already had a pretty good idea as to who might have been involved in the leakage. He must have known, if only from Cambridge days, of Maclean's views, but he also knew of other far more convincing evidence. Indeed he afterwards said that he had two 'professional' i.e., clandestine meetings with Maclean. Also General Walter Krivitsky, a Red Army Intelligence Officer who had defected to the West in 1937, had reported that the Head of the Soviet Intelligence Services in Europe had recruited a few years earlier a young man of good family from Scotland who had been educated at Eton and Oxford and had afterwards joined the Foreign Office. (Kim Philby realized that 'Eton and Oxford' need not be taken too literally but was an approximation for the kind of education Donald Maclean had enjoyed.) Krivitsky had said that the spy was an idealist who worked without payment for the Soviet Union. Nor was this an isolated report; for Konstantin Volkov, a Vice-Consul attached to the Soviet Consulate in Istanbul, who planned to defect to the West in August 1949 but was spirited away and disposed of before he could be interrogated, had declared in a preliminary statement to the British Vice-Consul in Istanbul that he knew the names of two Soviet agents working in the Foreign Office.

By the time Guy Burgess arrived in Washington on his final diplomatic mission, about a dozen reports had been circulated on the identity of 'Homer'. The names of several eminent British diplomats who had been stationed in Washington during the critical period were now considered—including Roger Makins (afterwards Lord Sheffield), the man who, it afterwards turned out, had been given the special task of reporting on Maclean's work. There was also Sir Paul Gore-Booth, later Head of the Foreign Office, who might have been considered an idealist since he was not only a Christian Scientist but also a teetotaller.

The inquiries, however, seemed to be proceeding with uncanny slowness. One reason for this could have been that since the offence had been committed on U.S. territory, the case was under the control of the Federal Bureau of Investigation, which was more interested in uncovering the misdeeds of Americans—as, for instance, Alger Hiss—on whom it could lay its hands, than in tracking a shadowy figure in a foreign embassy, who, perhaps, might already be out of the country.

Secondly, acting on past experience, both SIS and CIA had looked first for the kind of embassy employee they would expect the Soviets to bribe, threaten or flatter, rather than the sort of official who would work for the Russians without reward. They originally visualized the spy as someone who might indeed have access to important documents, but whose personality or position was sufficiently colourless for him to be free of suspicion. It is not necessary to suppose that the investigators were prejudiced by class-consciousness into believing that only lesser breeds drawn from the working classes would betray their country. But on the face of it a diplomat whose abilities and discretion had hoisted him to the upper ranks of his profession would be less likely to commit himself to the service of a foreign power.

One might also add, however, that in any organization, class-ridden or not, it needs far greater courage, other things being equal, to accuse a leading figure, recognized by the great majority of his colleagues as occupying a position of strength, than it does to investigate an employee who occupies a relatively obscure post.

But a third reason for the slow progress of the investigation could have arisen from the fact that soon after the tell-tale messages from the Soviet Consulate General had been decoded, the Russians appeared to change their cypher, and the messages became extremely difficult to unravel.

One pointer, however, could possibly have helped the sleuths. Lewis Strauss, pillar of the U.S. Atomic Energy Commission, discovered in 1948 that 'an alien' had a permanent pass that allowed him to enter the AEC building and to walk about inside unattended, a special privilege not even granted to General Groves, the man charged with carrying out the U.S. atomic programme. Strauss heard from Rear Admiral John Gingrich, the Head of AEC Security, that Maclean had been using his pass after office hours, several times a week and had been doing so over a period of months. (Security men usually distrust anyone who habitually works late when no one else is there to see just what they are up to.) Presumably he was getting worthwhile information there that could be obtained in no other way.

The pass was immediately cancelled. But the resentment that this aroused among the British helped to cover Donald's indiscretion, and perhaps hindered rather than helped the investigations that would have led to his exposure. The Foreign Office remained indulgent towards Donald, even when he made anti-American statements in public and, instead of looking more closely into his conduct, moved him to Cairo—with promotion.

But the British and American security sleuths, renouncing class consciousness, stayed on the trail, and one of them noticed, perhaps from the cables they had deciphered, or perhaps merely from the intervals between 'Homer's' reports and the questions that followed them, that 'Homer' was apparently in New York for two days in each week.

Then someone remembered that when Maclean was working in Washington, there were times when his wife was in New York, and that he went there for two days in the week. He also paid regular visits to the British Information Services in New York. It was the missing clue.

# 13

# Maclean's Countdown

Meanwhile Burgess, though recalled to London, showed no great eagerness to leave the shores of America where he felt so unhappy. Nor, in truth, was the Foreign Office in a pressing hurry to see him. They had almost certainly decided to ask him for his resignation and perhaps a few days' reflection on his part would make him more ready to give it. His passage home, not being a matter of urgency, was booked on the *Queen Mary* sufficiently far ahead to allow him to take a short holiday in New York.

The Russians in London would need a few days in which to plan Maclean's escape, and it would take time for the plans to be approved in Moscow and circulated to those who would have to put them into action. Burgess, of course, would have to be kept in touch with these developments and it would be easier to hold discussions with him in New York where he was not under the immediate eye of the Embassy than in Washington—or London.

Once aboard the *Queen Mary*, Burgess made friends with a young American 'an intelligent, progressive sort of chap' whom he introduced in London as Bernard Miller; he let it be known in London that this was an emotional relationship. Jack Hewit described Miller as a medical student who had come to London to study here, but other reports placed him as proprietor of a semi-political off-beat theatre in New York. While in London he stayed at the Green Park Hotel, which suggests that his income was that of a proprietor rather than a student.

After landing at Southampton on 7th May 1951, Burgess went to spend the weekend with his old friend Goronwy Rees, who was then living at Sonning-on-Thames, and Burgess would have gone to Sonning again for a second weekend if Rees had not put him off. The third weekend, in any case, was going to be different for Burgess.

For on Wednesday 23rd May he booked a cabin for two on the steamer *Falaise* which was leaving Southampton two days later, on Friday 25th May, for a weekend cruise, calling first at St Malo and then at Jersey. He gave the booking office his own name and told them that his fellow passenger with whom he was sailing would probably be 'Miller'.

In the meantime he had got in touch with Maclean. According

to Philby's account, he had told Burgess to see Maclean at the Foreign Office on the pretext of reporting on his experiences in the States. During the interview, he was to push a paper over the desk to Maclean telling him the time and place of a *rendezvous* where they could meet. Cautious as ever, however, Burgess thought it might be easier to contact Maclean direct at home, for telephone calls to the Foreign Office normally go through the Downing Street switchboard which might already be monitored. On 18th May, therefore, Burgess rang Lady Maclean, Donald's mother, to ask for her son's home number. But when Guy heard that Donald was living at Tatsfield, a small village reached through a manual exchange at Westerham through which calls could also have been monitored, he reverted to the original plan. The meeting, however, took place on a sofa in the corridor outside Maclean's office. There was nothing especially peculiar about this; indeed, it is a stratagem often adopted in the Foreign Office when a senior official wishes to have a confidential discussion uninterrupted by secretaries, messengers or telephone calls, and Guy must surely have used the technique himself. He suggested later that Maclean might have thought his office had already been 'bugged'.

Guy declared that he went to see Maclean as Head of the American Department not only to give him a report on the situation in America (which the Ambassador had refused to forward from Washington) but also to deliver 'innocent' messages from friends (for he had taken the precaution of seeing Donald Maclean's brother Alan, who was in New York, waiting to take up an appointment as assistant to Sir Gladwyn Jebb, Britain's representative at the United Nations).

Not so innocently, Burgess arranged to have lunch with Maclean later that very day at the Royal Automobile Club. (Burgess afterwards said that they had gone there because they could not get a table at the Reform. But they may also have thought that they were less likely to meet mutual friends there.)

According to Burgess, he and Maclean had at least two other meetings at which they perfected the arrangements for their flight. Theoretically, there were a number of different ways of getting Maclean out of the country. Burgess could simply have told him that he would have to make his own way to the most convenient Soviet Embassy on the Continent if he did not want to land in jail. But a Soviet agent of Maclean's standing had the right to expect better treatment, and in any case, since he might already be under suspicion, it might be extremely risky to leave the arrangements to him. If he was being followed, he could hardly go and buy himself an air or cross-channel ticket, and, if his Soviet friends bought one on his behalf, there would still be the problem of delivering it to him. Then there was also the possibility that Maclean, left to himself, and knowing that his wife was shortly expecting a child, might be unwilling at the last minute to desert his family, disrupt his marriage and jettison the only permanent emotional ties he had accumulated over the years.

Did it not need a stronger character to warn him what was likely to happen to him if he disobeyed orders and allowed himself to be taken—and questioned about what he had told and to whom? And would he not need an assurance, too, that he need not worry about leaving his family, that they would be looked after and, indeed, would be reunited with him at the earliest possible moment?

How convenient it was, then, that Burgess, courier extraordinary, who was available to convoy Maclean through the minefields of MI5, happened also to be planning to go on exactly the kind of cruise that offered Maclean the best chance of success. Burgess could draw the money for the journey and drive Maclean to the dockside. Maclean, at the last minute, could take the place of 'Miller'.

Thus it seems not improbable to suppose that Burgess in suggesting that he and Miller should go on holiday together was following plans laid down in New York by the Russians. It seems unlikely that he ever intended to take Miller—unless perchance Maclean was arrested and Burgess, having been seen with him at the RAC Club, also became a wanted man. In such an eventuality, he could use Miller and the weekend cruise as a fall-back plan to ferry himself to safety.

Burgess never accepted this interpretation of the facts. He told Tom Driberg in Moscow that it was ridiculous to suppose that he had ever been a spy. The idea of going to Moscow as a political refugee came to him, he said, when Donald Maclean told him that he had decided to go there himself but did not know how to evade the detectives, who had obviously been put on his trail, not because *he* was a spy but because he had been speaking too openly against Foreign Office policies.

Burgess said he felt that Maclean had made the right decision and this had persuaded him not only to help him but to join forces. He did not do so because of friendship for Maclean and added, indeed, that he had never been a close friend of Donald's. (This was true for, according to several of his friends, Burgess had once compared white wobbly Donald to Dame Nellie Melba, an invidious distinction intended to exclude him from Guy's inner circle.)

Philby, however, whose book *My Silent War* was published twelve years after Burgess's *apologia*, was permitted, being senior to the late Guy in the Soviet hierarchy, not only to deny his dead colleague's version of the facts, but to add his own gloss. As we have seen, he declared that Burgess was an agent and not a refugee.

One of Philby's main concerns in writing his memoirs after he had defected to Moscow (for he is not free from the human failing of vanity) was to excuse himself for the error he had made in accepting Burgess as his house-guest in Washington. The argument put forward in his book was that his hospitality to Burgess would not alone have been the clue that exposed him if Burgess had obeyed his (Philby's) parting injunction, as he saw Burgess off, not to accompany Maclean.

Philby did not accuse Burgess of having panicked and defected against the orders of his superiors. But he comes close to suggesting that the late Burgess in effect saved his own skin at the expense of his (Philby's) career. He affected to believe that Burgess need never have fled.

Philby could not, of course, offer this explanation to the bloodhounds of MI5 when they interrogated him. Instead, he said, he concocted an interpretation which he said fitted the facts and could be disproved only by reference to the three people concerned. He told the interrogators that he believed that Maclean must have known he was under suspicion and had taken the initiative in asking Burgess through his Soviet contact in London to help by making arrangements for him (Maclean) to escape. And why did Burgess go too? Well, the Russians had probably decided that as he was about to be thrown out of the Foreign Office he could not be of much further use and was more likely to be a liability if he was not taken out of circulation.

On the face of it, the second half of Philby's story, according to which the Russians took the decision to pull Burgess out, seems plausible. But the question has proved highly controversial to previous writers on the Burgess–Maclean story. Some have argued that the Russians would never have willingly compromised Philby by bringing Burgess in out of the cold. But even Philby admitted that by the time Burgess left Washington he himself was already a potential suspect. Others have reasoned that Burgess originally meant to return to Britain after a short holiday abroad. He had, for example, invited himself to dine the following Monday at Lady Pamela Berry's house at the same time as his old friend Sir Anthony Blunt, with a view to getting a job on the *Daily Telegraph*. It has been suggested that it would have been unnecessary to go to these lengths in bluffing the authorities, particularly since Burgess himself was not under suspicion of any kind.

But could he have been so sure of this? Since Maclean was being followed, he must have been seen with him when they went to lunch at the RAC Club. If the Russians knew this, and had already decided that Burgess—at large—could be a liability to them, and thus to Philby, they would surely have told him that he, as well as Maclean was running into deep trouble. And if Burgess, in turn, believed that he was under the surveillance of MI5, what better way could there be of proving to the sleuths (if caught) that he never intended

to leave the country for good than the word of his old friend Blunt
that he had arranged to meet him for dinner the following Monday?
Thus the decision that both Burgess and Maclean should leave
Britain with despatch is likely to have been taken at an early stage
in the proceedings. But how was it to be done?

In any scheme to get Maclean out of the country, much depended
on whether orders had already been given to stop him leaving the
kingdom. In this case, instructions would have been issued to im-
migration officers at all the regularly manned posts.

A weekend cruise ship on which passport facilities were handled
on board might, however, be a different proposition. Once aboard
the boat, Maclean's passport might still be examined, but at least
he would have the ready explanation that he had every right to
take a weekend cruise for the good of his health, that he had no
intention of leaving the country and that he would certainly be back
at his office on Monday morning.

But how would Maclean get to Southampton? It would be un-
wise for him to use his own car, the number of which would be
known or easily obtainable by the police. Another more compelling
reason was that by May, Donald was no longer in a condition to
drive himself. He was met and driven home from the station by
Frank Watson, proprietor of the local garage, who also drove the
Maclean children to school.

It was, in fact, a demoralized and unhappy Maclean that Burgess
had to shepherd back to the Soviet fold. For despite Dr Erna's hopes,
Donald had not recovered his mental balance. Indeed, according to
the late Cyril Connolly, still one of the major authorities on this
period of Maclean's life, Maclean returned to work in the Foreign
Office on 6th November, suffering from a hangover after a heavy
night's drinking. He must have dreaded the strains he would have to
bear when re-establishing himself with his Foreign Office chums
while at the same time preparing to betray their confidences to his
Soviet control.

No doubt it was very cosy to be back in Downing Street again at
the hub of affairs, but all diplomats returning to London from a
post abroad find themselves at a disadvantage. The allowances
granted to them to meet the expenses of representing their country
abroad are suddenly withdrawn. Few of them can afford to live in
London and most, like Maclean, have to find a house in the suburbs.

For a time Donald made the best of it and was apparently liking
the country. Christmas and New Year passed with only one
reappearance of 'Gordon', who after being left out in the cold was
said to be seriously considering going into partnership with 'Sir
Donald'.

But catching a slow train home becomes less and less attractive
to anyone attending a diplomatic cocktail party and is virtually

excluded for anyone asked out to dinner. It was not long before there were further signs of strain. According to Cyril Connolly, it was 'at the end of that winter', fairly early in the year, that a friend— it was actually Mark Culme-Seymour—came to consult Connolly about a problem. He was absolutely certain that Maclean had asked him:

> 'What would you do if I told you I was working for Uncle Joe?'
> 'I suppose I would be very embarrassed.'
> 'Well, wouldn't you report me?'
> 'I don't know. Who to?'
> 'Well, I am ... Go on, report me?'

Culme-Seymour felt confused. There was an awkward silence, and the subject was dropped.

But next day Culme-Seymour went round to see Cyril Connolly to ask what he would have done in the circumstances. They concluded after discussing the affair that Donald's confession was too preposterous to be taken seriously and must have been a try-on to see whether his friends would really stand by him if, indeed, he should prove to be the English Hiss. The possibility that Maclean might be speaking *in vino veritas* hardly occurred to them, and they dismissed it as Rees had dismissed Burgess's confession, believing, but with rather less reason than Rees, that if there was anything serious in it, MI5 would be on the scent already.

And, of course, by this time MI5 were on the trail, and from the time Guy Burgess arrived in London to warn Donald of this, his alcoholic bouts became more and more frequent. He was keeping a bottle of whisky in his desk at the office again. 'Donald's drinking followed an established routine,' Connolly wrote. 'The charming and amiable self was gradually left behind, and the hand which patted his friend on the back became a flail. A change would come into his voice like the roll of drums for the cabaret.' Then unpredictably he would pick quarrels with those whose political stance he disapproved of.

To his friend Robin Campbell, Maclean confided that he longed for 'a leap of faith' which would convince him that Communism was right. But, in fact, the only leap that he could have taken would have been, while still free from suspicion, to seek voluntary asylum in the Soviet Union as a political refugee, perhaps even taking his family with him. But as a spy who disobeyed orders, how would he be received in Moscow? His faith in Stalin was evidently not strong enough to set these doubts at rest.

Once more he took to alcohol as a pain-killer.

Early in May, Melinda's sister Harriet and her husband, Jay Sheers, came over from Paris to stay with the Macleans, and though it was less than five months since she had seen Donald, she noticed how ill and strained he looked. Harriet must have remembered with foreboding the events of the previous summer in Cairo.

He seemed to feel particularly strongly over the case of Alger Hiss, whose second trial in the United States had ended in January 1950 with a five-year prison sentence. Hiss had been accused by Chambers before a Grand Jury of stealing and passing to Whittaker Chambers, then a Communist, documents which Mr Sumner Welles, U.S. Under-Secretary of State, afterwards said would have put the security of the United States in peril if communicated to a foreign power. Evidently Maclean saw parallels with his own predicament. One April night in 1951 at the Gargoyle Club he became so incensed with Philip Toynbee, who had written an article not entirely unfavourable to Whittaker Chambers, that he pushed Toynbee into the bandstand, calling on several patrons of the club to buy him a drink as he was the English Hiss. Melinda and Toynbee's new wife were present at the time.

In some ways the comparison between Maclean and Hiss was apt. Hiss's career was also not unlike Maclean's to the extent that he was an extremely able diplomat, Harvard-trained, and had enjoyed a meteoric rise. Maclean, although not yet accused, had done much the same.

Like Maclean, Hiss had been guilty of actions which seemed very much harder to justify in the atmosphere of the Cold War than even ten years earlier. In the thirties, few considered the Communist as a real danger to the American way of life. They were mainly intellectuals—subversive, but without mainstream political leverage —and their views on poverty, 'social justice' and Hitler were not far removed from those of the promoters of President Roosevelt's 'New Deal' for the 'common man'. Maclean, if he had lived in the United States, would have been attracted to Communism for the same reasons as Hiss.

One of the theories which, according to Alistair Cooke, was being aired at the time of Hiss's trial, was that Hiss had been a Communist and had reneged from the party and that Chambers, still a Communist, had been ordered to denounce Hiss, as a warning to others of what might happen if they broke faith. This thought probably entered Donald's mind during his darker moments.

Another weird similarity about the two dramas lay in the characters of the leading personalities. Hiss, presentable, at home with diplomats and statesmen of all kinds, was being denounced by Whittaker Chambers, socially unacceptable, a man who confessed in court that he had been a Communist, that he had lied and stolen in his time and even gone under a false name. Did it not, perhaps, occur to Donald that Burgess who, in his way, was just as disreputable and socially unacceptable as Whittaker Chambers had been,

would be just the person to claim that he, Burgess, having given up
his Communist beliefs, felt it his duty to denounce Maclean. At
any rate, Donald used to tell friends that he regarded Burgess as 'his
black shadow'. 'Something dreadful always happens to me when
he descends on me,' he used to say.

But nothing terrible seemed to be descending when Donald got up
on Friday 25th May, the morning of his thirty-eighth birthday. At
any rate, Sylvia Shrubb who came from the village every day to
help in the house—and afterwards became the family nurse—noticed
nothing out of the ordinary. Donald raced through his breakfast of
bacon and two eggs, with two cups of tea, as he always did and
rushed upstairs as usual to give Melinda a kiss before leaving for
the office, she said. He even found a moment to water the cyclamen
plant his wife had bought for him.

He was meeting Robin Campbell and his wife, Lady Mary Campbell, for lunch that day. Mary had become one of his special con-
fidantes and he had revealed to her, as he had to Philip Toynbee,
his dual personality. He admitted to her how ashamed he was of
the incidents when 'Gordon' the beast took control of his thoughts
and actions; he relied on her as a penitent relies on a confessor and
after unburdening himself to her, he felt the relief of the sinner who
has been shriven. He called her his 'rock'. She had seen him in
moods of despair when he was so depressed that a single incautious
word would touch off a tirade of disapproval of the Americans, the
Foreign Office and, worst of all, himself.

So often had this happened that Mary had devised a code so that
she would know when meeting Donald what kind of state he was
in. On days of gloom, when feeling 'prickly', he would turn down
the brim of his hat (diplomats wore them in those days) and when
he had the world on a string, he would turn the brim up all round.

Clearly 25th May was one of his good days for when Lady Mary
drove up to the steps of the Foreign Office in her jeep she saw that
the brim of the Maclean hat was unsnapped. It was going to be a
gladsome birthday celebration. They started off with oysters and
champagne at Wheeler's, a rickety-staired but luxurious fish haunt
in Old Compton Street, Soho—and Maclean, although he was no
longer an expense-account man, insisted on paying the bill himself.
It left him with only small change in his pocket. After this, the
three of them decided to eat something more substantial at Schmidt's
in Charlotte Street—a restaurant well-known for its solid German-
style dumpling, red cabbage and goose dishes, as well as its modest
prices.

On the way they encountered Cyril Connolly who was on his way
to the very much more fashionable Etoile, a restaurant in the same
street favoured by such *literati* as Ian (James Bond) Fleming and
his circle.

Meeting Maclean was a source of some embarrassment to Connolly who, about ten days earlier had received a visitation from Maclean at his Regent's Park home when he was in one of his least endearing alcoholic moods. Unfortunately, Connolly happened to have had guests at the time. Maclean, after insulting those who did not match up to his own high-minded standards, collapsed on the floor of the hall and lay there semi-conscious. He had to be put to bed. To Connolly's eye, Maclean still looked 'rather creased and yellow' but on this occasion he seemed relaxed and in no way truculent. The moment of uneasiness passed.

Before they parted, Connolly suggested that Robin and Mary should join him for coffee after their lunch.

At Schmidt's, the Campbells found Maclean almost his old self. He talked a good deal about the future. Though he was not thrilled with his present job, he was, he said, thinking of asking for a transfer to something more interesting. Then, since Melinda would soon be in hospital waiting to have her Caesarean operation, he asked if he could come and stay with the Campbells, at Stokke Manor, the house they then lived in in Hampshire, over the weekend of 8th June. He told Mary that he had now got over the infatuation he once had for a negro porter at the Moonglow nightclub, and added that above all, he did not want to get involved in any escapades which could bring shame on his family, or to Melinda who had stood by him through all his misfortunes.

After lunch, the Campbells went on to the Etoile and Maclean to his club, the Travellers, in Pall Mall where he cashed a cheque for £5—a portion of which he spent on a couple of large scotches, before returning to his desk at the Foreign Office.

From his attitude at lunch and from the fact that he afterwards drew only a small cheque, the Campbells concluded that, at the time they saw him, Donald did not then know that he would be leaving the country later that day for ever. They believed that it was only that evening that Burgess, in a telephone talk, told him there was now no more time to spare.

It was understandable, of course, for old friends to wish to give Donald the benefit of the doubt. But, even if for a moment we discount Philby's version of the whole affair, such wishful thinking scarcely stands up to analysis. For already on Thursday 24th May Donald had been talking to Melinda about his friend 'Roger Styles' who would be coming to dinner the following night. Thus, if Melinda had been speaking the truth, the timing of his escape could hardly have been a last minute decision. Later, Mary wrote to Donald to ask whether he knew when he talked about coming to stay with them in June that he would be fleeing the country that evening. His answer was 'Yes'.

And so, for the last time, he made his way home to Tatsfield.

# 14

# And So Farewell

Burgess's day was not quite so untroubled as Maclean's, but it began reasonably smoothly. Soon after nine o'clock Jack Hewit, who in fact acted as a kind of factotum in Burgess's household, made him a cup of tea, and Guy, who had no need to put in an appearance at the Foreign Office, lay in bed reading the morning papers at leisure. He rang Stephen Spender's wife at home to ask for Auden's address in Ischia—and so perhaps spread a false report that if by any chance he had not returned from his weekend cross-channel jaunt, it was because he had gone on holiday to Italy.

Guy appeared quite unruffled when Hewit left for work soon after nine. He was still lying on the bed smoking and reading a book. 'See you later, Mop,' he said as Hewit got up to go. (Mop, it seemed, was Burgess's pet name for Hewit.) They intended to have a drink together that evening before Burgess left for France with Miller. 'Don't do anything I wouldn't,' Hewit riposted as he closed the door behind him.

Burgess completed his toilet and made at least one more telephone call before taking the short walk along Piccadilly to the Green Park Hotel where he had arranged to meet Miller at half past ten. Then the two of them walked across to Green Park where, incidentally, their conversation could not be overheard. Miller afterwards described Guy's manner as nervous, and some people have concluded from this that something had occurred during the morning to put him on edge. He may, of course, have heard via Philby the news that Maclean was shortly to be questioned and this would undoubtedly have added to the strains of the day. But it would not have affected the escape plans which could hardly be brought forward and most certainly could not now be postponed.

Nevertheless Burgess's interview with Miller must have required a considerable amount of delicacy. For he had to break to Miller the fact that they might not be going on holiday together after all. This alone could have been an emotional occasion if, as Guy's friends believed, Guy had achieved a close relationship with the young American. Naturally Burgess could not risk telling Miller that another man was going abroad in his place, for besides breaking security, that would have led to an enormous row. Nor could Burgess afford to quarrel irrevocably with Miller, for if by any mischance Maclean were arrested that day, then Burgess would still need Miller as the alibi for his trip abroad. He therefore told Miller that he might not after all be able to make the trip as a young friend of his at the Foreign Office was in great trouble and that he (Burgess) was the only person who could help him.

Burgess added that he would not know his plans for certain until later but would let Miller know either way by eight thirty in the evening. To tell Miller about the Foreign Office was a gratuitous error on his part when there must have been other plausible stories he could have invented. But if we accept that Guy had already decided he was leaving Britain anyway, then it was a marginally less serious slip, for it was not likely that Miller would be quizzed before Burgess was safely overseas. He could, of course, have led the unfortunate Miller still further up the garden path by telling him nothing about any change of plan, and pretending to arrange to pick him up at, say, eight thirty in the evening. But there was a very good reason why this pretence could not be kept up.

If Burgess had been definitely committed to arrive at the Green Park Hotel at eight thirty to pick up Miller, Miller would undoubtedly have telephoned Burgess's flat at once to know what was amiss and Hewit, already disconcerted by the events of the day as we shall see, would have become even more disturbed. As it was, Miller did not telephone until several hours later.

The next record we have of Burgess's movements was at 2 p.m. when he called at the offices of Welbeck Motors in Crawford Street, London, W1, and hired a self-drive car—a cream coloured Austin A70 model numbered VMF 196. He paid £25 cash in advance—£10 deposit and £15 for the hire. He signed his own name and gave the Reform Club as his address. Then he went and did some shopping at Gieve's, the naval tailor, whom in former days he must almost certainly have patronized as a cadet. He bought a new light-weight suitcase and a white mackintosh—a garment he had never been known to wear in the past.

Then he homed back to the Reform Club from where he could be certain of telephoning without the conversation being bugged. At this point he seemed to be under considerable stress. He rang up Mrs Goronwy Rees and told her in a monologue lasting for nearly twenty minutes that he was about to do something which he felt was right but which would shock many people. He said that the Rees's would not see him for some time—even for a very long time, but perhaps that would be for the best as he and Goronwy no longer agreed on politics. However, in the style of the maudlin alcoholic, he felt that Goronwy would understand what he was about to do and was the only one of his friends who would.

Guy sounded confused and strange, and Mrs Rees concluded that he might have been trying to tell her, through a haze of liquor, that he had accepted a job on the *Daily Telegraph*, a paper with whose views he would be in strong disagreement.

The next news of Burgess's day came from Hewit, who arrived back at the flat from work soon after five o'clock and found Burgess in the midst of packing. The telephone rang and Hewit believed that the caller was Donald Maclean. Burgess seemed disconcerted at receiving the call—possibly because he believed that his home telephone was bugged and feared that Donald might say something indiscreet. However, the moment passed, Burgess completed his packing and left the flat with scarcely a word to Hewit. Nothing was said about the drink they were to have had. It was the last they saw of each other and a casual way to end a partnership that had lasted for fourteen years.

From this point on, however, the story becomes less easy to follow. Later that afternoon, Burgess was seen at the Reform Club where he asked for a map of the North of England as if to put his pursuers off the scent.

According to Melinda's story, as told to Geoffrey Hoare, Donald caught 'his usual train' that night, the 5.19 p.m. from Charing Cross to Oxted. But in fact Donald never went to Oxted or Sevenoaks but habitually used Woldingham, which, though about five miles away, was the most convenient station. He was usually met there and driven home by Frank Watson. He could have reached Woldingham in two ways, either without change in a steam train from Victoria or from Charing Cross with a change at East Croydon. Neither station offered a train to Woldingham starting at 5.19 p.m.; but the 5.24 p.m. from Charing Cross arrived at East Croydon at 5.47 p.m., ten minutes before the connection onwards to Woldingham, and this might help to explain how Maclean was able to telephone to Burgess at his flat (to say he had shaken the dust of Whitehall off his feet?) at a time when he was thought to be already aboard his train.

The 5.24 p.m. train would get him to Woldingham at 6.18 p.m., just in time to receive Guy (Roger Styles) Burgess when he arrived for dinner.

But Melinda also said that Roger Styles arrived at 6.30 p.m., about half an hour after her husband. Donald, in other words, was home about six o'clock, in which case he would have had to take the direct 5.09 p.m. train from Victoria, making his telephone call from Victoria, before boarding the train.

Later, Melinda confessed to a 'vague feeling' that Burgess and her husband had travelled to Tatsfield together in Burgess's car. Donald might have preferred this and might even have rung Burgess to say so on Friday afternoon. But if Donald was being followed in London by MI5 men, where could he have met Burgess in safety?

Furthermore, Frank Watson recalls driving Maclean from Woldingham to Beacon Shaw as usual that night.

Another puzzling aspect of the affair is that, according to Melinda, Burgess and Maclean drove off for Southampton at about 9 p.m. in Burgess's hired car with Guy at the wheel. (He had always liked thrilling motor drives at night.) But, in fact, Frank Watson remembers driving the two men after dinner to Woldingham Station in Maclean's dark green Humber Snipe, in time to catch a train that would take them both back to London. Furthermore, he does not remember seeing Burgess's white Austin or any other strange car at Beacon Shaw that night.

One possible explanation for this discrepancy is that Burgess decided to lay yet another false trail. He could, for example, have driven south from London in his car, and picked up Maclean by arrangement at East Croydon. From there he could have taken Maclean as far as Woldingham Station, leaving him to wait there to be fetched by Frank Watson, while he himself parked the car in a nearby side road near the station, so that they could get into it again later the same evening for their drive to Southampton. Then he would have taken a taxi from Woldingham to Tatsfield, arriving, as Melinda said, about half an hour after Donald. It seems strange —though not inconceivable—for Melinda not to have known in which car her husband left for Southampton. But why did Burgess think it necessary to call at Beacon Shaw at all? He could have picked up Maclean at Woldingham Station and have taken him straight to Southampton. But he may have thought he would be safer in the privacy of Beacon Shaw than if he re-appeared at Woldingham at a time when the 'dicks' might have decided, after all, to keep tabs on Maclean.

Dinner at Beacon Shaw proceeded, as we know, without incident, but although 8.30 passed, Burgess, for reasons we have guessed, did not think it necessary to ring up Miller in London to tell him that their jolly jaunt together was now cancelled.

As the clock ticked on, however, it must have been difficult for Burgess, knowing that they had less than three hours to motor nearly 100 miles to Southampton in a family car, to conceal his impatience, and Burgess claimed that it was only because he knew the Southampton docks area well that they were able to board the *Falaise* before she sailed at midnight. 'My word, they're cutting things fine,' said one of the passengers standing by the ship's rail. 'What about your car?' shouted a seaman on the dockside. 'Back on Monday,' was the reply as the two men vanished into the ship.

Here, once more, the evidence begins to conflict. According to one witness, Maclean, smartly dressed and carrying a small briefcase, and Burgess, hatless and wearing a mackintosh, were met at the gangway by a man in a Homburg hat. The same witness, Mr William John Lyons, a sixty-five-year-old London produce merchant, said that when the ship arrived next morning, 26th May, about 10.30 at St Malo, the rain was coming down so heavily that none of the passengers thought of going ashore—except Burgess, Maclean and their friend. Moreover, they were met by a smart black taxi which took up its stand not on the usual taxi rank but opposite the forward part of the ship. The three men got into the cab and were driven away. But another account says that the three men were the last to leave the boat. MI5 eventually accepted that the men went ashore at a quarter to twelve. A taxi driver took them to St Malo Station, and then to a hotel to change money, and on to Rennes where they would have been able to take a fast train for Paris.

The investigators were not able to identify the man in the Homburg hat who apparently rejoined the ship with the other passengers before she left St Malo on Saturday night.

Burgess, in his role of political refugee, denied this version of his exodus. He said that no man in a Homburg hat had met them on the boat. According to him, Donald suggested that it might be a good idea for them to make for Prague because there was a Trade Fair on there and the Czechs would be ready to give visas to foreigners wishing to go there. The first step would be to proceed to Rennes which, the railway time-table showed, was the junction for Paris. They took a taxi from St Malo to Rennes—an ordinary one off the rank—and were in time to catch the 1.18 p.m., the fast train to Paris. When they got to Paris, they found from the time-table (it was important not to draw attention to themselves by asking questions) that there was a train to Berne leaving about midnight. They booked berths on it, had dinner first in a café and travelled the night through to arrive in Berne about six o'clock on Sunday morning. The next day Maclean called at the Czech Embassy and on the strength of being a diplomat, they both got visas for Prague. Planes flew there from Zurich, but not on Mondays, so they had to wait for another day; there was a motor rally in Zurich and Guy, as an enthusiastic car-fiend, could not stay away; but he survived unrecognized.

On Tuesday 29th May, they reached Prague and presented themselves at the Soviet Embassy there. There was no reaction for a week, Burgess said. The Russians, he was told, would have to get instructions. But even at this late date, according to Burgess, he had still not decided definitely to go to Moscow 'at once'. It was the news that hundreds of security men were looking for him which finally helped him to make up his mind. Until then he had still been considering the holiday he had tried to arrange in Italy with Wystan Auden, and it was in that mood that, after fleeing with Maclean, he had sent the message to his mother telling her that he was embarking on a long Mediterranean holiday. At the time he left Britain it could still have come true, he argued. He had no idea why the Russians had sent the message from Rome. But when the story of their flight became public, the Kremlin reacted. They were told to catch one of the regular flights to Moscow and were met when they arrived there. They were boarded in a hotel for a day or two, and then in a flat, while Soviet experts 'debriefed' them on the latest Foreign Office thinking. Then the 'authorities' sent them to Kuibishev—where foreigners were unlikely to see them—while they considered their future.

There is one small detail which makes the above account unconvincing. Train passengers with sleepers normally surrender their passports to the sleeping car attendant so that when the train crosses the frontier e.g. from France to Switzerland during the night, the formalities can be completed without waking the passengers. But none of the sleeping car attendants remembered seeing Burgess or Maclean—or their passports.

A later account of the escape given by Vladimir Petrov also mentions Paris and Prague as stopping points for Burgess and Maclean on their way to Moscow, but, of course, Petrov confirmed that the escape was no haphazard affair cobbled together by Burgess the brilliant amateur motor-rally man and time-table wizard, but master-minded in the Kremlin by F. V. Kislytsin, one of the Soviet Union's top subversive intelligence agents.

As a result, it would take the British MI5 and the American CIA a powerful long time to recover their balance.

# 15

# Losing The Scent

It was Jack Hewit who first set the alarm bells ringing. Late on Friday evening he was rung up by Burgess's friend Miller who had been expecting to hear by 8.30 from Burgess one way or the other about their trip, and now already it was nearly midnight. Miller wanted to know what had gone wrong. Now Hewit became uneasy, too. Of course Burgess had often decided to stop away the night on the spur of the moment without telling Hewit. But perhaps something in Burgess's manner had been different this time. Also, it must have occurred to Hewit that Guy's absence could not be just an impromptu affair, because, when Hewit arrived back from work, Guy had been packing clothes into a new suitcase. Moreover, he had offered Hewit no explanation of where he intended going. Never before, or at least not for fourteen years, had he gone on holiday without Hewit knowing where.

Next morning, Saturday 26th May, with still no word from Burgess, Hewit rang Goronwy Rees's house at Sonning as he knew Guy liked going there. Rees was away in Oxford for the weekend and Mrs Rees had no idea where Burgess might be. Had he gone abroad after all, Hewit wondered? Perhaps he would have left a note somewhere. He looked through Guy's things. And when he found what was missing, he was still more upset.

Guy had gone off with two large bundles of notes, one of £125 and one rather larger, both of which he had brought back from America—the proceeds, he said, of a black market deal. He had also removed Savings Certificates worth £40 or £50 which he had held on to for years. The black Foreign Office briefcase which Burgess sometimes took to work was missing too—and a large suitcase, together with a green and brown Irish tweed suit, a biscuit-coloured American light-weight suit, some nylon shirts, two pairs of blue jeans and a pair of shoes. This hardly looked the sort of luggage Guy would take for a mere weekend trip. But if Guy was really going further afield, why had he not said a word to Hewit? Surely, the explanation must be that he was once more working for the Security Services on something about which his lips were sealed? So Hewit decided to ring Guy's old friend Anthony Blunt, who

Burgess at home in Russia

The last picture that Burgess
sent home to his mother
before his death, 1956

Philip Toynbee, Maclean's companion in London, Paris and Cairo

(*Left*) Sir Frederick Warner, Burgess's former colleague at the Foreign Office, and (*right*) Goronwy Rees, whom Burgess tried to recruit as an agent

had worked with Guy in the Intelligence Service during the war, who could doubtless find out, if he did not already know, Guy's plans, particularly since he was due to meet him at dinner the following week.

Meanwhile Rees, too, had become worried. He recalled Guy's rather distrait manner during his weekend visit a fortnight earlier, he remembered Guy's strongly slanted anti-American views, also his perplexing telephone conversation on the previous Friday with Mrs Rees in which he said that it might be a very long time before he saw Rees again, and finally he took note of Hewit's acute anxiety about where Guy could be. Adding all this together, he came to the conclusion that, preposterous as it might seem at first, Guy could have gone to Moscow. So on Sunday night Rees, too, got in touch with someone he knew in the Secret Service, and revealed his fears.

Thus, from the start, the case of the missing diplomats was handled by MI5 rather than by the regular police force, and MI5 had very good reasons for ordering a clamp-down. MI5 men follow the general principle that you never show the other side the cards in your hand; you never tell the enemy how much you know—or do not know—about his methods of espionage. But in this case it was even more important not to break silence. For MI5 was just beginning to rumble the truth about the super spy Kim Philby who, having sheltered Burgess in Washington, was now a marked man. Also, they did not want a public row with the Americans about what secrets might or might not have been sold to the Russians. Nor were they certain whether they could safely tell all to the French authorities.

They had, at the time Burgess and Maclean left, no conclusive evidence of their spying activities. Would any Soviet agent have been as avowedly anti-American as Maclean had been—or as indiscreet as Burgess? Nor were they in a position to arrest either man. So it was much better that Burgess and Maclean should be referred to as missing diplomats—whatever the Foreign Office might think —rather than as spies.

The newspapers were happy to conform. They bore in mind the fact that both Burgess and Maclean might conceivably have been kidnapped, though the fact that the Foreign Office suspended them for leaving the country should have indicated an official belief that they left voluntarily. Or they might have gone into hiding. In either of these two cases, they would be in a position to sue for many thousands of pounds if they were described without reason as traitors.

Also, as Rees might have suggested to his contacts, and as the

I

Special Branch hinted to Percy Hoskins of the *Daily Express*, the two men might have gone to Russia for 'idealistic reasons'.

John Price, who was now serving in the Embassy in Paris, thought it unlikely that any of the above theories would fit. Like many others, he thought that the two topers must have gone somewhere on the spree, and yet even this sounded improbable since they were not known to be close friends.

About other aspects of the case, however, the media were less satisfied. On the day the story broke, the News Department of the Foreign Office had unfortunately arranged to throw a bun and lemonade party—sherry for the grown-ups—in their offices for Foreign Office mothers and children who had been watching the ceremony of Trooping the Colour on the royal birthday. Not all correspondents appreciated this kind of competition. They also resented the fact that the Foreign Office had no photographs available of the missing men. They wondered if the story of the escape would ever have been divulged at all by the Foreign Office if the *Daily Express* had not discovered the facts.

It was the French authorities who, as an act of co-operation, released the text of the two telegrams sent on behalf of Maclean to his wife and mother—revealing, incidentally, to the newspapers just where they could get hold of his relatives. Only then did the Foreign Office release the text which they already had of Burgess's telegram to *his* mother.

Editors in the U.K. were irked by a 'D' notice issued by the Voluntary Censorship Board enjoining them not to refer to Burgess's wartime Secret Service activities. The reporters on the case concluded that there could only be one reason for concealment—that there was something to hide.

There were various other ways in which reporters felt themselves baulked by secretiveness which seemed to them not only obscurantist but positively unpatriotic. Thus if photographs of Burgess and Maclean had been issued on Monday 28th May when officials first knew that they were missing, the chances of catching them would have been greatly improved. Papers not only in Britain but in France and elsewhere would have been glad to help with 'Have you seen These Men?' pictures. Frontier guards and Customs officers would have been put on the alert or at very least would have remembered seeing the two men. A French official at Rennes was warned on Saturday 26th May that two passengers aboard the steamer *Falaise* who had weekend return tickets to Britain had not returned aboard when the ship sailed homewards from St Malo. But it was ten days before he was given reason to believe that the two weekenders were in fact the missing diplomats. No doubt the escape had to be passed first to the French Foreign Office and by them through the French

Ministry of the Interior, to the DST (Direction de la Surveillance du Territoire), the French equivalent of MI5.

It must also have occurred to the more percipient British reporters that if, as they have been led to believe, Burgess and Maclean had gone to the Soviet Union for idealistic motives, that is as political refugees, the Soviet Union could have been expected to announce the fact and given it the greatest possible publicity. For, indeed, it would have been a triumph if two Foreign Official men had left Britain for no other reason than that they considered that life in the Soviet Union was preferable. But the Russians could not be sure that MI5 had nothing more than suspicions in their files.

Another difficulty—both for the Press and for the authorities— was that both Burgess and Maclean moved in circles where personal loyalty was at a premium. On 7th June Harold Nicolson wrote in his diary:

> I come back to Neville Terrace and am horrified to read headlines in the evening papers that Donald Maclean and Guy Burgess have absconded. If I thought that Guy was a brave man, I should imagine that he had gone to join the Communists. As I know him to be a coward, I suppose that he was suspected of passing things on to the Bolshies, and realizing his guilt, did a bunk. Apparently he and Maclean went off by car to Southampton and took the night boat. I fear that all this will mean a witch-hunt.

Yet, in an interview given later to the *Daily Express*, Nicolson said:

> He [Burgess] publicly announced his sympathies with Communism, and yet he heartily disliked the Russians. He thought they were cruel and spoiled a great deal. He was a most indiscreet talker. He said anything that came into his head, and cared nothing about who heard him. Of course he was a heavy drinker. He drank anything in any order, and when he had too much his eyes went out of focus.... When Burgess was sober, he was charming, jolly, and a magnificent talker. When he was drunk he drooled foolish nonsense. He was a kind man, and despite his weaknesses I don't think he would do anything dishonourable or mean.

Other friends of Burgess—including his former housemaster— took much the same line. Hector McNeil, formerly one of his sponsors, said in a television interview: 'I should not imagine it was likely he was a dependable spy of a high rank or reputation.'

Later, speculating in his diary on the possibility of being called on by the authorities to give evidence in Burgess's favour, Nicolson wondered what he would be able to say, knowing, as he did, Burgess's drunken habits and sexual promiscuity. ' "Do you mean to tell the Court," the Attorney-General would thunder at me, "that although you knew what sort of man he was, you continued to see him?" As a matter of fact I had rather dropped him because he was a bore with his drunken habits, but I couldn't say that in court.' Donald's relatives and friends were no less loyal—in fact probably more so.

But despite these handicaps, the reporters had fun. They traced in the Reform Club the call that Burgess had made—and not paid for —to Mrs Rees. They pondered why the milometer on Burgess's hired car showed 210, at least 30 miles more than was to be expected, from the trip via Tatsfield to Southampton and back. They learnt from the police that Burgess and Maclean had left their clothes behind on the boat—probably to encourage anyone told to arrest them to wait to do so until they got back to the boat or possibly to convince the authorities, if they were taken when landing, that they were not escaping but had intended to return on the *Falaise* to Britain. Perhaps the white mackintosh that Burgess had bought at Gieves on the day of the flit was the most interesting garment. Guy had never owned a mackintosh before, and its true purpose may well have been to identify him quickly to someone waiting to meet him aboard the *Falaise*. Alternatively the various garments, including a dinner jacket (he would not need that in Moscow) may have been included as false trails for the trackers. In due course relatives came to Waterloo Station to claim the clothes of the missing men. Alan Maclean had little difficulty in recognizing Donald's, but Colonel Bassett appeared less than enthusiastic over some of the garments included in his stepson's luggage.

The reporters visited Burgess's flat, and subjected it to a lengthy examination. Hewit was described—his blue nylon thread suit, blue suede shoes and his rimless plastic-lensed spectacles. The heavily-curtained bay windows, the splintered Worcester pottery, the charcoal sketches made during that wild trip to Tangier, the two-foot pleasure steamer made of sardine tins, the silver teapot presented to his mother by the ship's company of *Hebe* in January 1915, his books—Trotsky's *Karl Marx*, Gooch's *Annals of Politics and Culture*, Sandys' *History of Classical Scholarship* and biographies of Salisbury, Bentinck and Morley—all were noted and assessed.

One reporter watched Hewit take a plate from the larder on which lay a slim, brownish looking object—a smoked eel bought for Burgess's supper on the night he left. 'It's time it went,' said Hewit as the creature slid off the plate into the dustbin.

One unmentioned relic left behind by Burgess (who, unlike

Maclean, possessed no effective furnace in which papers could be burnt) was a large trunk which was seized by MI5 bloodhounds before reporters could get wind of it. It contained notes and character studies amassed for Burgess by one of his friends who afterwards joined the Foreign Office. These records were intended to serve as a register of potential recruits for the Communist party and set out in meticulous detail not only the political leanings of each prospect but also the dates and social occasions on which each had been met. Although the information had been assembled in the thirties, it caused trouble for a lot of people in the fifties one former investigator remembers.

On 6th July the *Daily Express* carried the story a stage further by publishing a report quoting a man of repute whose name was withheld to safeguard his friends in Prague. The man said:

On 3rd June, which was a Sunday, I drove with my wife about twelve miles outside Prague to the Hotel Réné, a pleasant little two-storey place among the pinewoods and a couple of miles off the main road.

At Réné's, which has half a dozen luxurious rooms, a saucy-pictured bar, and a rustic-styled restaurant, you escape the feeling of being spied on that we all get in Prague.

Western diplomats often go there for lunch or tea. When everything was nationalized the Communists made the owner keep Réné's going, mainly for foreigners.

My wife and I arrived about 2.30 which was late for lunch. Only one table was still occupied—by two Englishmen and two Czech girls.

The Englishmen were strangers to us, and in Czechoslovakia these days you can count the British here. We know them all.

The girls were pretty, and smartly dressed, the type of girls who are paid to show foreigners a good time, and keep an eye on them.

The Englishmen took little notice of the girls. They were finishing a bottle of red wine with a Bulgarian label, and talking to each other in clear, educated voices.

We wondered who they could be. Obviously not trade unionists sampling 'other people's democracy'—the Press would have heralded such a visit anyway.

Not diplomats; we know them all and meet most of them for cocktails every week.

Not business men—there is no business to be done. English fellow-travellers? Again, the Press would have made a fuss of them. It always does. The taller man, sitting about six yards away from us in the empty restaurant seemed to resent my scrutiny.

He drained his wine, then the four rose. I did not see a bill presented.

Through the wide window I saw them go off in a chauffeur-driven Buick, sky-blue, with ordinary Czech number plates—foreigners in Prague get distinctive plates—yellow with red numbers.

I had not heard of Burgess and Maclean then.

A week later, we saw an English newspaper and we recognized their pictures with a shock. The tall man in Réné's was Maclean, the other was Burgess.

It is dangerous to discuss such discoveries on the phone, so I went round to a British diplomat, a friend of mine in Prague, and, sitting in his bathroom—with the tap running in case there was a microphone about—I told him what we had seen.

He knew Burgess and Maclean and said they were exactly as I described them.

I went back to Réné's once or twice in the hope of running into them, but they did not show up. The belief in Prague is that they have 'gone on' to Warsaw.

This accorded with information received by the French police by an informer working in the Czech Embassy in Paris that two men, answering to the description of the diplomats, had been seen entering the Embassy in Avenue Charles-Floquet on the left bank 'between 28th May and the first two days of June'.

It also linked up with a snapshot of Maclean found on the seat of a train to Paris. At the time it was regarded as a clue planted by an agent to mislead security men. A legitimate conclusion, perhaps, if the snapshot had been deliberately left on the seat. But Maclean could have dropped it carelessly, face downwards on the floor where it would have lain undisturbed until some other idly curious passenger picked it up and left it conspicuously displayed to view.

Meanwhile what about Melinda?

At one end of the spectrum you have her own story as originally told to MI5, the Press Association and Geoffrey Hoare. According to this, she knew nothing of Donald's activities, and would never believe, without proof, that he was a traitor to his country or even politically unreliable. 'My husband had no reason to go away,' she told one reporter. 'I know no more than any of his friends. I don't believe people who say he was a Communist. What else is there to say?' From this it follows that she had no idea on the night when 'Styles' came to dinner that her husband was about to leave her. When she talked to her mother on the morning of the 27th May she said she believed Donald had gone off drinking again, in which case he would turn up soon enough.

And then, at the other end of the spectrum, is the statement made later in Moscow, as we shall see, by Maclean that it was only his wife's pregnancy which prevented her from leaving Britain at the same time as he did. Melinda even told Mark Culme-Seymour, whom she met with Donald in Leningrad, that she had known she was going to Russia from way-back—long before Donald defected. By this, Melinda might have wished to convey that she had not become a convert to Communism by force of circumstance, i.e., because Donald had left her (which would have been 'opportunism') but through long-standing devotion to Communist principles. And another more compelling reason for Melinda's attitude will become evident later.

There was, furthermore, the story in the *Daily Mail* of 20th October 1955 by Gordon Young, the paper's foreign correspondent, who was known to have extremely good contacts with intelligence sources. His informant, whose papers indicated that he had occupied 'a highly responsible position in foreign communist circles' told Young that some time after Russia had entered the war on the side of the West, Maclean told his 'contact man', a Hungarian Communist spy, that he had taken his wife Melinda into his confidence and that she was helping him in his work.

Let us examine this part of the story first. There can be few agents who do not have problems about how much to tell their wives, and how much to conceal, and Donald was no exception. The general practice is for wives to be told only as much as they need to know, namely that their husband's work is confidential and must remain so in the national interest. And this is a precaution taken to discourage the more inquisitive wives from employing private detectives to shadow their husbands.

Melinda might well have been told less rather than more than other wives. Throughout their marriage, she had shown little interest in Donald's political work and it was most unlikely that they would have had discussions in depth on the affairs of the day. And if he did not think it worth talking about his day-to-day work, he would hardly have brought her into his day-to-day espionage activities, an indiscretion which would have added considerably to the risk of discovery.

On the other hand, it would have been difficult for Melinda, as an American-born wife in the United States, to have remained completely untouched by the conflicts there between the liberals and hard-liners, the 'China-lobby' of Chiang Kai Shek and the non-interventionists, and between those who wanted bigger and better atom bombs and others who wanted no atom bombs at all.

Donald's views on these questions must have been as well known to Melinda as they were to his friends, and there are reports that even in Washington she had made some 'anti-American' statements.

It is just possible, therefore, that Donald, who felt strongly on these matters, had set about converting his wife to his own political views, and that she was helping him in his work by 'educating' the children, one of whom told Mrs Dunbar that his daddy was 'fighting for peace'. Indeed, in a romantic letter written by Melinda to Donald after he had absconded and shortly before the birth of her third child (but never sent) she avows that she not only loves him but is proud of him. This could only mean that she understood and sympathized with his flight. But there would have been absolutely no point in Melinda duplicating the espionage work that Donald was already doing for the Russians. Nor would it have served any useful purpose to give her information or let her know the details of his contacts or of his meetings with other Soviet agents.

But did he actually tell her in advance that he was going to leave her? And had he already promised her before he left that one day they would be together again? Were his words in his telegram: 'Don't stop loving me' a declaration of intent rather than just pure sentiment? It is hard to be sure.

If Melinda knew in advance that Donald was to abscond, then the whole story of 'Roger Styles', for which the authorities had her word alone, must have been a fabrication. The story Melinda told of the events of the crucial Friday evening was a muddled one. At first she seemed certain that Donald had caught 'his usual train' from London, but later she qualified this by adding that she had a vague feeling that Donald and 'Styles' might have travelled down together. But in that case, why should they have arrived at the house at different times? The discrepancy must have puzzled the MI5 investigators who would have been entitled to think that Melinda knew more about 'Roger Styles's' movements than she had admitted.

Another more serious discrepancy in Melinda's story arose through Frank Watson's statement that after dinner Maclean and Styles had not left Beacon Shaw in a white Austin car but that, on the contrary, he had driven Styles and Maclean to Woldingham Station in Donald's car.

This, if it had become public knowledge at the time, would have been harder to explain. Melinda would almost certainly have seen Styles and her husband drive away from the front door. So she would almost certainly have known in which car they left. Yet why, if they were at all likely to be staying away overnight, should they be setting off with Watson who would presumably not want to sleep away from home, when they had Burgess's car available? And how would this have matched with the fact that they arrived at Southampton in Burgess's car? What perfectly innocent explanation could there have been of this apparently senseless procedure?

Thinking back afterwards, Sylvia Shrubb was also of the opinion that Melinda must have been warned in advance of Donald's departure. 'She was so calm when she told me the morning after "Mr

Maclean isn't here". She must have known.' Nevertheless in the opinion of the investigators the weight of evidence appeared to show that Melinda was not privy to Donald's escape plans. One reason was that Donald believed that he was being shadowed by MI5 men and had already confided his fears to friends other than Burgess. So why should he take unnecessary extra risks with his own skin at this critical time by taking Melinda into his confidence when he had never done so before? Secondly, the risks of a second miscarriage would be increased if he told Melinda that he was leaving her behind.

It was in any case the worst possible moment for Donald to leave his family, with its members just about to gather for his thirty-eighth birthday party and his wife shortly to have a baby. One of the boys was down with measles. It would be a terrible time for Melinda. It was probably a minor sacrifice for Donald to leave behind him all but his overnight clothes. He probably worried more deeply about the lies he had been forced to tell his small son. But, the domestic scenes with Melinda would be very much less serious if the problems were exposed to her gradually and in the course of time and not *en bloc* in advance. And, of course, the questioning that would ensue after Donald's departure would be less gruelling if it could appear that Melinda knew nothing before-hand about her husband's plans. Moreover Donald's escape depended entirely on Burgess, who no doubt insisted that secrecy must be maintained throughout the operation. And, as Burgess probably pointed out to him, the disgrace and worry to his family, as he himself half-hinted to the Campbells at lunch, would be so much greater if he stayed on and was exposed, than it would be if he left before he was caught.

Melinda, meanwhile, was under sedation and was not cross-questioned until Wednesday 30th May when she came to London to see her doctor. William Skardon, 'the man who broke Fuchs', was the chief interrogator. The interview took place in the privacy of the flat of Lady Maclean, who was then living at Iverna Court, near Kensington Gardens. During the interview, Melinda suggested that Donald, who had now been absent a mere five days, might soon turn up at home again. The MI5 man, although he knew from the background of the Maclean affair that this was improbable, followed the 'softly-softly' tradition and did not argue the point at the time. He appeared to accept Melinda's hope as the natural optimism of an innocent wife.

On 12th June, Melinda's sister Harriet and her husband arrived at Beacon Shaw and the next day Melinda went into hospital for her Caesarean operation. It was successful and a fortnight later she left hospital with her new baby girl.

As far as possible the Foreign Office security men kept to the compact they made with Melinda that if she co-operated with them —and gave no interviews to the Press—they in turn would protect her from 'harassment' by reporters. And so a policeman was stationed outside the padlocked front gates of Beacon Shaw, while the unmown grass grew and grew on the lawn and the children's toys lay about the place unrepaired.

But if the security authorities were prepared to accept, for the time being, that Melinda knew no more than she had said about Donald's double life, they believed nevertheless that Donald might try to get his family to join him behind the Iron Curtain.

Towards the middle of June, just about the time Melinda was emerging from hospital, Larry Solon, still in Paris, received a visit from an English visitor dressed in tweeds 'who stroked a small bristly moustache, and said that he would not give his name'. He declared he wanted a friendly chat. He was a friend of Mrs Maclean but he had come to see Solon on his own initiative. He had also been a friend of Donald's, though they had had their differences. His interest was, he said, to see that Melinda was treated fairly. He told Solon that he was wasting his time looking for Maclean in Paris. (Hewit, a source used by the *Daily Express*, had been over in Paris, seeking clues at the Café de Flore.) 'You should really drop all that nonsense,' the stranger said. 'It does no good. Mrs Maclean knows her husband is not in Paris *because she knows where he is.*'

Solon asked: 'Why doesn't she tell the police?'
The reply: 'Would you expect her to? She's his wife.'
Solon: 'I don't see how keeping it secret helps anybody.'
The reply: 'It might certainly interfere with her plans.'
Solon: 'Plans? What plans?'
The reply: 'My dear fellow, surely a wife who loves her husband would want to keep in touch with him, wouldn't she? Besides, she is being hounded enough as it is. You chaps ought to let her alone.'

The mysterious visitor evidently wished to help establish some form of communication between Maclean and Melinda, and feared that the Russians would interfere with it if there were too much 'snooping' by the Press. No doubt the stranger's encounter with Solon had as little effect as the original telephone call that had first put Solon onto the story. Nevertheless, the official investigators were on the right track in supposing that Maclean was alive and would get in touch again with his wife.

The first move came six weeks later on 3rd August when Mrs Dunbar, who was still living at Tatsfield with Melinda, received two registered letters posted in St Gallen in Switzerland two days earlier. One contained a draft on the Swiss Bank Corporation, London, for £1,000 payable to Mrs Dunbar, and the other was a draft for the same amount, also payable to Mrs Dunbar, drawn by the Union Bank of Switzerland on the Midland Bank, 122 Old Broad Street, London. Both drafts had apparently been sent on the orders of a Mr Robert Becker who paid for them in cash over the counter, gave his temporary address as the Hotel Central, Zurich and a permanent address in New York. Mrs Dunbar, who had never heard of Mr Becker, at once got in touch with the authorities who, however, were no more successful, even with the help of the Swiss police, in establishing his identity. Both addresses Mr Becker had given proved to be false.

Two days later, however, on 5th August, Melinda got an affectionate letter from Donald, posted locally in Surrey. It was he who had sent the two drafts, for convenience, to Mrs Dunbar as he remembered her banking arrangements. But they were really for Melinda to repay her for the deposit she had put down out of her own money for the purchase of Beacon Shaw. The letter, according to the account given to Geoffrey Hoare, told Melinda no more about where Donald was or why he left, though he said she must know in her own heart that he had to do what he had done. She concluded from the style that he had been given strict instructions about what he might or might not say.

Here, then, was just the kind of lead that the security forces in the U.K. were looking for. The letter must also have been of great encouragement to Melinda for it told her firstly that Donald still cared about her in the romantic way she had always hoped. Secondly, it was a sign that his protestations of love were not mere words. Thirdly, the fact that her resources had been restored would make her less dependent on her mother, and so more willing to listen to advice from Donald, and fourthly, the remittances were evidence that Donald was now a man of substance who was not only earning a great deal more than he had at the Foreign Office, but was also able to dispose of it exactly as he wished. The letter was carefully phrased to hint that Donald had left for ideological reasons.

Melinda showed the letter to the Foreign Office Security Branch man with whom she normally dealt and, in due course, it was returned to her. It was a treasure which she carried everywhere with her thereafter, and it influenced her life permanently.

Mrs Dunbar was disposed to tear up the two cheques; but it was pointed out to her that as from 1st June 1951 Donald had been suspended from the Foreign Service and there was no salary for Melinda to draw on. Nobody could be certain that the £2,000 had come from behind the Iron Curtain, or, if so, that it had been dishonestly come by, nor had Mrs Dunbar the right to dispose of money sent by her son-in-law to his wife. (Also, it would not have helped the Security investigators if the lure of £2,000 had been refused, since what they wanted was more communication between Donald and Melinda, not less.)

On 15th August, Lady Maclean, who, like Melinda, had been keeping her private correspondence from the knowledge of the Press, had also received a letter from Donald. It had been posted in Herne Hill and had taken four days to arrive, a delay for which the Security Branch might or might not have been responsible.

But their examination of the four communications sent through the post to Mrs Dunbar, Lady Maclean and her daughter-in-law must have convinced them that they were unlikely to discover in Britain what they most wanted to know, namely, the exact chain of communication between Melinda and Maclean.

Two days after Lady Maclean's letter arrived, Melinda, her mother and the children departed to France on holiday. Who knows? Perhaps Donald would make a more direct approach when not directly under the eyes of MI5.

# 16

# The First Cover-Up

Meanwhile an intensive post-mortem had been taking place with the Foreign Office. MI5 had to explain to the Americans why Kim Philby, Burgess's old friend, had been sent to Washington as Head of the British Intelligence Service. In addition, the Foreign Office, who were now aware of the almost priceless information which Maclean had showered on the Russians while in Washington, had now to find out what else he had been passing out from London.

Maclean's work as Head of the American Department was not, as it happened, concerned only with the affairs of the United States.

Indeed, his department was alleged to have spent more time in Latin-American affairs than on North-American. It was also claimed by Government ministers that the American Department did not deal with issues of high U.S. policy but concerned itself with routine matters such as the welfare of U.S. troops in Britain, facilities for important U.S. visitors and the like. The key issues concerning the U.S. were, it was said, dealt with regionally. That is, the Northern Department would deal with U.S.-Soviet relations, the Far Eastern Department (where, incidentally, Burgess had been stationed up until the summer of 1951) with the war in Korea, and the Japanese Peace Treaty, and the NATO Headquarters, then in Paris, with matters of joint defence.

But as we shall see, top secret papers which could hardly have concerned only 'routine matters' were circulated to Maclean and he would thus have known not only what had been decided, and by whom, but the considerations that led to those decisions. And it was only at the beginning of May that arrangements were made to see that he no longer saw documents of exceptional importance or confidentiality. known in those days as 'Blue Folder' papers.

At that time there were at least three major problems jointly exercising the minds of the British and United States Governments. The most longstanding and, as it proved, intractable of these questions concerned the signing of a peace treaty with Germany. The negotiations for a general settlement covering countries which had fought on the side of the Axis had been pursued ever since the autumn of 1945. But the peace treaty with Italy—which Maclean, while in Washington, had helped to draft—together with those for Finland, Bulgaria, Hungary and Rumania were not signed until February 1947, and the Big Four Foreign Ministers, who met in Moscow the following month, had been unable to agree on the future of Germany and Austria. In November 1947 a new conference of Foreign Ministers in London again failed to make progress, and, not long after, the Russians tried to settle matters in their own way by the blockade of Berlin.

In May 1949 after the siege of Berlin had failed, the Foreign Ministers met once more in the hopes of reaching a settlement on Germany and Austria—again without making progress. And in 1951 the Deputies of the Foreign Ministers who, it was hoped, would be more interested in practical details than in making propaganda speeches, met in Paris at the Palais Rose. They were no more successful.

The Soviet bloc countries pressed for East and West Germany to be merged under an all-German Constituent Council, equally split between East and West, whose task would be to prepare the way for an 'all-German, sovereign and democratic, and peace-loving provisional government'.

The Western view was that, on the contrary, democratic government could be set up in Germany only on the basis of free elections under international control, which would extend to the Russian-controlled area. Western 'Position Papers' for the Palais Rose conference were being prepared in the early part of 1951. They covered the causes of tension as well as the German and Austrian peace settlements, and it was, of course, vital for the Russians to find out whether the West would have a 'fall back' position to which they would retreat under pressure, and if so, what it was.

'There go the tripartite (i.e., British, French and U.S.) files of the Big Four Deputy Foreign Ministers' meetings,' said a State Department official when he heard of Maclean's defection. 'He knew everything,' commented Dean Acheson. Information about Anglo-American relations under a British Labour Government was all the more vital to the Russians because of the side-effects of the war in Korea. Korea, like Germany, had been divided into two areas: North and South, the North under a Communist regime and the South under an American-supported government. When the North Koreans invaded the South in the summer of 1950, there was considerable alarm in West Germany about the possibility that the Russians, who still occupied North Korea at the end of World War II but had since withdrawn, might be considering a similar Communist adventure in Europe. The Russians still had twenty-two divisions along the border between East and West Germany, at a time when the West had four Anglo-American divisions and a scrappy Air Force contingent.

Obviously Western Germany could not be left defenceless and open to political threats from the East. But ought she be permitted to have her own defence force or should the West German Federal Republic, created the previous year, be integrated as part of the Western community, by economic, political and therefore military ties? The United States was in favour of doing so. The French, overrun by Germany in two World Wars, were less enthusiastic. The British appeared not to have come down on either side, but again, it was vital for the Russians to know how the balance of opinion lay in the Foreign Office.

Two months after the North Korean invasion, Winston Churchill, speaking in Strasbourg at the Council of Europe, urged the creation of a European Army, including a German contingent. In September 1950 Ernest Bevin, shortly before a meeting of the Western Foreign Ministers in the Waldorf-Astoria Hotel in New York, had said that 'Germany naturally must be brought back into the family of nations, but giving weapons to German troops is not the right way to achieve that object'. So the political balance in Britain was even. But the U.S. Secretary of State Dean Acheson, of whom Bevin had a high opinion, agreed to send substantial reinforcements of American troops to Europe only if Germany were allowed to raise an army. So Bevin gave way. In December the NATO Council meeting agreed, amid the snow and Christmas decorations of Brussels, to open negotiations with West Germany's Chancellor Adenauer on integrating (Bevin preferred his own word 'integrating') Germany into a common defence effort and to discuss changes in the occupation arrangements which would have to follow the creation of German defence forces.

This second problem fitted in very well with Maclean's return to the Foreign Office in November 1950. In the case of a trusted agent like Maclean, it might not have been necessary for the Russians to see photographs of the documents.

A third aspect of Anglo-American relations on which the Russians needed information concerned the role in the Far East of General MacArthur. Following the North Korean invasion, the United Nations requested the United States and other member nations to send aid to South Korea. Sixteen nations, including Britain, did so. By the end of the summer of 1950 the U.N. forces under MacArthur had pushed the invaders back over the frontier and up into North Korea.

Truman had already been embarrassed by the visit which MacArthur had paid in July to the Island of Formosa, to which Chiang Kai Shek had retired after the Communists had driven his forces from mainland China. Soon after the Korean war began, Chiang Kai Shek had offered to throw 30,000 troops into battle on the side of the United Nations. Truman had rejected the offer— partly because Britain, who had already sent troops to Korea, had already recognized the Chinese Communist Government, and wished, no more than the United States, to reopen the conflict on the Chinese mainland. Now he was afraid that MacArthur was working with Chiang to reverse his ruling and bring Chiang's troops into battle.

The President's anxieties were renewed when, on 3rd October, the Indian delegate to the United Nations passed on a warning from China's Foreign Minister, Chou-en-Lai, that China would send troops to the Korean frontier if U.N. or U.S. troops (as distinct from South Korean troops only) moved north of the thirty-eighth parallel of longitude, which lay about half way up the Korean peninsula. MacArthur disregarded the warning and sent U.S. troops across the parallel without specific authorization from the President.

Truman, in an effort to regain control of the situation, flew in mid-October to Wake Island in the Pacific for a conference with MacArthur. The President, realizing that a delicate stage in the conflict would be reached as U.N. troops approached the Soviet and Chinese borders, asked what were the chances of Soviet or Chinese interference. MacArthur pointed out that the Chinese might have perhaps 125,000 troops along their side of the Yalu River, which formed the frontier between the two countries; he said there was no Chinese Air Force to speak of, and that consequently it was unlikely that Red China could put more than 60,000 troops into the Korean battlefield. The Russians, he said, had no ground troops available for Korea and since the winter had almost begun, their mobility was limited. The war would probably be over by the time a Russian division could arrive at the front. The Russians could give air support to the Chinese but there appeared to be little or no military liaison between the two Governments.

MacArthur also assumed that neither the Chinese nor the Russians would be likely to commit large forces in Korea because this would invite the U.N. to retaliate with heavy bombing raids on Communist airfields and lines of communication as well as on troops.

But at that very moment a unit of the Twenty-fourth Communist Chinese Army was crossing into Korea. MacArthur asked to be allowed to bomb the bridges over the Yalu River or at least to make reconnaissance flights over the area. Both requests were refused. By the end of November some 200,000 regular Chinese were in the field. During the three months that followed, MacArthur asked for permission to engage in the right of hot pursuit of enemy

Philby in Moscow,
clothed-capped and
inconspicuous, 1968

Philby with Melinda
in Moscow

At the funeral of Burgess, 1963: (*left to right*) Donald, Melinda, Georgy Stetsenko (a colleague of Burgess's from the Moscow Foreign Languages Publishing House) and Nigel Burgess, Guy's brother

Melinda in the U.S.A., visiting her mother, 1976

planes when they retreated into Chinese airspace. This, too, was refused.

He asked for an economic and naval blockade to be imposed on Communist China, which the U.N. after all had by now branded as the aggressor. But the President withheld his consent. It was apparently more important for Truman to be able to deny with conviction that the U.N. troops had any intention of crossing the Chinese border.

In December, the President, apprehensive about MacArthur's intentions, had published a ruling that military commanders (including MacArthur) must clear any statements on military policy with the Department of Defence before issuing them, and refrain from direct communication on military or foreign policy with newspapers, magazines or other publicity media in the United States.

But on 20th March MacArthur wrote a letter to Joseph Martin, Leader of the Republican Opposition in the House of Representatives, advocating, once more, the use of Chiang Kai Shek's troops in Korea. The letter was not confidential and on 5th April Martin read it out on the floor of the House. Five days later MacArthur, hero of the Pacific and the Japanese war, was summarily dismissed.

There was, of course, no shortage of protests led by Republicans and the China lobby in Washington. MacArthur, they said, had not blundered in his estimate of the Chinese threat. For one thing, he had been forbidden to make the reconnaissance flights which might have told him what was happening. He had been compelled to fight with one hand tied behind his back because of the privileged sanctuary to which China's planes could retire whenever they were attacked.

Britain's premier Attlee, who had flown to Washington to urge restraint on Truman, was among the scapegoats and blamed for the fact that U.N. forces were not allowed to clinch their victory but were compelled to fight on with needless loss of American lives.

The birth of NATO led to complaints that, once again, the U.S. Pacific theatre was being neglected in order to give first priority to Europe.

But the special condemnation of MacArthur's supporters was reserved by a chain of reasoning for the two defectors and the people who let them go. MacArthur had reckoned that the Chinese, for fear of retaliation, would not commit large numbers of troops to the Korean battle front. Then why did they do so?

Somebody must surely have told them for certain that the Americans were not going to retaliate. The Chinese were evidently so sure of themselves that they did not even bother to enforce a black-out on the Yalu River bridges at night. Someone must have leaked the instructions given to MacArthur not to undertake border reconnaissance or engage in hot pursuit. And who might that have been?

Clearly those British spies, one of whom had worked in the Far East Department of the Foreign Office and the other as Head of the American Department, must have had something to do with it. Perhaps the odds were on Maclean as the Chinese 'volunteers' first began to arrive in large numbers shortly after Maclean resumed his work in the Foreign Office.

The timing of Maclean's departure was most unfortunate for the Foreign Office. For although Maclean had become the principal suspect by 1st May, it was not until 25th May that an application was made by Sir William Strang, Permanent Under-Secretary to the Foreign Secretary, in the presence of G. A. Carey Foster, Head of Foreign Office Security and the 'Foreign Office Adviser', the Under-Secretary who acted as a liaison officer between the Foreign Office and the Intelligence Service, to Herbert Morrison who had succeeded Ernest Bevin as Foreign Secretary on 9th March to interrogate Maclean.

It has been suggested that a decision to question Maclean was postponed while Ernest Bevin was still in charge because the Permanent Under-Secretary and others did not wish to burden the Foreign Secretary, already suffering from angina and circulation troubles, with yet another problem, and because there was some unwillingness among Maclean's colleagues in the Foreign Office to believe that one of their number could be a traitor. Certainly there was disbelief at first at the highest official level and this may have caused delay. But if we believe the official post mortem account, it was not until mid-April—at least a month after Morrison took over from Bevin, that the number of suspects, of which Maclean was one, had been narrowed to three. It is, however, conceivable that some officials may have been in favour of allowing Morrison a little time in which 'to find his feet' at the Foreign Office.

Yet even by 25th May there was not enough evidence for Maclean to be prosecuted under the Official Secrets Act.

Here was the dilemma. It could be risky to question Maclean without anything firm to go on. A premature inquisition might merely alarm him without yielding anything new. So, if possible, MI5 had to try for tangible evidence. Maclean's house could be searched in the hope of finding purloined Foreign Office documents, hidden radio transmitters or—more likely—photographic equipment, but it would be better to wait to do this until Melinda, whom the Foreign Office knew to be pregnant, would be away in hospital. (But even this plan would not have been foolproof since Harriet and her husband, who were looking after the children, the children themselves, Sylvia Shrubb, and the odd-job man all came in and out of the house from time to time.) Donald was indeed shadowed. But this could not be done by the highly experienced Special Branch unless a legal basis existed for such action. Until that point had been reached, the shadowing had to be done by MI5's limited staff.

Their men could probably cover Maclean's movements by day but three times as many men would be needed if he were to be watched twenty-four hours a day. In any case, it would be difficult to keep Donald under surveillance in an isolated village such as Tatsfield without his followers becoming conspicuous. Even in London, Donald claimed that he spotted two men shadowing him in a car which ran into the back of his taxi. From early May specially confidential documents normally circulated in Blue Folders were withheld from Maclean. But the longer the inquiry was delayed the more likely it was that Maclean's suspicions would be aroused by the absence of his 'Blue Folders'.

The decision to withhold the 'Blue Folders' was not taken lightly. It was not merely a matter of isolating Maclean from secret papers. Confidential papers can be of only marginal value to a foreign government if they are drafts liable to be altered later, or if they deal with events which are likely to have taken place before the Foreign government has been able to profit from the information.

On the other hand, documents harmless in themselves could allow Maclean and his Soviet contacts to realize which cyphers were known to the West and must be changed, and which were not.

An attempt had been made to solve the problem by seeing whether Maclean's work—which should have been suffering owing to the fact that he kept a bottle of whisky in his desk, had deteriorated to the point where he could be taken off the American desk, or even off all work, altogether.

As Lord Reading, then Minister of State in the Foreign Office put it: 'A very experienced Under-Secretary who supervised the Department was watching him [Maclean] with special closeness towards the end of the time before his disappearance just to see whether there was anything which indicated that Mr Maclean was not performing his duties satisfactorily at that moment, and he came to the conclusion that there was nothing to which exception could be taken.'

The Under-Secretary, according to the Foreign Office, was Sir Roger Makins, who later became Ambassador in Washington, though Mr Macmillan later denied that Sir Roger had undertaken an inquiry. (True enough if he had merely been exercising a stricter than normal supervision and not conducting a cross-examination.)

In any case, Maclean had something more to go on than suspicions. Burgess had told him the brutal facts. And Philby afterwards admitted that he had told Burgess. He excused himself to the British investigators by explaining that while in Washington he had received a stack of routine FBI reports filled, for the most part, with unsubstantiated rumours—including one which he considered especially ridiculous—mentioning Burgess as a suspect. Burgess came into his office just after he had read the report and Philby told him about it. 'Can you imagine what nonsense the FBI is putting out now,' he said. 'They're claiming you're a Soviet spy.' Burgess received the news with complete calm and joined in the incredulous laughter that followed.

Philby said he had mentioned Maclean's name to Burgess as being suspected too—because he remembered that Burgess had known him at Cambridge.

This rather lame explanation served to infuriate still further the security-minded MI5 against the laxness shown by the MI6 (espionage-promoting) branch of the Intelligence Service in which super-spy Philby had found his life-work. If Philby had never intervened, then the slow-paced stalking technique which MI5 adopted towards Maclean might yet have paid off.

It is, of course, just possible, if we disregard most of Melinda's story about Roger Styles, that Donald Maclean had no idea at lunch time on Friday 25th May that he was about to abscond and that he was warned only later that afternoon that the decision to question him had been taken that very morning. This is what Robin and Mary Campbell believed.

Philby would probably have been told that permission to quiz Maclean had now been given in order that he could pass on the news to the Americans and he might have slipped a message through to Maclean sometime on the critical Friday afternoon. But on this theory Burgess, who had already been planning Maclean's escape, had concealed the plans for their escape from Maclean until a few hours before they were due to leave—a considerable risk.

In any case, a last-minute warning to Maclean could not have affected his time of departure one way or the other. His journey had already been arranged for Friday evening.

Burgess, who could have settled the point, was unfortunately not to hand, but Herbert Morrison, at least, could be cross-examined. There was no reason why the Morrison appointment should not have been a success. Morrison had been successful first in local government and later at the Home Office and the Ministry of Home Security. He had shown a sense of public relations and considerable organizing ability. Attlee had appointed him Lord President of the Council and Deputy Prime Minister, but he evidently thought that he would be able to cut a dash as Foreign Secretary, and had been pressing Attlee to give him the job with more and more insistence as Ernest Bevin's health declined.

A few weeks in the Foreign Office were enough, however, to show that Morrison was unfit for it. His interests continued to be centred on home politics and on profiting from the success of the Festival of Britain, to which he had devoted much of his time. Unexpectedly, during Attlee's illness, he had also had to fulfil his duties as acting Prime Minister, at a time when Aneurin Bevan and Harold Wilson were working themselves up to resign over the charges for National Health false-teeth and spectacles dispute.

Never having previously interested himself in events outside his own country, he found it burdensome to acquire such knowledge at the age of sixty-three by reading the briefs provided for him by ambassadors abroad and officials at home. Nor did he seem able to master those briefs that he did read. It was not long before his defects were noticed and commented on on all sides in the House of Commons.

I am worried about Morrison, [Harold Nicolson wrote that summer]. Dick Law told me that his speech on Foreign Affairs on Monday was absolutely deplorable. Everybody squirmed in agony. He pronounced the first syllable of 'Tigris' to rhyme with 'pig', and called the Euphrates the 'You Frates', in two separate words. Now, I do not mind people pronouncing foreign names incorrectly, but to pronounce the Tigris and Euphrates in that way indicates not only lack of education, but also the fact that one has never heard the Middle East discussed by men of experience. It is that which is so terrifying.

(The mistake was not a Churchillian-style anglicization by Morrison but, as Roderick Barclay reveals, a genuine error by the Foreign Secretary's staff who normally provided him with the suggested pronunciation of exotic names, but supposed in this case that it would not be necessary.)

It was also distasteful to Morrison to have to defend in Parliament an institution whose staff's attitude to their work he did not approve. Senior Foreign Office officials, he found, would address one another by Christian name in the presence of a Minister, disregarding distinctions of rank which would have been considered fitting at the Home Office. He may have concluded with some bitterness that if you were already one of the élite, then the difference between one civil service grade did not matter very much—even in the presence of a Minister. 'This easy-going familiarity (within the Foreign Office) is not wholly restricted to one level, it exists among all ranks and crosses the usual barriers between seniors and juniors,' he complained, adding with a back-handed slap at Bevin that even

Secretaries of State had been known to address Foreign Office Civil Servants by their Christian names. His prejudices about the Foreign Service were enshrined in a simple sentence penned some time later. 'I did not meet Burgess so far as I can recall,' Morrison wrote in his memoirs. 'I gathered that he was an intelligent and rather bumptious young man—a typical young career diplomat.'

We have seen the various reasons which led first Maclean's friends, then the Embassy in Cairo, then the Foreign Office, and next the Security Services to say as little as possible about the Burgess and Maclean affair. But lips in the Cabinet tightened too as the time drew near when a public statement would have to be made in the House of Commons.

The Labour majority in the House was already slender, and the prospect of an autumn election—in which the Government was to fall from power—was already casting its shadow over the Ministers. Herbert Morrison could see better than most that a scandal in the Foreign Office would rub off to some extent on Labour, just as in the sixties the story linking Christine Keeler, Profumo and Captain Yevgeni Ivanov, Assistant Naval Attaché of the Soviet Embassy, would rock the Tory administration of Harold Macmillan. In addition, Morrison had no wish to anger the left-wing of his own party by accusing their Soviet ally of uncomradely activities.

Thus Morrison was content to shield the Foreign Office from scandal not only because he was pressed to do so by MI5 but also because it protected his own reputation and, with it, that of the Government.

His first serious interrogation in the House took place on 11th June, seventeen days after Burgess and Maclean had left the country but only four days after the public first heard about it. Before being questioned, Morrison made a two-minute statement to the House:

I have little to add to the Foreign Office statement issued on 7th June. The absence abroad of Mr Maclean and Mr Burgess was established on Tuesday 29th May. Mr Maclean had asked for and been granted permission to be absent from duty for private reasons on Saturday 26th May. Mr Burgess was on leave pending a decision as to his future.

The matter was at once placed in the hands of the appropriate authorities who are receiving full collaboration from my department in their inquiries. On the same day, 29th May, it was found that they had left Southampton, ostensibly for a weekend cruise on the night of 25th May. They disembarked at St Malo on 26th May but no further confirmed information has been received.

Mr Maclean, as has already been stated, suffered from a breakdown in Cairo a year ago owing to overstrain. When he recovered he came to the Foreign Office as head of the American Department. Mr Burgess had recently been recalled from the Embassy in Washington owing to his general unsuitability in the position he held, and the question of his future employment in the Foreign Office was under consideration.

Mr Burgess is not a member of the senior branch of the Foreign Service but he held the temporary and local rank of second secretary in His Majesty's Embassy at Washington for a trial period. Neither Mr Maclean nor Mr Burgess has been dismissed. They have been suspended from duty pending the results of the inquiries which are being made. The question of their dismissal will depend on the result of these inquiries.

The security aspects of the case are under investigation and it is not in the public interest to disclose them.

But despite its brevity, his exposé contained a remarkable number of under-statements, evasions and half-truths. Thus Morrison said that Burgess was 'on leave pending a decision as to his future' when, in fact, he had already been suspended with a view either to his resignation, or, if this were not forthcoming, probable dismissal after he had been heard by yet another disciplinary board.

Again it was not quite true to say that the matter had been 'placed in the hands of the appropriate authorities' since it was MI5 which had drawn Morrison's attention to the security leak and not the other way round. Similarly, MI5 had already heard of Burgess and Maclean's departure *before* the Foreign Office reported it to them.

However, Morrison's main difficulty was to protect the Labour Government from the suggestion that its Foreign Secretary had condoned the infiltration of Communists into the Foreign Service, a possibility to which the Tories were fully alive. Mr Somerset de Chair, for instance, asked if there had been any systematic check on the loyalty and the affiliations of members of the Foreign Service, like Mr Burgess, who joined the Service during the war when we were fighting allies of the Soviet Union. Morrison's reply: 'Yes, sir. Security checks are made on members of the Foreign Service on their appointment, and if it proves necessary, from time to time.'

Mr Duncan Sandys wanted to know whether, when the last security check-up of officials took place, the Foreign Office were satisfied that Burgess had no Communist associations.

Morrison avoided answering the question: 'I did not imply that there is a regular and systematic week-by-week check-up of all Foreign Office officials,' he said, 'and I should not like it to come to that. Indeed I do not think the Department deserves such a check-up.'

Brigadier Head returned to the earlier question. He said it had been pointed out that, when Burgess went to the Foreign Office,

Britain and Russia were allies and the question was whether subsequent events had caused another check-up to be made. Burgess
had made little or no secret of his extremely left-wing political views
and was it not curious that no check was made subsequently
regarding them.

Morrison: 'I am not aware of that, but if the implication in the
question is that we have one test of suitability for office in the
Foreign Office according to whom we are in alliance with or at war
with at the time, then I am bound to say that these are not considerations that would influence my mind.'

A gallant effort was made by Mr Chetwynd, the Labour MP for
Stockton-on-Tees, to keep both the Foreign Office and the Soviet
Union out of trouble. Had Mr Morrison, he asked, yet discounted
the theory that the absence of the two gentlemen is connected with
their private lives and has nothing at all to do with their Foreign
Office connections?

But Mr Morrison did not snatch at this straw nor at one offered
by Mr Paton who asked: 'Is my Rt. Hon. Friend in possession of
even a shred of real evidence which could connect the disappearance
of these men with Soviet Russia?'

'I would impress on the House,' Mr Morrison said, 'that it would
be premature to come to a conclusion one way or the other. That
is the only position one can adopt at this stage,' he opined.

Mr George Wigg, the Labour MP for Dudley, asked whether Mr
Morrison would institute inquiries into a suggestion made in a
London newspaper (it was the *Sunday Dispatch*) that there was
widespread sexual perversion in the Foreign Office, and, if the
inquiries proved the allegations unfounded, would he consult the
legal officers of the Crown with a view to instituting proceedings.
(As already mentioned sex between consenting male adults was at
that time a criminal offence in Britain.)

Morrison's reply drew the first laugh of the afternoon: 'I should
not like to answer the question about legal implications on the spur
of the moment. I can only say that perhaps I have not been long
enough at the Foreign Office.' He added: 'In any case, I should
think that any such implication was unfair and irresponsible. The
writer of the political stuff in the Sunday paper referred to is not a
gentleman to whom any of us need pay too much attention.'

Other questions followed about the treatment given to Burgess
after he had joined the Foreign Office. Sir Jocelyn Lucas pointed out
that a Sunday newspaper mentioned earlier in the House, namely
the *Sunday Dispatch*, 'says quite openly that Mr Burgess had
admittedly strong Communist tendencies and hated America.' In
that case, why was he sent there, Sir Joceyln wanted to hear.

But Mr Morrison, who evidently had not studied the matter with

as much care as the *Sunday Dispatch*, had no explanation ready.
'If that was by the same author to whom my Hon. Friend referred,
with great respect, I would not take any notice.'

Mr Godfrey Nicholson, a solid Tory from Farnham, turned the
discussion away from Burgess's sex life to Maclean's drinking spells.
He asked was the conduct of Mr Maclean in Egypt at all times
consistent with the high level required of Foreign Office officials,
because, he said, there were rumours, to say the least, and to put
the matter as carefully as possible, that he was of a highly erratic
nature. This sally appeared, however, to be ignored by the Foreign
Secretary.

A week later, however, the Tories returned to the attack—this
time with Mr Kenneth Younger, Minister of State, standing in for
Mr Morrison. Once more on dangerous ground, Younger said that
a security check had been made on Burgess 'some time ago' and it
was negative in its result.

Brigadier Head: 'When Mr Burgess was taken on as a permanent
member of the Foreign Office staff, was he screened before he
entered this confidential employment?'

Mr Younger: 'I do not think so. Frankly, I do not see why he
should have been. That does not seem to me to have been a
particularly appropriate moment. He had already been in the
Foreign Service and other forms of Government employment some
time before that. His establishment did not give him an any more
confidential position than he had before, and I do not think that
a check was made at that time.'

Mr Sandys asked Younger if the 'highly Communistic' views
which had been widely expressed by Burgess could by any stretch
of official tolerance be regarded as consistent with holding a position
of confidence in a Minister's office?

Mr Younger: 'I do not know to what particular views the Right
Hon. Gentleman is referring as he has not explained it to this
House. To try to make this a little more precise, perhaps I might say
that what the Prime Minister said when we were discussing this
matter some three years ago was that it was the policy of the
Government that no one who is known to be a member of the
Communist Party or to be associated with it in such a way as to
raise legitimate doubts about his or her reliability is employed in
connection with work the nature of which is vital to the security of
the State.'

And so in the House, at any rate, the story for the moment went
off the boil.

# 17

# Holiday For Melinda

Mrs Dunbar, it will be remembered, had already decided, even before Donald had disappeared, to take Melinda's two small boys Fergus and Donald junior away with her on holiday, while Melinda was in hospital. Now, she insisted, with reason on her side, that Melinda should come too. She discounted the anxieties of the Foreign Office about the undesirable publicity that such a trip would inspire.

Beacon Shaw, she insisted, was no place for a convalescence. Rumours were still pouring in from almost all over the world that the missing diplomats had been seen here, there and everywhere. And Melinda was considered to be the person most likely to know whether every latest 'find' was true or false. The Foreign Office, who were not averse to hearing the latest reports the day before they would appear in the newspapers, told Melinda to refer all inquiries to them, which removed some of the strain, but reporters, when led up a dead end, endeavoured to get news from other sources. They waylaid the Maclean children on their way to or from school to question them and take photographs. Sylvia Shrubb, the children's nurse, was interviewed and propositioned. Reporters lurked round the drive gate and sometimes even behind bushes in the garden.

In the meantime MI5 had been pursuing their investigations. Where possible, the interrogations, most of them by William (more usually known as Jim) Skardon, were conducted in a low key. Both Alan Maclean and Mary Campbell say that they asked the interrogator many more questions than they were asked—the sign, probably, of an acute interrogator. The same held good in the early stages for Melinda, who appeared most anxious to discover the real character and background of 'Roger Styles'.

In leading Melinda towards the confession which they hoped to get, the interrogators could not very well confront her with what they knew about Donald. They could not take it for granted that she would not pass it on elsewhere, and in any case most of what they knew in the early phase of their investigations was sensitive material on nuclear weaponry which they had received from the Americans. It was not theirs to disclose.

Nevertheless, they could not help thinking that Melinda must know *something*, or at least suspect something. For example, she had been present at the Gargoyle Club when Donald Maclean had said before witnesses that he was the English Alger Hiss. Looking back, could Melinda really believe that this was Donald talking drunken nonsense? He had so often disagreed with the Foreign Office policy on Spain, the Middle East and Korea. Could it really have been a surprise to her that he should one day abscond to the Soviet Union? And the £2,000 that Donald had sent her, could she really believe, as some people seriously suggested at the time, that he had become a gigolo and embarked on an affair with a foreign millionairess?

Could she really under these circumstances be speaking the truth when she rejected any suggestion that her husband might have been a Communist agent, or even a Communist? Could they believe her when she said that Maclean had no reason to leave the country?

As time went by, they must have become less certain of Melinda's complete loyalty. At any rate, shortly before she was due to leave on holiday, according to her account given to Geoffrey Hoare, the MI5 man who was conducting the investigation in softly softly style, telephoned and said that he would like to see her again. Later he telephoned again and said that he was prevented from coming because he had a bad knee and would like to send a colleague instead. And the substitute who arrived at Tatsfield in mid-August wasted no time on niceties. He suggested that Melinda must have known that Donald was a Communist, was probably a Communist herself, and was planning to join him. Melinda, however, was able to say that nothing had been proved against her husband, and until it was, she would never believe that Donald had betrayed the interests of his country.

The lie detector, first introduced in the United States in the mid-thirties, was not tried out in this case. The MI5 men reasoned that you might get a positive reaction from an innocent man or woman who was suddenly confronted with circumstantial evidence. Nevertheless to Mrs Dunbar, Melinda said almost in tears that perhaps it was possible to be married to a man without really knowing anything about him at all.

This must have been music to Mrs Dunbar's ears. In any case she could now show the Foreign Office and the world that her daughter was no longer under suspicion and was free to go where she pleased. She had taken a house, La Sauvageonne, owned by a Monsieur Gosselin, at Beauvallon, a village on the north shore of St Tropez Bay, surrounded by pine and cork trees at the foot of the Maures Mountains. It had a garden of its own and enough rooms to take not only Melinda and the children but also her sister Catherine, now Mrs Terrell. But Mrs Dunbar was mistaken if she supposed that Melinda would be able to find peace and quiet by the sea.

Her departure from Northolt Airport did not escape the notice of the Press, particularly as she was seen off by Donald Maclean's brother Alan, and Lady Maclean who, it will be remembered, had received a letter from her missing son only two days before. The reporters apparently took little notice of Lady Maclean's statement that 'It's purely a holiday. Mrs Maclean is making no attempt whatever to find her husband while she is in France.'

Once more, newsmen, as far as they were able, laid siege to the Macleans. They suspected—rightly, as it turned out—that agents from the other side were seeking to contact Melinda. She was watched when she hired a water pedalo on the beach, when she went out to dinner in St Tropez, and when she escaped from the watchers to drive to a lonely fort of La Garde-Freinet high up in the mountains. Some reports claimed that she was away for the two nights of 21st–22nd August and 25th–26th, though Melinda denied this. Perhaps the agents were frightened off by the publicity on the Côte d'Azur, or perhaps they got a message to Melinda saying in effect 'later but not here'. What was not generally known at the time was that Melinda, towards the end of her holiday, escaped to Paris where she was not known and where 'the other side' had a far better chance of contacting her. At any rate, after almost exactly a month, Melinda and the children came back to Tatsfield as if nothing had happened for another winter of discontent.

Just before Melinda returned from holiday, Francis Marling, Mrs Dunbar's first husband and Melinda's father, arrived in London. Under pressure from Mrs Dunbar, he appeared at the Foreign Office and urged them, if they did not know or were not prepared to reveal the whereabouts of Donald Maclean or declare him to be guilty of treachery, to pay his salary to his wife. The Foreign Office, however, kept their counsel and their money.

Meanwhile matters in Britain had not stood still. Kim Philby was asked to resign from the Foreign Service, though it was four years before this was published. Alan Maclean resigned, at his own request, with rather more publicity. The Foreign Office was unwilling to condemn his brother, and it was certainly not up to him to do so. On the other hand, he had no desire to earn martyrdom by quarrelling with the Establishment in public over his future in the Foreign Service. These considerations were publicly implied in the hand-out released by the Foreign Office News Department in which he had once worked. A report in *The Times* of 22nd August 1951 read:

Mr Alan Maclean, a younger brother of one of the two Foreign

Office officials who disappeared in May has tendered his resignation from the Foreign Service in which he has been a temporary officer for four years.

Accepting his resignation the Foreign Office thanked Mr Maclean for the excellent services he had rendered in the various capacities he had filled in the Foreign Service.

The Foreign Office letter (accepting his resignation) 'takes note of the fact that Mr Maclean offered his resignation on the understanding that there is no suggestion whatever that he is in any way implicated in the disappearance of his brother or that he believes him to have unwittingly taken any step injurious to the security or interests of the country'.

Mr Alan Maclean who served in the 11th Hussars during the war was afterwards seconded to the Control Commission in Germany. Later, he served in the Foreign Office in the German Department and the News Department. A year ago he became secretary to Sir Gladwyn Jebb, Chief British Delegate to the United Nations, and recently he was appointed Information Officer of the British United Nations Delegation.

He was summoned home before he could take up his new job.

Lady Maclean maintained a dignified silence but visited Tatsfield at least once and her eyes filled with tears as she recalled the happy memories of days gone by, and found in the sunken garden at Beacon Shaw the medals that Donald had won for athletics and given to the children to play with. When she died in 1962 she left Donald an equal share of the family inheritance.

Donald's friends remained inhibited by past loyalties, and most, after consultation with each other, decided that neither the newspapers nor MI5 had the right to criticize their choice of friends or to question their patriotism—or their gullibility.

After the Tories came to power in October 1951 there was a period of comparative calm in the House of Commons, if only because those who had been asking the awkward questions while they were in Opposition now had to answer them. However in July 1952 it was announced that Burgess and Maclean had been finally sacked, and the sceptics stirred again.

One of them was the indefatigable Lieutenant-Colonel Marcus Lipton, a left-of-centre socialist uncharitably described by commentator Andrew Roth as a 'news paragraph snatcher'. He asked Mr Anthony Nutting, Under-Secretary at the Foreign Office: 'Can the Hon. Gentleman explain the reason for this extraordinary delay of one year in finally deciding to dispense with the services of these two men?'

Mr Nutting: 'It is because the search for them was continuing. Indeed the search is still continuing. But, having been absent without leave for a year, my Right Hon. Friend has considered that as a disciplinary measure their appointments should be terminated and that they should be dismissed the Service.'

Lieutenant-Colonel Lipton: 'Is it to be understood that disciplinary measures can be applied to absconding Government civil servants only after they have absconded for 12 months? Is that an essential qualification which must be taken into account before people are given the sack?'

Mr Nutting replied that it was not. And there for the time being the matter ended.

But less than a fortnight later on 15th July 1952 the Press Association issued a statement on behalf of Melinda to all newspapers and agencies. It read:

Mrs Donald Maclean is shortly proceeding to France with her children to spend a holiday of some weeks there.

Mrs Maclean later in the year, it is understood, contemplates taking up residence either in France or Switzerland.

In accordance with the practice she had adopted since the disappearance of her husband, Mrs Maclean has notified the Foreign Office of her intentions.

She is hoping, it is learned, by changing her residence, to ensure a degree of privacy for her family of young children.

In a report published the following day, the *Daily Express* quoted Mrs Maclean as saying among other things: 'I have waited for over a year for news of my husband. Now I am starting a new life for my children ... I may come back to this country to wind up my affairs, but I shall never come back to live.' Had she any regrets about leaving Britain? Mrs Maclean smiled ... 'I would rather not answer.' (George Joyce, the interviewer, was criticized for reporting a smile, which he could not have seen down the telephone, rather than a chuckle he might have heard.) Asked whether she would sell Beacon Shaw, Mrs Maclean said: 'That is not really settled, I hope to.'

Her mother, who had been helping the housekeeper with the packing, said: 'I am going, too, with the children. Going to Switzerland is my daughter's affair. Where she lives is her business and mine. No explanations ... All I can say is "Goodbye".'

There could have been perfectly innocent reasons for Melinda's decision. First, her mother had decided that the time had come for her to make a new life. She had held the purse strings ever since the Foreign Office had stopped paying Donald Maclean's salary, and his dismissal from the Foreign Office in June 1952 destroyed the last hope that he would be reinstated. Mrs Dunbar would have preferred Melinda to divorce Donald and remarry. But in Britain with a British passport it would be three years before she could be free. In the United States, however, the process only took two years. But to get a divorce in the U.S. she would need to regain her American passport which she had lost when she married Donald, and her prospects for doing so would be greatly reduced if she continued to live in England.

Melinda's feelings towards Donald must have varied. In October, a month after she came back from holiday, she wrote to Harriet:

Life goes on and gradually a pattern seems to emerge out of the swamp. Oh, I can't tell you how completely shipwrecked I feel. Like a drowning man my past seems to rise up and confront me and I couldn't be more horrified. I made the fatal mistake of reading old letters (1939 ones) not Donald's and as far as I can see I never wrote and answered any of them and altogether behaved so bitchily or unconsciously it isn't true. I can't tell you how shocked I am. I feel like writing to them all now and saying please forgive me for not having answered your letter before, I would like to meet you for dinner when you come to Paris, etc. Wouldn't they all be shocked out of their wits, as would their respective wives and offspring. If I had ever learned to answer letters perhaps I would be among the ranks (of the wives I mean). Don't despair. I haven't gotten as far as that yet, nor have I lost a particle of faith in Donald, but, Oh God, why is life quite so difficult.

Was this just the letter of an unrepentant coquette? Of a woman still in love with her husband? Or of one merely afraid to accept the fact that her world had been shattered for good?

Her hopes may have dwindled during the long period of waiting during which, so far as is known, no more messages came from Donald. In the spring she went into a London hospital for three weeks for a minor operation, and at that time declared that she no longer loved Donald and that she was glad that the pretence of marriage was now over.

Not all of this could have been due to post-operational depression. Life in the country during the winter would not have been ideal. Beacon Shaw, which they had chosen because it was outside London, seemed more remote than ever. It stood on the brow of a hill and caught the wind; it was chilly and could not provide the normal American standards of comfort. It needed a man there to pump the water, carry the coke and take the ash out of the furnace.

Melinda must also have sensed a thinly veiled atmosphere of hostility around her, not from the villagers of Tatsfield but from others—even if nothing much was said. MI5 had clearly suspected her earlier of knowing that Donald was a Soviet agent. Then she must have felt that Lady Maclean, who had never considered her good enough for Donald, held her in some way to blame for his disappearance, and thus indirectly for Alan's resignation from the Foreign Service.

On the other hand, Melinda certainly had a weakness for putting off decision-making, whether it was giving notice to a servant or marrying Donald or leaving Beacon Shaw. She was delighted with her youngest child Melinda junior, called 'Pinkers' partly because she looked like a pink rose, but also because of the pink rose pattern Melinda had chosen for the nursery wall paper. Beacon Shaw was the first home she and Donald had owned and leaving it would be a wrench.

Two considerations helped her to make up her mind. One was that the two boys needed a more advanced education than could be found in the neighbourhood. Fergus would be eight in September 1952 and would then be too old to continue with Donald junior at the primary school in Woldingham. The second factor was that, like Melinda, the boys resented being exposed to unwanted publicity —like a goldfish in a tank. According to Mrs Dunbar, they had been frightened by reporters who they believed had come to take their home away. One day according to Geoffrey Hoare's account, Mrs Dunbar said she saw Fergus crawling into the bushes at the edge of the garden. She asked him what he was doing and he said: 'I'm going to shoot the reporters who are making Mummy unhappy.' Schoolchildren followed the Maclean children after class with taunts of 'Your father's in prison', and led by militant girls, threw stones at them.

A swarm of reporters had descended on Tatsfield again on 25th May, the anniversary of Donald's disappearance, and had once more tried to photograph and interview the boys on their way to school—which gave Melinda the feeling that the Press were never going to let the story die.

Even so, Melinda did not feel like being completely uprooted and the final plan agreed with her mother was that they should both go on holiday in France, and afterwards they would settle down in Geneva where the boys could go to the International School. But she had not yet decided—or said she had not yet decided—to sell Beacon Shaw. There may have been the thought at the back of Melinda's mind that once she re-crossed the Atlantic back to the United States she would never be able to get in touch with Donald again.

A few days before they were due to leave Britain, the senior MI5 investigator telephoned to Mrs Dunbar and asked her to see him. She said that she would be going to Victoria to buy the tickets and agreed to ring MI5 when she got there. She did so and the investigator met her in the office of British European Airways and took her to a nearby café. But he had nothing to tell her about Donald's whereabouts and would give no pledge to inform Melinda first if he heard anything—a further indication that his suspicions had not been entirely lulled. He told her, however, that she and Melinda would not be under police surveillance in France, as they had been at Beauvallon the previous year.

Within a week of the Press Association announcement the three Macleans, Mrs Dunbar and the children's nurse had left Britain for good. Melinda spent a few days in Paris with Harriet and her husband at the flat at 7 Avenue de Segur before driving down to a farmhouse in the countryside behind Deauville which Harriet's husband had found for them. But the house turned out to be uncomfortable and remote, and not even Calvados, the apple-brandy tipple so dear to the people of Normandy, could banish the damp and the cold. So they cut their losses and returned to Paris to stay in a hotel. Lees Mayall, who was then stationed at the Embassy in Paris, remembers meeting Melinda again and finding her a rather pathetic figure, dependent for ever, it seemed, on her mother.

But about this time she seems to have decided that if she was not going to hear any more from the Foreign Office, it was up to her to make up her own mind. She would go with her mother and the children to Geneva, return to England after all to sell Beacon Shaw and Donald's car, and then come back to Geneva to live there, and even, once more, look for that ever elusive job. She would talk to solicitors about getting a divorce and recovering her American passport. She told Geoffrey Hoare that she had no intention of marrying again, but added coquettishly (for despite her three children she still had a slim, almost girlish figure): 'Who would marry a notorious woman like me with three small children?'

Early in September she drove from Paris to Geneva in a new car that her mother had given her and the family settled into a hotel while they looked around for a flat. In October they found a furnished flat over a fur shop, in the Rue des Alpes, a semi-commercial street in the centre of Geneva, containing a number of medium-priced hotels, suitable for those who wished to be near the station rather than the airport. One living-room had a view over the lake.

The Director of the International School, set up originally under the League of Nations, forerunner of the United Nations, was helpful. He raised no objection to enrolling the children of this 'notorious woman' Melinda Maclean, and about a month after the term had started, Melinda returned to England to settle her affairs. She saw her doctor, her solicitor and her bankers, without, however, making much progress towards recovering her passport or filing a petition for divorce. Nor did she sell Beacon Shaw.

She enjoyed herself, nevertheless, and got back to Geneva only two days before Christmas, which she spent quietly with her mother with a bottle of champagne in front of a miniature log fire. Towards the end of January, Mrs Dunbar, feeling that Melinda was now happily settled in, left Geneva for Paris, where she spent ten days with Melinda's sister Harriet, and early in February took off for the United States. She did not return to Geneva until mid-May, so that Melinda was by herself for about three and a half months.

She did not, however, find life too monotonous. In early spring, she took her children to Saanenmoser, then a small village with three or four hotels and a few private villas, but easily reached from Geneva or Montreux, where she joined up with an English friend and her two little girls for a fortnight's ski-ing. She made other friendships with parents at the International School.

When her mother returned, Melinda told her that she would like to accept an invitation from some American friends to take the whole family in as paying guests in their house at Majorca for the summer holidays, which began at the end of June. The offer had come the previous year from an American, Mr Douglas McKillop, whose wife, a friend of Harriet's, had died about a year before. McKillop had been a security officer in the Marshall Plan offices in Paris but had given up his job and settled in Majorca, and had a large house at Cala Ratjada at which he would be delighted to put them up for as long as they could manage to stay. Cala Ratjada was then a small village on a bay of the rocky east coast of the island, with an artists' colony.

In the war Douglas McKillop was recognized as an expert on the interpretation of air reconnaissance photographs. He told friends that one of his regrets was that his marriage had produced no children. McKillop was the odd man out in a colony of married couples, and he told a friend of his, Harrison Elliot, that he hoped to remarry while he was in Majorca.

So Mrs Dunbar got ready to sublet the flat while they were away from Switzerland. At the last minute, however, Melinda changed her mind. She said she needed mountain air rather than sea air and took the children away once more to Saanenmoser, meaning to stay there for a fortnight.

Melinda's sudden change of plan led to a family row. The children had been looking forward with great enthusiasm to going to the sea and would be heartbroken if their trip was cancelled, Mrs Dunbar said. They had enjoyed ski-ing at Saanenmoser in the winter but there would be no snow there now and practically nothing to do. Mrs Dunbar, who hated the mountains, as Melinda very well knew, said she would be happy to take the children on to Majorca without Melinda, who could join them later. But Melinda would not agree to this. She wanted to take the children with her and in the end Mrs Dunbar gave way. The bookings were cancelled and Melinda drove off with the children into the mountains.

But after five days at Saanenmoser she came back to Geneva; the weather had been poor and, after all, she decided that the original plan of going to Majorca was better.

So on 9th July Melinda went back to the travel agency to re-book five tickets to Majorca, but by now the planes were booked up until 23rd July and so three weeks of the holiday was lost.

Once she got there, Melinda enjoyed herself, and Mrs Dunbar had hopes of a romance for her daughter. Melinda and her mother often dropped into the small hotel owned by Mrs Peggy Carnrick and when she left she gave a farewell party for twenty-five American friends.

But Melinda achieved no special relationship with her host. She seemed to pay more attention to an artist, a naturalized Briton, born in Austria, married, a tall fair-haired man who had a remarkable resemblance to Donald Maclean—a likeness which Melinda noticed and commented on. It was in this mood that she returned on 7th September with Mrs Dunbar and the family to Geneva.

# 18

# Reunion For Melinda

On Thursday 17th September the Manchester *Guardian* led its front page with a story from its Geneva Correspondent, Clare Hollingworth. 'Swiss Search for Mrs Maclean' the headline ran 'Kidnapped or Gone to Join her Husband?'

Mrs Maclean, the wife of Donald Maclean, the British diplomatist who disappeared in 1951 has now disappeared with her three children [the report read]. The Chief of the Geneva Police says she may have gone to join her husband behind the Iron Curtain, or she may still be in Switzerland, and all police and frontier officials have been ordered to look out for her. He discredits the idea that she may have been kidnapped. Her mother, Mrs Dunbar, reported her disappearance to the British Consulate here and to the Foreign Office in London.

The paper noted that Mrs Maclean had never previously taken her youngest child, little over two years old, with her on her 'not infrequent' weekend trips.

Mrs Dunbar had become worried when her daughter failed to return home on Sunday night after a weekend visit. Melinda had left no address and had apparently taken only a weekend case with her, and, when there was still no sign of her by noon on Monday, Mrs Dunbar rang the British Consulate to report the matter and ask for advice. But apparently Consular officials were so busy with the visit to Geneva of the Lord Mayor of London that she was unable to get much response from them. She was told that she would not be able to see anyone until after 2 p.m. All the senior officials had already left for the airport to meet their distinguished visitor, and even after lunch there seemed to be no sense of urgency. London, she was told, would be informed 'through the usual channels' which could have meant whenever the next diplomatic bag left. So on Monday afternoon Mrs Dunbar telephoned direct to the Foreign Office in London.

At noon on Wednesday a post-office messenger boy was seen entering the house in which Mrs Maclean had been staying with a telegram which, however, was intercepted by the police officer on duty. The paper's diplomatic correspondent made the point that Mrs Maclean would not have needed a visa to enter any of the countries bordering Switzerland.

Meanwhile the Swiss police had found Mrs Maclean's black Chevrolet car GE 10514. She had left it at 6.30 on the evening of Friday 11th September at the Garage de la Gare, Lausanne, and had told the receptionist Marcel Micheli: 'I want to leave the car here for a week.' She seemed calm and composed. She gave her name as Dunbar—possibly to delay the police in their search, or to help Mrs Dunbar to reclaim the car later. For the same reason, perhaps, she left the certificate showing that she had paid both the tax and insurance. There were French maps, which by some coincidence covered the area round St Malo where her husband had landed in France on the morning after he disappeared. (Was this a hint to Mrs Dunbar that Melinda had done the same? Or a reminder from the Russians to the Foreign Office of how Maclean had outwitted them?) There was also a new map of Switzerland showing details of the German and Austrian frontiers, together with the Triptyque, the document which records for Customs purposes all the journeys in and out of Switzerland. It showed that during the previous twelve months Mrs Maclean had made sixteen journeys over the Swiss border—although to anyone living in Geneva almost alongside the French frontier and within reach of French ski-ing resorts there need be nothing unusual about this.

Some children's toys were still in the car, and, on the front seat a book belonging to seven-year-old Donald Maclean jr: *Little Lost Lamb* open at a page which read:

> Oh wind, blow softly over my sheep,
> Away from the lion, and over the lamb,
> Blow softly.

Melinda had left the flat in Geneva about half past three for a car journey to Lausanne which should not have taken longer than an hour and a half. How, then, did she fill in the spare hour and a half which she had on her hands? Did she take the children and give them a solid meal or had she some last minute shopping to do—or did she meet her contact who briefed her on the arrangements for the rest of her journey?

From the garage the police moved on to the station nearby and found that before leaving the car, Mrs Maclean had fetched Louis Papeaux, a porter from the station, and left the luggage with him. Mrs Maclean and her children arrived only a short time before the train was due to depart—no one remembered seeing her buy a ticket. Nor are tickets examined before passengers board the train.

Professor André Guignard of Lausanne, who was on his way to Fribourg to deliver a lecture, was one of those who, nevertheless, noticed the Maclean family.

I was thirteen minutes early for my train at Lausanne station and so I walked up and down the platform. I saw in front of a newspaper stand a woman in a light costume—grey or beige [light blue would have been more accurate]—standing with a child of about two on her arm. Huddled close to her were two boys whose hair was fairer than any you see among the Swiss—almost white.

As I walked, I continued to look at this group and noticed a porter arrive with two light-coloured suitcases, a bundle of comic books and a toy rifle. He put down the whole load in front of her and said: 'I found something to tie the books together.'

She said: 'I beg your pardon' in French, and then spoke in English. Another porter came up, saw the boys with the rifle and said jokingly: 'Present arms!'

The train arrived and the woman entered a carriage ahead of me. She stopped and looked round. She looked very frightened. The two boys had run along the coach and entered at the other end.

She lost sight of them for a moment and it seemed to me she became almost hysterical. But this was the only time that she showed any nervousness at all.

The train left Lausanne for Zurich travelling roughly north-eastwards across Switzerland and the family arrived at Zurich at 11.16. There they changed into the Arlberg Express that travels almost due east across the Swiss frontier into Austria and on to Vienna.

Paul Glauser, the ticket collector, remembered the Macleans too. There were only a few passengers that night on the Arlberg Express from Zurich. Mrs Maclean, he noticed, had pulled down the blind of the compartment and had put the baby girl in the corner seat. The child was fast asleep. All three children were asleep when the train left Saargans shortly before the train crossed the Swiss frontier into Austria. Mrs Maclean looked pale and her hair was ruffled as though she, too, had tried to sleep. Her tickets—first class one full fare for herself, and two halves for the boys (Melinda junior travelled free) took her only as far as Buchs on the Swiss-Austrian border. The conductor warned her five minutes before the train reached there, so that she would be ready to alight, and he noticed that Melinda had begun to comb the boys' hair. Glauser left the train at the frontier, so he did not then know that Melinda and her family had continued their journey without leaving their carriage. She had a second set of tickets taking her to Bad Gastein, a resort about half way across Austria and thirty-five miles south of Salzburg. Thus she had laid two false trails, each designed to throw the trackers off the scent away from her real rendezvous. Both sets of tickets, it was discovered, had been issued in Zurich.

To get to Bad Gastein the family would have to change trains again at Schwarzach St Veit, a railway junction which they reached about nine o'clock the following morning (Saturday). But when they got to Schwarzach they stayed there.

An American officer who travelled on the same train as Mrs Maclean and her children shared a first-class compartment with the family. The Macleans were only too easily identified from his description—the two boys in their grey flannel suits who told him they went to school in Geneva; the luggage—the expanding suitcase and two raffia hold-alls from Majorca, and Melinda in her bright blue three-quarter length coat—were unmistakable. The officer saw Mrs Maclean in the courtyard outside the station. The children still had their comics and their pop-gun with them.

Peter Gruber, a station porter, remembered the American lady. 'She looked very tired and nervous when she got off the train with her children. I asked her where she was going, and she said in English: "Someone is meeting me in a car." After twenty to forty minutes, during which the Macleans ordered breakfast in the station restaurant, I saw an American car drive up, and a man got out. I asked him: "Have you come to meet someone?"

'He seemed terribly startled and said: "Why do you ask that?" I think he was angry. I said there was a lady and children waiting for a car and he said: "Yes, that's them." '

And there the trail ended. Until October 1955, Austria was occupied by British, American, French and Russian troops and the country divided into zones, the most easterly of which was under Soviet control. It was assumed that the Maclean family were driven from the American Zone in which Schwarzach St Veit lay, into the Russian Zone, probably to Neunkirchen, an industrial town south of Vienna.

The car was a newish black or blue-black Ford or Chevrolet, a private car with a Salzburg number plate. The driver was a well-dressed man, aged thirty-five or forty, with receding medium-fair hair. He spoke English, and German with an Austrian accent. Meanwhile the two MI5 men most concerned with the Burgess and Maclean affair had flown out to Geneva to see Mrs Dunbar.

MI5, as is their wont, had already suggested to Mrs Dunbar on the previous Tuesday that she should say nothing to anyone about Melinda's departure (it would save her from being pestered by reporters and would help the Swiss police with their inquiries). So why, they asked, had the story leaked out? It was an accident,

Mrs Dunbar explained. She had telephoned her daughter, Mrs Terrell, in New York to tell her that Melinda had vanished and her call came through when Mrs Terrell had a visitor—a woman who lived in the same block of flats. It never occurred to Mrs Terrell to conceal from her friend that the call was from her mother in Geneva, or that it brought the bad news that Melinda was missing. Perhaps Catherine Terrell had forgotten, or had never known, that the friend's husband worked for a New York newspaper and was also a 'stringer' or tip-off man for one of the big news agencies.

After that had been cleared up, Mrs Dunbar told MI5 the facts leading up to Melinda's disappearance. On Friday morning, Melinda had been to the weekly market for fruit and vegetables and had come back in unusually good spirits. She said she had met a friend from Cairo days by chance in the market, and he had invited her and the children to spend a weekend with him and his wife at their villa at Territet—a suburb of Montreux almost at the other end of the Lake of Geneva. They had an English governess for their children, Melinda said. And because the villa was not easy to find, the friend said he would meet Melinda at 4.30 that afternoon in the lobby of a hotel in Montreux, the name of which Mrs Dunbar could not remember for certain. She had asked Melinda the name of her friend and thought it sounded like Robin Muir.

Fergus and Donald junior were due back at school early on Monday morning after the holidays and Mrs Dunbar therefore expected them home at about six o'clock on Sunday evening. When there was no sign of them, she thought they had decided to come early on Monday morning to avoid the weekend traffic.

Then there was the telegram, which the policeman at the door had intercepted. It had been sent from Territet on Wednesday 16th September at 10.50 a.m. and read:

TERRIBLY SORRY DELAY IN CONTACTING YOU UN-FORSEEN CIRCIONSTANCES [*sic*] HAVE ARISEN AM STAYING HERE LONGER PLEASE ADVISE SCHOOL-BOYS RETURNING ABOUT A WEEKS TIME ALL EX-TREMELY WELL PINK ROSE IN MARVELLOUS FORM LOVE FROM ALL MELINDA

The telegram said nothing about the invitation which Melinda had very recently accepted to a cocktail party on 17th September.

It had been handed in by an English-speaking woman of about the same age as Mrs Maclean who came into the post office with the telegram form already filled in, and as it had been handled by several people, her finger prints had become too smudged to be identifiable.

The spelling mistake made it clear that the message had not been written by Melinda—even though the reference to 'Pink Rose' (Melinda junior's nickname) showed that it was composed by someone who knew the family well.

It was, indeed, rather like that badly written telegram that Donald was supposed to have sent to Melinda shortly after he had disappeared. Perhaps Mrs Dunbar recalled now the time when Melinda had exclaimed 'Maybe you can be married to a man for a long time and really never know him at all.' Now she had to ask herself if she had known her daughter at all.

For evidence showed that Melinda had been making secret plans to deceive her mother and take the children away with her for at least four months. In the first place, she had new photographs taken of the children, one of which of the two boys she had enlarged up to passport size, but not the size used in the British passport with which Melinda travelled. The photographs had been ordered in the name of Smith, and Melinda had called and paid for the enlargements soon after Mrs Dunbar had returned from New York to Geneva. Yet she had said nothing to her mother about them and had never shown them to her.

Secondly, there was the fact that Melinda had taken not merely summer weekend clothes with her, as Mrs Dunbar had first thought, but almost all that she possessed. Either the suitcase held more than it appeared to, or Melinda had packed her other clothes in the boot of the car at lunch when Mrs Dunbar was putting Melinda junior to bed for her afternoon nap.

Finally, there was the evidence of the garage receptionist who had noted on the form that Mrs Maclean wanted to leave her car at the garage for a week.

Thinking back, Mrs Dunbar could remember other incidents which might have warned her what to expect. For instance, there was Melinda's sudden trip to Saanenmoser, and the fact that she had spent most of the night walking up and down her bedroom before she broke the news to Mrs Dunbar that she wanted to go there. There was the complete disinterest that Melinda showed latterly in Geneva about her mother's efforts to get a divorce for her and recover her American passport. Once or twice during those last few weeks, Melinda had suggested, with suspicious insistence, that her mother should fly to London for a change of air, or to Paris to buy some new clothes, neither of which propositions happened to fit in with Mrs Dunbar's plans. And when Mrs Dunbar said that she might go to Paris a little later on, after Fergus's birthday, which was on 23rd September, Melinda said: 'Oh that will be too late.' 'Too late for what?' her mother asked. Melinda did not answer.

Also, Melinda had seemed in more of a hurry than usual, after they got back from holiday, to have her clothes cleaned. She took three of her frocks to the cleaners right away, and spent the afternoon of the day before she left at the hairdressers having a cut, wash and set. She also bought a new jersey dress for herself without showing it, as she normally would have, to her mother, and also a new woollen jacket and shoes for 'Pinkers'. All the kind of things one might expect from a woman who was going to show herself and the children off to a husband she had not seen for more than two years.

MI5 had no success in tracing Mr Robin Muir's appearance in the lobby of any of the hotels at Territet, nor, indeed, the whereabouts of the villa in which Melinda was supposed to be going to stay. And the MI5 men departed after a few days for home while Mrs Dunbar sought refuge from the photographers behind dark glasses and a trip under an assumed name to Paris. The Foreign Office issued a statement according to which 'Mrs Maclean is a free agent and is under no obligation to inform the authorities of her movements'.

And Melinda? Well, some of the authorities believed that she must have known or guessed almost from the start where her husband was and was hoping to get in touch with him with a view to joining him.

Such, at least, was the view of the unknown gentleman with the bristly moustache who came to see Larry Solon less than a month after Maclean had disappeared and told him that Maclean's wife knew where he was. Had he perhaps thought that Paris was the place where Melinda was most likely to be contacted? The MI5 interrogator who came to see Melinda shortly before she left Britain for good also apparently thought that Melinda knew more than she admitted.

If so, Melinda's talk of divorcing Donald was a pretence—a step which she never intended to take. And the reason she left England would have been that she realized that as long as she stayed there, the Russians were not going to risk contacting someone whom they suspected might be closely watched. On the other hand, a divorce and the recovery of her American passport was something that Mrs Dunbar felt was vital to Melinda's happiness and at times she was able to convince Melinda that this was the only course for her to take. And it would hardly be surprising if once in a while Melinda did not echo the things her mother was constantly dinning into her.

She may equally have left England because she felt that nothing was being done there or would be done there to trace her husband: that all the authorities wished to do was to forget the whole affair.

And if that was so, the main reason for staying in the United Kingdom—namely to get news of Donald—was no longer a valid one. And this was in addition to the other disadvantages of living in the United Kingdom—the publicity and the pressure at school on the boys.

Robert Kee, the writer and broadcaster, who knew both the Macleans very well and was stationed in Geneva for some of the time that Melinda lived there, made a very valid comment when he said that most accounts have over-simplified Melinda's attitude —and 'made the whole thing too easy'. People are not all of a part, he feels, and have not always decided to be one thing or the other. They tend to slide about a bit. And this is very likely what happened.

Donald, for his part, was extremely fond of his children. He believed that he was now at last engaged on work of value to the human race in a position of considerable importance. Melinda must surely realize this and agree that their children must be brought up not in the environment of decaying capitalism but in the Communist world of the future.

In the Soviet Union, where Donald was 'fighting for peace', the children would have a better education than they could get at home. But he had first to persuade the Russians that Melinda was not still working for the British as she appeared to be doing when she showed them each letter or telegram that came from him. He could have pointed out that Melinda already knew that he was the English Hiss, and that she had nonetheless helped him to return to the Foreign Office (and this in turn would help to account for Melinda's subsequent statements that she had always known about Donald's work as a Communist agent; she was in fact 'stuck with the story' which was her passport into the Soviet Union). Donald could even have added that she knew too much to be left at large to marry some American to whom she would tell all once she had forgotten Donald.

Most defectors, as a Western agent who has handled many of them told me, are awkward customers to deal with. They are no more use, yet they have to be kept contented. So it would not be surprising if the Russians sought to keep Maclean happy by bringing his wife and children to Moscow especially if this would embarrass the West.

So far so good. But next there was the problem of making sure, first, that Melinda was willing to come and if so, how to arrange for her journey to Moscow. Convincing Melinda might not have been too difficult. For although she had a fairly amusing time in Geneva, it would not have been too difficult to suggest to someone as hungry for admiration as she was that she had no real place in its society—that she was unwanted not only in Switzerland but even in her own country. Furthermore, the life she was leading was clearly a superficial and materialistic existence and would continue to be so as long as she had to live under her mother's eye. Everywhere she went in the West she would be watched—perhaps even reviled. So would her children. Once in Moscow, she would have no difficulty in accepting other people's views as her own, as she had always done in the past.

Some steps would have been taken to make sure that Melinda did not change her mind and decide at the last minute to stay at home with Mummy. Most probably she was induced to write to Donald without telling the authorities or her mother. It has also been suggested that Melinda might have received threats that if she did not go willingly to the U.S.S.R., her children would be taken from her. But this seems not only unlikely but quite unnecessary, because, as the agent sent to see her would soon have found out, Melinda was still in love with Donald and not all the parties and flirtations which came her way since he disappeared had blotted him out of her mind.

There has been a good deal of speculation as to who contacted Melinda and how this was done in such a way as not to arouse the suspicions of her mother. There is, of course, a fairly large diplomatic colony in Geneva because, in addition to the various consulates, there are a number of United Nations agencies established in the old League of Nations buildings. There is also a large commercial community. There would probably be more than one contact. There could even have been a delicate approach from a mother at the International School, with a hint that if the British were not doing enough to discover Donald's whereabouts, there were other ways of getting in touch. A second contact would offer to take a letter—through unofficial channels—and gradually Melinda would be disciplined to keep in touch at certain times and certain places with other agents whose names she must have known were code names. Exciting—perhaps even dangerous. For who could tell what would happen once she was in Soviet hands. There were others who had not lived to tell the tale.

But as Donald and some others believed, a new era had begun after Stalin's death early in 1953, and though neither the West nor the Russians had officially accepted that Burgess or Maclean still existed, their prospects were bound to improve.

# 19

# Petrov Blows The Gaff

On 3rd April 1954 Vladimir Petrov, a tubby, bespectacled official of the Soviet Embassy in Canberra defected to the West—and stirred up a new cloud of suspicion about the Burgess–Maclean affair.

Petrov, who was officially described as Third Secretary and Consul in the Embassy, was, in fact, Head of the Australian branch of MVD, the Soviet spy network. While in Australia, he had been promoted to the rank of full Colonel in the MVD, and his wife, thirty-five-year-old honey-blonde Evdokia, who was nominally the Embassy book-keeper, held the rank of Captain in the same organization, and acted as her husband's cypher clerk. It was the normal kind of arrangement in Soviet Embassies abroad. Messages for Petrov were sent in the ordinary diplomatic bag, marked on the envelope with initial letters standing ostensibly for 'Office of Weights and Measures'. Those were the envelopes that Petrov picked out for himself. They contained undeveloped film, wrapped in light-proof paper. Petrov developed the films and his wife then decoded the instructions they contained.

Two developments helped to bring about Petrov's defection. First, there was trouble within the Embassy—and even fears that the Australian security authorities were going to raid it. Petrov was asked to find hiding places outside the Embassy for the most sensitive documents, but at least two of the caches he suggested were considered unsafe by Moscow. Both he and his wife were accused of inefficiency and disloyalty, and Petrov became afraid that they would soon be sent back to Moscow in disgrace, after which who knows what might have happened.

Even then, however, Petrov might not have defected but for another coincidence. While visiting Sydney he had already begun to cultivate a doctor Michael Bialoguski, a Russian-born emigrant who had settled in Australia, as one of his agents. Bialoguski was a member of the committee of the Russian Social Club of Sydney, and appeared sympathetic to Communism, and Petrov had received permission from Moscow to recruit him as a local agent.

But, strange to relate, that is exactly what Bialoguski was planning to do to Petrov. They got on first name terms with each other, and, eventually, the time came when Bialoguski thought it safe to let on to Petrov that he was not, as a matter of fact, all that keen on Communism after all. And that was the very time that the same thoughts were running through Petrov's own mind. Petrov dropped a hint that not everything was going smoothly at the Embassy just then. It was enough. Soon afterwards, Bialoguski who was, of course, working for the Australian Security Services, put Petrov in touch with a Dr Becket who suggested in his blunt Australian way that the best solution to Petrov's problems would be to stay in Australia for good. And so the deed was done.

Petrov was, of course, an extremely valuable catch for the Australian Security Service and its morale was boosted still further when the Russians tried and failed to force Mrs Petrov to fly back with them to the Soviet Union. She was rescued in the nick of time while the aeroplane was waiting to take off.

Both Petrov and his wife talked freely to their new hosts and, since their revelations involved Australian citizens, a Royal Commission was set up in Australia to report on their disclosures. The Commission accepted Petrov's evidence and produced a report, published on 14th September, which ran to 100,000 words, based mainly on his evidence. But while Petrov told the Australians all they wanted to know about the Soviet spy network in Australia, he was not obliged to disclose what he knew about Burgess and Maclean.

This was a purely British affair and he had no special obligation to the British Security Services. He preferred to sell his story to the Sunday newspaper *The People*. Petrov knew a great deal about the Burgess–Maclean case because one of his officials then in Canberra, named Filip Vladimirovich Kislytsin, had not only arranged the details of the Burgess–Maclean escape in London but also, before being posted to Australia, made the preliminary arrangements for Mrs Maclean's escape from Geneva.

In 1945 Kislytsin had been posted as cypher clerk to the MVD in the Soviet Embassy in London and handled all the material that came from Burgess. Burgess, he said, passed briefcases full of Foreign Office documents to a Soviet MVD official. After meeting Burgess the official used to arrive back at the Embassy with his clothes spattered with mud, which suggested to Kislytsin that their meeting place must have been somewhere in the country. Most of the documents were photographed before being returned to Burgess, but in cases of urgency Kislytsin encyphered the text and had it sent by direct radio to Moscow.

Kislytsin was recalled to Moscow in 1948 and put in charge of the English section of the MVD reference library, part of which was filled with Foreign Office documents received from Burgess and Maclean. There was so much material that, even three years later, some of it had not been translated—or even sorted.

News that Petrov had talked freely about Burgess and Maclean began to reach Britain before the end of April 1954 but the Foreign Office temporized and on 3rd May that year Mr Selwyn Lloyd told the House of Commons: 'The interrogation [of Petrov] is at present in progress, but such information about Messrs Burgess and Maclean which has so far been elicited is of a limited and general character, and it is not yet certain whether it is based on Petrov's personal knowledge or on hearsay.'

But Petrov's revelations, when *The People* began to publish them on 18th September the following year, were anything but limited and general, and half way through the series, the Government published its own White Paper. The Foreign Office might well have preferred to maintain a sceptical attitude to Petrov's revelations in *The People* which, as he mentioned himself, had been put together after he had studied Western official records on the case.

As late as April—a year after Petrov had defected—a Foreign Office spokesman said: 'We have not yet received a full account from Australia of the evidence produced by Petrov. In these circumstances any hearsay evidence which Petrov may produce must be treated with some reserve and cannot be regarded in any sense as conclusive, or to justify statements made in the Press, [it was the *Daily Express* at it again] this morning.'

On the other hand, the British would have committed a costly blunder if they had tried to discredit Petrov's evidence after the Australians had accepted him as a witness of truth. British incredulity would be misunderstood in Australia—perhaps even by the Australian Government—and the U.K. Government would have faced accusations in Britain that once again they were trying to smother the truth. The Russians, in turn, would have pointed out with glee that defectors to the West cannot count on being trusted, and that Petrov was considered by the British to be as unreliable as he had been traitorous to the Russians.

Michael Foot, however, had no such inhibitions and declared on 25th September with his accustomed assurance of infallibility that 'the thing was a big hoax and the Petrov evidence not worth the paper it was written on'. Mr V. A. Zorin, one of Russia's Deputy Foreign Ministers, said that same week: 'Burgess? Maclean? Never heard of them,' while Konni Zilliacus, the left-wing MP, declared that Burgess and Maclean were 'being used as a spanner to throw into the works of peaceful co-existence.'

Meanwhile, as soon as the White Paper* on the disappearing diplomats was issued, as the Government spokesman said 'for open debate and free discussion', the Foreign Office News Department received instructions that *they* were not to answer questions

* The full text appears in the Appendix, pages 237–246

arising out of it as the document was to be laid before Parliament and therefore did not officially exist until Parliament reassembled a full month later on 25th October. When that event occurred, it would be the responsibility of Ministers to answer any questions it might provoke.

And what were Petrov's revelations with which the Government in its White Paper felt obliged to concur?

They were contained in one paragraph (23) of the White Paper and amounted to this: that Burgess and Maclean had been long-term Soviet agents. They were recruited independently while they were still at Cambridge. That 'one or the other' had realized that they were under suspicion and had asked their Russian contact to arrange for their escape. That the Russians had agreed to do so and had flown them to Moscow, probably from Paris via Prague. That they were now working for the Russians as specialists.

The White Paper said:

> In view of the suspicions held against Maclean and of the conspiratorial manner of his flight, it was assumed, though it could not be proved, that his destination and that of his companion must have been the Soviet Union or some other territory behind the Iron Curtain. Now Vladimir Petrov, the former Third Secretary of the Soviet Embassy in Canberra who sought political asylum on 3rd April 1954, has provided confirmation of this. Petrov himself was not directly concerned in the case and his information was obtained from conversation with one of his colleagues in Soviet service in Australia. Petrov states that both Maclean and Burgess were recruited as spies for the Soviet Government while students at the University, with the intention that they should carry out their espionage tasks in the Foreign Office, and that in 1951, by means unknown to him, one or other of the two men became aware that their activities were under investigation. This was reported by them to the Soviet Intelligence Service who then organized their escape and removal to the Soviet Union. Petrov has the impression that the escape route included Czechoslovakia and that it involved an aeroplane flight into that country. . . .

Previously the furthest point reached by the Government was a statement made on 25th January 1954 by Mr Selwyn Lloyd, then Minister of State at the Foreign Office, who told Colonel Lipton, a persistent questioner in the House: 'If you were to presume they are behind the Iron Curtain you would probably be right.'

Now, the White Paper not only accepted Petrov's evidence that the missing diplomats had landed in Moscow but that they were working for the Russians: 'Upon their arrival in Russia, Maclean and Burgess lived near Moscow. They were used as advisers to the Ministry of Foreign Affairs and other Soviet agencies', the White

Paper said. In fact, Petrov in his revelations had been rather more specific. He said that Burgess and Maclean were acting as advisers especially on questions affecting Russia's relations with Britain and America—a glimpse, perhaps, of the obvious which it did not suit the authors of the White Paper to follow.

The White Paper—entitled 'Report Concerning the Disappearance of Two Former Foreign Office Officials'—was an eight-page leaflet of about 4,000 words and twenty-eight numbered paragraphs. It was long enough to conceal those facts which the authorities felt they had to state but to which they did not wish to give too much prominence, and the style was soporific in the extreme.

Many of the facts stated in it had been known for months, if not years—for example, the date when the diplomats left the country, the milestones in their respective careers, the known details of their flight, the letters received by their families with dates, and the departure of Mrs Maclean from Geneva, and so on.

*The Times* said:

'Two points call for comment' says the White Paper on Burgess and Maclean. That is typical of its primness and defensiveness. There are not two but a dozen points that call for comment, and the White Paper throws little new light on them.

Appearing as it does scandalously late four and a quarter years after the two men fled the country, the whole paper might have been expected to give many details hitherto unknown.

*The Times* added:

There is very little doubt that, but for the knowledge that Mr Petrov was going to make his evidence public, the Foreign Office and the security authorities would not have decided to publish a White Paper even now.

Throughout the past four and a quarter years, the pattern has been almost invariably the same. A Press report has been followed by a reluctant and often tendentious admission in the House or at the Foreign Office. Official statements were made which are now seen to have been misleading.

Only two new items impressed *The Times* leader-writer. One was the news that Burgess had been asked to resign as a result of reckless and careless conduct in the United States; and the other was that Morrison had given permission on 25th May, the day when Burgess and Maclean fled, to question Maclean.

The paper noted the White Paper's statement that 'Espionage is carried out in secret', that 'Counter-espionage equally depends for its success upon the maximum secrecy in its methods', and that it was not 'desirable at any moment to let the other side know how much has been discovered or guess what means have been used to discover it'. The paper's leader-writer agreed that reticence was an excellent principle but wondered how it applied in this case. 'The Foreign Office needed no elaborate means to "discover" that it had asked Burgess to resign, or that it was closely watching Maclean; and the Russians already knew—otherwise they would not have helped the two men escape.'

After speculating why the security men who suspected Maclean and were about to question him, cut themselves off from his movements over the critical weekend when he was out of London, *The Times* went on to draw attention to the sentence in the White Paper, Paragraph 26, which read: 'The second question is how Maclean and Burgess made good their escape from this country when the security authorities were on their track.' Was Burgess then also being watched? *The Times* asked.

> There is nothing else in the White Paper to suggest it. The evidence produced is simply that he had been asked to resign after the Ambassador in Washington had reported on his personal behaviour. The authorities cannot have it both ways. If there was suspicion of espionage in his case, the evidence should be in the White Paper. If the authorities had no such suspicions, they evidently had been caught napping. The mystery is deepened by the fact that it was now believed that both men were 'long term agents' for the Soviet Union. Petrov said so and his testimony is accepted, but on British evidence the part of Burgess has not been brought to light.

The *Daily Mail* called the White Paper 'alarming. Alarming for its admission. Alarming for its omissions'. The *Daily Telegraph* said: 'The White Paper is only remarkable for its total failure to come to grips with the real questions in the public mind.' Whitewash or no, there was certainly a good deal of hedging on previous official statements.

The most obvious of these occurred early in the document in Paragraph 3 which said: 'In May 1950, while serving at His Majesty's Embassy, Cairo, Maclean was guilty of serious misconduct and suffered a form of breakdown which was attributed to overwork and excessive drinking.' This was a definite advance on the original Foreign Office statement which said: 'Mr Maclean had a breakdown a year ago owing to overstrain' and contained nothing about 'serious misconduct' or 'excessive drinking'.

Mr Morrison in his statement to the House on 11th June 1951 had used the same words about overstrain and no more.

Another doubt was raised by the wording of Paragraph 13, according to which: 'Immediately the flight was known all possible action was taken in the United Kingdom, and the French and other Continental security authorities were asked to trace the whereabouts of the fugitives, and, if possible to intercept them.'

By using the word 'immediately' at the beginning of the sentence, the White Paper conveniently skated over the delay that actually took place in putting the French security authorities on the trail. Also, what did the word 'intercept' mean? If it meant anything, it meant that the two men were, if possible, to be arrested or held by the security authorities for questioning. But how was this to be reconciled with Paragraph 26 which read: 'Both men were free to go abroad at any time. In some countries no doubt Maclean would have been arrested first and questioned afterwards. At the time there was insufficient evidence.' If Maclean could be 'intercepted', i.e., arrested first and questioned afterwards, on foreign soil, presumably he could have been held all the more easily on British soil.

The authorities, of course, could argue that the diplomats' journey to France was all the evidence needed to justify their detention. But then if leaving the country was to make the difference between arrest and non-arrest, it would have been much simpler—as Richard Crossman afterwards suggested—to tell Maclean that he was under suspicion and wait to see what happened—provided, of course, that precautions were taken to see that he did not leave the country without being 'intercepted'.

Petrov also took an uncharitable view of Melinda—though he admitted that conclusive evidence on her motives was lacking. He believed nevertheless that Melinda knew all about her husband's plan to flee and that, 'at any rate', soon after her husband's departure, she was co-operating in plans for her own flight. MI5 had got nothing out of her, Petrov said, and so convinced were the authorities of her innocence that they raised no objection when she took the children away on holiday to France only three months after her husband's disappearance.

According to Petrov, Kislytsin was hoping to arrange for an MVD agent to get in touch with Melinda either in London or at Tatsfield, but this was considered to be too risky. Instead it was decided to contact her somewhere outside the range of British security agents. Petrov suggested that the contact was probably arranged while she was on holiday in France, for, although a French guard was placed outside the house, she was able to slip away for two whole days without apparently being followed.

Similarly when she was in Geneva the Swiss intelligence service did maintain some kind of surveillance over the flat in the Rue des Alpes, but, according to Kislytsin, an MVD agent in Geneva was able to make the arrangements for Mrs Maclean and the children to leave without anyone knowing about it in advance.

British readers would have wished to know whether Petrov's assessment was right or wrong. But 'the authorities' evidently took the view that it was not worth wasting time on her because any information that she might have had came to her through her husband. And after his flight she had no more to give.

There were other glossings over which irritated those who already knew most of the facts. The White Paper did not reveal the details of Maclean's revels in Cairo, nor those of Burgess's holiday adventures in Tangier and Gibraltar.

> Early in 1950, [it said] the security authorities informed the Foreign Office that in late 1949 while on holiday abroad, Burgess had been guilty of indiscreet talk about secret matters of which he had official knowledge. For this he was severely reprimanded. Apart from this lapse, his service in the Foreign Office up to the time of his appointment in Washington was satisfactory and there seemed good reason to hope that he would make a useful career.

The White Paper did not go into the reasons which made this assumption possible.

Yet some entertainment was provided for the cynics during the period of suspense while their legislators were at play. A fine display of righteous indignation was affected in and around Whitehall about the number of people who said that *they* had known, even if MI5 had not, that Burgess and Maclean were spies. In particular, in the ITV programme 'Free Speech' broadcast on 25th September, the discussion in which Michael Foot had endeavoured so dramatically to discredit Petrov's evidence drew unfavourable comment.

Robert Boothby, then still a House of Commons MP, said during the broadcast that he knew Burgess and 'would not have trusted him with half a crown [12½p.]'. 'What I want to know,' Boothby added, 'was how they were able to get away with it. Their records! Their characters!'

Professor Alan Taylor, the Oxford historian familiar with the workings of the Foreign Office, said that he had met Maclean in 1950. 'If you had asked me if he was a Soviet agent, I would have said it stuck out a mile ... If I had been asked: "Is Maclean telling the Soviet Union everything we do" I would have said "Yes" without the slightest doubt.'

Maurice Webb, former Socialist Food Minister, told *The People* in October 1955 that he had known Guy Burgess was a Moscow agent as long ago as 1944. At that time, Burgess was working in the BBC and helped to produce talks that Webb gave from time to time, mainly on the Overseas Broadcasting Service. Burgess, according to Webb, took little interest in his work, except when the subject of Communism came up. Then he reacted swiftly in a way which aroused Webb's suspicions.

One evening, Burgess, partial as ever to liquor, suggested that, if Webb had some cash on him, the two of them might go over to a pub near Oxford Circus for a quick drink. As they were talking, a man wearing a gaberdine overcoat came into the far corner of the saloon. Thereupon Burgess's manner became tense. 'He's one of our chaps,' Burgess said as he went across the room to speak to him. A few seconds later he came back and told Webb that he would have to leave at once. Webb followed Burgess and his companion to the door, and was interested to see that they went back not to the BBC but into the Oxford Circus tube station. Webb was interested because he recognized Burgess's friend as one of the organizers of a Communist-sponsored pacifist People's Convention Webb had attended four years earlier.

Later, when Burgess pressed Webb at the House of Commons for introductions to important contacts and for confidential reports on War Conferences that were shown to journalists, Webb did not respond. In fact, he denounced Burgess to the BBC, and was relieved when Burgess left that organization.

But that was not the end of the matter. In 1948 Webb arranged a Sunday meeting in his Bradford constituency at which Hector McNeil was the co-speaker. The two met at a hotel and McNeil's first words were: 'Can I get some cigarettes for my personal assistant?' Webb got the cigarettes and went out with McNeil to his car. There, sitting in the back seat was Guy Burgess.

Webb was astonished. Turning to McNeil, he asked: 'Why didn't you consult me before you took him on?' Burgess said nothing. Neither did McNeil. Back in London, Webb raised the matter once more with McNeil but gathered he had not the slightest idea that Burgess could be a Communist agent. When Burgess was kept on in the Foreign Office, Webb came to the conclusion that he might be working as an anti-Communist counter-spy on behalf of MI6.

In view of Webb's experience, it was difficult to take seriously the bureaucrats and, later, the Ministers when they suggested that friends and acquaintances ought to have tabled their suspicions about Burgess's reliability and Maclean's loyalty on the desk of the Security Services (wherever that might be), thus impugning both the efficiency of MI5 and the sincerity of Ministers who declared how heartily they abhorred 'witch hunts' and how great their faith was in the infallibility of the Security Services.

Meanwhile, it was too much to expect that the public disquiet over the Burgess and Maclean affair, which had been repeatedly expressed during the four years which followed their defection, would have subsided within four weeks of the publication of the White Paper.

And two weeks after Parliament's reassembly the Prime Minister Sir Anthony Eden and his Foreign Secretary Harold Macmillan had to agree to a highly distasteful debate in the House of Commons.

# 20

# The Second Cover-Up

On 6th November, the night before the parliamentary debate in the House of Commons on the Burgess and Maclean affair, Harold Macmillan, the Foreign Secretary, had been dining in Geneva as the guest of Mr Molotov, the Soviet Foreign Minister. At the end of the meal, as Macmillan relates in his memoirs, Molotov asked him why he had to go back to London. It was for the debate, Macmillan said. 'What about?' Molotov asked. Macmillan answered: 'On a subject where you can really help me, if you would —on Burgess and Maclean. Can you tell me where they are?' Molotov answered with apparent seriousness: 'That's a matter that would require investigation.'

Macmillan, as Foreign Secretary, had to open the debate and tell the House how far the British investigations had now gone and why they had not progressed further. He began his address in a tone of regret. Rarely had a Minister had to unfold 'so painful a story' as the one concerning people he referred to as the 'two traitors'. At last all but the very tip of the cat's tail was out of the bag. The Foreign Office, said Mr Macmillan, felt the case as if it had been a personal wound 'as when something of the kind strikes at a family or a ship or a Regiment'. It had been a profound shock to the House and to the public, he added.

After some words about 'the horrible crime of treachery', he said there had been suggestions that security should be taken out of the hands of the Foreign Office altogether and turned over to a central security authority. But this, he said, would be a mistake. If the Foreign Office or any other Government department had no security section of its own, there might be a danger of its relaxing its watchfulness on the ground that security was no longer its own responsibility.

Referring to Maclean's entry into the Foreign Office, Mr Macmillan continued: 'I have heard it said that the Civil Service Commission Board who interview all candidates ought to have known of Maclean's reputation for extreme left-wing views while he was an undergraduate.' (They could have, too, if they had read, for example, Maclean's letter to *The Granta*, the undergraduate magazine, in which he spoke of the 'economic exploitation of the student' at Cambridge, and the 'reactionary and valueless teaching in every faculty'. He called for 'student protest' and 'student demands to be put forward alongside the workers' demands at the National Congress of Action' in phraseology which even in those days was recognizable as Communist jargon.)

'In fact,' said Mr Macmillan, 'Maclean's college authorities gave him an exceptionally good report in which no mention was made of his left-wing views.' There was hearty laughter among MPs when they heard this, but Mr Charles Pannell, the Labour MP for West Leeds, sharply rebuked Mr Macmillan. 'Left-wing is a connotation for this side of the House. I ask you, therefore, Mr Speaker to ask the Foreign Secretary to use plain English and say "Communist-affiliations" when this is meant, and not "left-wing affiliations".'

But, even if the (Civil Service) Examining Board (before whom Maclean appeared) were to have reported that Maclean had showed Communist sympathies as an undergraduate, would it have been right, Mr Macmillan asked, to exclude him automatically from the Foreign Service? (A number of MPs were heard to say 'No').

Then Mr Macmillan defended the Foreign Office decision to act as any good employer would in the circumstances when an employee fell ill, by giving him a second chance, as they did in the case of Maclean.

His pleadings about Burgess were, however, rather less convincing. His suggestion that Burgess might have been considered respectable because he had worked for six years in the BBC was, for some reason, apparently well understood at the time, greeted with more loud laughter. On Burgess's war effort, Macmillan said: 'We now know that his work with the war-time department had been unsatisfactory. During the war many departments did not keep good records about temporary staff. Neither the Foreign Office nor the Civil Service Commission Board knew (in 1945) of Burgess's failing.'

Mr Macmillan then said that after his holiday in Tangier and Gibraltar Burgess had been severely reprimanded and told that he would be transferred and that his prospects for promotion were diminished.

(Here the sharp-nosed critic might notice a distinct hint that Burgess was being transferred, as a punishment for being indiscreet to a less influential post, and not, as has been suggested in the White Paper and at the Foreign Office, that he was being sent to Washington to get experience abroad at a time when 'there seemed good reason to hope that he would make a useful career'.)

There was much discussion, Mr Macmillan said, as to his future. It was desirable to send him to a post where his general suitability for the Foreign Service could be tested. It was, therefore, decided to send him to Washington for a period of trial on routine work. In other words, it was a case of giving him enough rope to hang himself.

Another elucidation was one that Macmillan may not have felt able to offer—namely that the Foreign Office Personnel Department, which dealt with postings, was divided into two almost autonomous sections: 'A' Branch dealing with senior 'A' Branch officials, and 'B' Branch, which coped with the smaller fry.

Burgess, despite his ambitions, had not been promoted to 'A' Branch (he was still in the fourth grade of 'B' Branch) and his posting was, therefore, handled by 'B' Branch which worked, as it were, in the foothills of the Foreign Service and seldom needed or asked for advice from higher up. It would, of course, have been a very serious matter for 'B' Branch, as the junior partner, to have initiated proposals for dismissing Burgess, who had been inducted into the Service at top level, and had not yet been given any opportunity to serve as a regular officer abroad.

Then Mr Macmillan came to one of the more difficult passages in his address. He had to convince the House that the Government had no power to stop either Burgess or Maclean from leaving the country before the Executive was ready to bring a charge against them.

It was an issue about which there was a good deal of misunderstanding. Most MPs believed that the authorities could have prevented Burgess and Maclean from leaving the country by confiscating their passports. Mr Macmillan argued (wrongly) that, though a passport was Crown property, it could not be withdrawn without a Court order, and other groups of MPs muddied the issue with other equally irrelevant questions as to whether Burgess and Maclean could have left the country without a passport, whether they could have landed in France without one, and whether Foreign Office personnel, like serving officers, needed permission to leave the country.

Pursuing his 'do you want a police state here?' line of argument, Mr Macmillan quote a newspaper article: 'It is said that the authorities had no legal right to stop Mrs Maclean leaving the country,' the article read. 'There is no law. Could they [the authorities] not have found one?'

On this Mr Macmillan commented: 'There you have the very nub of the problem. Hitler would have found one. Mussolini would have found one. Stalin had got one.' The Government had taken these kind of powers in wartime and had dropped them it was hoped for ever as soon as the war was over.

He believed that the new system of positive vetting which called for a diligent search into the school and university career of anyone recruited for confidential work would make a recurrence of an affair like this exceedingly improbable—if not impossible.

'But these security measures cannot go beyond the letter and spirit of the law [cheers]. Before these limits are altered, Parliament should weigh the balance of advantage and disadvantage. It would be a tragedy if we destroyed freedom in an effort to preserve it.'

On the whole, Macmillan had made a good show and was unlikely to run into too much trouble, if only because most of the damage occurred under the previous (Labour) Government. However, a fair number of MPs on both sides of the House had prejudices they wished to air and hearsay they wished to repeat at some point during the debate.

Colonel Alan Gomme-Duncan (Perth and East Perthshire) recalled that while in Paris in 1938 Maclean had made no secret of his sympathy for the Spanish Communist Party, and that in 1940 he had associated with the Tass man in London.

He wondered, too, if there had not been some contact between Burgess and Otto John who had defected from West Germany to the East in 1954. Otto John had been Chief Legal Adviser to Lufthansa before the war and a member of the Canaris Group which had plotted the death of Hitler. When that failed, John's brother had been executed and John had escaped through Spain and come to London at the end of 1944 and had worked for the BBC. He had then become a close associate of Guy Burgess. 'They had all too much in common outside their public duties,' Colonel Gomme-Duncan recalled.

After the war, John, with British and U.S. approval, had been appointed President of the Federal Office of the Constitution—the security machine responsible for reporting neo-Nazi activities, and in his work he employed agents, some of whom also worked for the Russians. It seemed plausible that while Otto John was still in a position of trust or even afterwards there might have been some contact between the two old friends.

On the plus side, Gomme-Duncan was able to say that he had seen the new Foreign Office F.2. forms on which annual reports on senior staff had now to be made out. He was gratified to notice that the forms now had spaces for reports on 'Reliability', 'Contact with Foreigners', 'Social Behaviour' and for a 'Detailed Pen Picture' of the official reported on. Furthermore, contrary to the practice in the armed services, the forms did not have to be signed by the rapporteur or shown to the official reported on. So the rapporteur had greater freedom to be frank.

There was some anxiety over the fact that, although Maclean became suspect in April 1950, his previous background, according to the White Paper's Paragraph 4 was not investigated until *after* he had disappeared.

The sentence in Paragraph 10 of the White Paper, according to which 'suspicion had been narrowed by mid-April to two or three persons' also provoked some curiosity. One of the suspects was Maclean and the other two were not Burgess; who could they be?

Mr Charles Pannell who, as we have seen, had been taking an active part in the debate, made capital out of the fact that a screening procedure to exclude Communists had been applied to 'members of the working classes' and Trade Unionists wishing to join the Ministry of Supply factories producing classified weapons, but not apparently to the gentlemen of the Foreign Office, and Mr Alfred Robens (Blyth) asked if there was to be one law for Communist sympathizers from Cambridge and another for a Communist sympathizer from Cambridge University.

Behind this was a general belief that the togetherness which led diplomats to cover each other's mistakes arose from the fact that the members of the Foreign Office staff were all members of the same élite class. But suggestions that this complaint could be cured by merging the Foreign Office with the rest of the Civil Service did not get very far—it being pointed out that what separated the two was the willingness and ability of the diplomats to serve abroad. Besides, there was already a shortage of recruits for the higher branches of the Civil Service and the scarcity would be greater still if those who wished to apply for foreign service were obliged in future to take the ordinary Civil Service examination without the assurance that they would be able to embark on a diplomatic career.

Nevertheless at least one Member, Mr Malcolm MacPherson (Stirling and Falkirk) seemed to think it was more important that people in the Foreign Office should not be considered as 'different from our own people' than that it was for them to be able to get on with other foreign diplomats (who presumably were).

But Mr Godfrey Nicholson (Farnham) thought that they *were* different and that those who committed indiscretions, made unfortunate marriages or entertained questionable friendships should be transferred from the Foreign Office to another Civil Service Department.

Mr Herbert Morrison contributed something fresh by reading from a letter that he had received from a man whose name he would give in confidence to the Foreign Office only if requested. It was from a respected friend of Morrison's who had lunched with Maclean on 24th May—i.e., the day before Maclean had lunched with the Campbells. Morrison's letter read in part:

On that day I am sure that he [Maclean] had no intention of

leaving England in the way he did. He spoke to me so normally about his private affairs, his wife's confinement and his plans for the immediate future, that I am convinced he was not intending to leave the country. This makes me feel that, subsequent to his meeting me on 24th May, Maclean received some warning that he was under suspicion and immediately left the country with Burgess.

It may be therefore that someone in the Foreign Office told him on 25th May that you had authorized him to be questioned and of course it was not only the Foreign Office who knew. It was the Security Service as well.

And Maclean had obviously been working hard that week to discredit both of them.

The Commons Debate was wound up by the Prime Minister, Sir Anthony Eden. After dealing with the reforms which he helped to introduce in the Foreign Office, he tackled the question of what he would have done if he had been Foreign Secretary at the time of Maclean's drinking bout in Cairo. He said that the Foreign Office as employers had been faced with an appallingly difficult decision about Maclean. Was it wrong, he asked, that this man who had a brilliant record should be given a second chance?

He said that the methods of positive vetting which now had been in force since 1951 were disagreeable, but inevitable.

I am convinced as Prime Minister that the Foreign Office is now following correct and careful security procedure and that its standards are of the very highest in this or any other country.

It does not guarantee us against future disaster, but it does give the strongest assurance that I can give to the House with all the responsibility that rests on me that we have done all we think we can within the law.

Sir Anthony then took off his glasses and put away his notes. He was about to make a special appeal to the House.

Would the House agree that the law should be altered to allow any British subject to be detained on suspicion? (There were murmurs of 'No'.) Well you have to face these questions when there is no evidence on which the man could be judged. Would you be willing that people should be held indefinitely by the police while evidence is collected against them? Of course not.

In this case detention would have been justified. But British justice over the centuries has been based on the principle that a man is to be presumed innocent until he can be proved guilty. Have we abandoned that principle?

Worst of all, are we to make an exception for political offences? The last thing I would wish to see in this country is the Security

Service having the power to do some of the things which some of our friends in the Press do not seem to realize would flow from such a policy.

If we had that power under the law Burgess and Maclean would not be where they are today. What would have been the consequences to British freedom and to those rights which this House has always defended?

I would never be willing to be Prime Minister of a Government who asked those powers of this House,

Sir Anthony concluded.

And on this basis the Government survived. But a few days later (22nd November) there was a debate in the Lords where the speeches were rather better and more entertaining.

Lord Astor, who opened the debate, first apologized for his difference of opinion with the Party Whip who would have preferred to omit the debate on the disappearance of Burgess and Maclean and pass on to the reappearance of rabbits, the next subject which their Lordships were due to discuss. However, he said, the debate in the Commons had been so unsatisfactory that he felt he could not do otherwise than retain his Motion on the Order Paper.

Lord Astor said:

I think it is particularly unfortunate that in the House of Commons the Minister of State, Mr Anthony Nutting, should have used the phrase 'witch hunt' for those who were trying to find the truth about Burgess and Maclean. The term 'witch hunt' got into disrepute because the existence, let alone the prevalence, of witches was a highly hypothetical and uncertain matter. On the other hand Communists are not uncertain and hypothetical. Nor are traitors, any more than murderers or burglars. To try to uncover treason is as much a duty as it is to prevent burglary, and the honest attempt to clear up these matters should never have been stigmatized by the highly questionable phrase 'witch hunt'.

We then had the White Paper, which was like the magistrate, in the sad affair of young Albert and the lion, who seemed to come to the conclusion that 'No one was really to blame'. If the Government had come forward with honest apologies and had said that great mistakes had been made, it would have been far better than that curious White Paper which was criticized by all the organs of the Press, including those most favourable to the Government . . .

It is ridiculous to pretend that the American Department deals only with sending ballet dancers to Bolivia: it is a most important department. The head of a great department in the Foreign Office sees the flow of papers on all subjects, and this ridiculous 'playing down' of the matter did no credit to anybody. What was curious was that after this gentleman had had this very bad record in Egypt, not only was he appointed to an important department but he had continued that extraordinary standard of conduct in this country. He used to go out in the evenings and get disgustingly drunk in a certain club. He twice engaged in drunken brawls with former left-wing friends in one of which they were rolling on the floor. This was the head of the American Department of the Foreign Office. In each case, the cause of his attack on these gentlemen was that they had betrayed their former extreme left-wing opinions.

The question I want to ask is: Did the Foreign Office know of this conduct and tolerate it, or were they ignorant? If they were ignorant, it is hard to believe that they live in such an ivory tower. Can one imagine the colonel of a regiment, the general manager of a bank or the head of a university not knowing about such conduct among important subordinates about whom they had already been warned? I am one of the few people who never knew Guy Burgess, and apparently I missed a lot. By all accounts he was one of the most amusing and clever conversationalists there was, who charmed a great many people. But he was drunken, dirty and a sexual pervert. He had been ever since his school days. He made no pretence about it either in his conversation or his conduct. Did the Foreign Office know about his peculiarities and tolerate them? Or were they the only people who did not know about them?

At no moment was it said in the House of Commons debate that people with this unfortunate habit [i.e., homosexuals] are not suitable for confidential positions in the public service or to go abroad in a representative capacity.

I am not one of those who takes the view that the homosexual is a criminal. Those of us who are lucky enough to be normal should, I think, have nothing but pity for people in that situation. But when it is a crime, when it brings a country into disrepute or lays a person open to blackmail, surely it should be laid down quite clearly that people of these characteristics should not be used in the Foreign Service ...

The only thing that might be said as a result of some inquiry is, of course, that 'More care must be taken that people of left opinions do not get in'. That is all wrong. No sensible person should say that civil servants should all be Conservatives; but what we can say—and it should be pointed out to the Civil Service Commission—is that character is as important as cleverness ...

Lord Astor went on to say that the British delude themselves about the real nature of the foe:

In Communism we see an expression of Russian nationalism or of agrarian reform in China. We say that surely the third generation are looking after their comforts and their vodka and are not devoted to theoretical Communism—as if people who have known nothing but theoretical Communism, who have been stuffed with it educationally from their youth, could not be as strong Communists as their predecessors . . .

But those people are dedicated enemies with no standards of honour, no patriotism as we know it, no possibility of compromise. They despise socialists even more than they despise capitalists; and the first thing they do in any country is to put all socialists and trade union leaders into concentration camps. We have to recognize that, for the first time since the reign of the first Queen Elizabeth, we have a fifth column that has penetrated, apparently, the highest ranks of the Civil Service, the scientists and even the Church.

Some apt interventions followed. Lord Conesford, a former Tory MP barrister said:

I believe that if a man employed by any business or industrial concern behaved in this way he would have been instantly dismissed altogether from his employment. I believe that the same is true of the fighting services. If I am wrong in the assumption that he would have been dismissed altogether, I submit that one thing is absolutely certain: he would not have been given a new post without searching inquiries into all that was known about him, and into the probable cause of his breakdown—if breakdown it was that caused the misconduct . . . Incidentally, was it wise to treat the post of head of the American Department of the Foreign Office as of minor importance? There are two disadvantages in such a course: first, the Americans will not believe us, and, secondly, they would be very much insulted if they did.

It really will not do to say that the Foreign Office acted as a good employer in giving him a further post of responsibility without searching inquiries. It simply is not true that a good employer places kindness to a servant before public safety.

And, rather as the attack had been above the standard in the Commons, the defence, despite or perhaps because the Labour Peers had refused to take part in the Debate, was well below.

Lord Reading, the Minister of State, was testy and at times sarcastic in his justification of the Government's position. To Lord Salter, who had intervened when it seemed likely to him that Reading was about to be evasive, the Minister said:

The noble Lord asked those two questions [about Maclean] in his original speech and I was about to embark on the answer to them when he asked a second time—not that I complain at all.

Lord Reading continued:

After Maclean had come back, on the basis that this had been a breakdown in health and in the light of all the reports that we had had upon him from the Ambassadors in charge of the various posts in which he had been employed, no inquiry was made further back into the past. Frankly, I do not see any reason why, in those circumstances, there should have been any such inquiry. During the time that elapsed between his appointment as head of the American Department and the moment of his disappearance he was working in London and living in the country and doubtless was going to a number of parties. It may be true, as the noble Viscount, Lord Astor said in opening, that during that period he indulged in certain drinking bouts, but certainly we did not know. I would ask your Lordships this: How could we tell? What are you to do with a man living a normal social life in London and the country? Are you to have people posted to watch him at every party he attends, and detail them to report back what he says and does ... ?

But, of course, if the Foreign Office had seen fit to tell MI5 about Maclean's drinking sprees in Cairo—which, astonishing as it may seem, they had not, this, too, could have been put right.

At one point in the Debate in the House of Lords, Lord Reading made so bold as to say that up to the time of Maclean's disappearance 'we had no evidence of any kind that he was in any way affected by homosexual impulses'. So Maclean's instinct in insisting on being treated by his own psychiatrist paid off.

Lord Sherwood remained unconvinced. Why was it, he asked, that during the period when this man was clearly on probation to see whether he could make good, no watch was kept by the Foreign Office? It is no good asking for ordinary people to come forward and say that he was doing this or doing that. One would have thought that he would have been watched to see what sort of character he was manifesting after that assault.

But this suggestion did not please Lord Reading.

I thought I had already dealt with that point, [he said] but perhaps I did not deal with it sufficiently for the noble Lord's purpose. The point I have been making all the time is that the view was that this was not a case of bad conduct, a case of a man being on probation and needing to be watched. The view taken, quite genuinely, was that this was a case of ill-health and that the man had been cured. It is extremely difficult, if not impossible, to have someone in this position constantly watched in that way. I think that if one looks back upon all the circumstances of the time and bears in mind what we knew and what reasonably we could be expected to know, it was not by any means an unjustifiable risk, or, indeed, thought to be a risk at all, to give him further employment.

(The Peers had forgotten already the Government's admission in the White Paper that Maclean had been guilty of 'serious misconduct' in Cairo.)

Later in the debate, Lord Reading again found himself involved in a clash, this time with Lord Astor, who said:

> I was a member of another place for eleven years and have been a member of your Lordships' House for three years. I have never heard a winding-up speech more chivalrous and gallant in an effort to defend some very indefensible things than the one we have just heard ...
>
> The noble Marquess [of Reading] who has answered, is not the only person in this House who knows perhaps a good deal more than he chooses to say. Most of us know a good deal more of what happened, but we did not want particularly to air more dirty linen in public than was necessary. The vast majority of the Foreign Service disliked the type of conduct which these two officers indulged in and were shocked that such a long rope was given by their superiors to these two individuals.

Lord Reading: 'What does the noble Viscount mean by "disliked that type of conduct which these two officers indulged in?" '
Astor replied:

> I refer to the constant series of incidents in Egypt, more than those mentioned, if any noble Lord cared to investigate. I do not propose to air any more dirty linen than has been aired already because there is no point in doing so, but everybody knows that there was not just one incident but a good many. I say only this. A member of the women's Services happened to find herself in an aeroplane in Egypt with Maclean, and his behaviour towards her in various ways was extremely rude and unpleasant. She mentioned it to some other member of the staff who said: 'Oh yes; that is Maclean, of course. He is notorious for that type of bad behaviour.' That is just one incident.

Both in the Commons and the Lords, the Government was fighting with one hand tied behind its back. One reason was that Hector McNeil, the man responsible for taking on Burgess as his assistant, had died of a stroke the previous month aboard the *Queen Mary*. Any attempt to blame him for retaining Burgess would have been categorized as cheap and unworthy.

The second weakness arose from the fact that although the Government was not sure whether or not Burgess and Maclean had fled because they had been tipped off, yet it felt obliged to exonerate the Foreign Office completely from the suspicion that one of its staff could have warned the traitors.

Macmillan said that the authorities took the possibility of a tip-off very seriously and were still looking into it. But he completely cleared Philby of any responsibility. Philby, he said, was temporary First Secretary at the Embassy in Washington from October 1949 to June 1951, had known a good deal about the investigation of the leakage. He had been an undergraduate friend of Burgess at Trinity College, Cambridge, and had had Burgess as a guest in his house from August 1950 to April 1951. It was also known that Philby had Communist associations during and after his university years.

Against this background he had been asked to resign from the Foreign Service.

> From that date on [Mr Macmillan said] his case has been the subject of close investigation. No evidence has been found that he was responsible for warning Burgess or Maclean. While in the Government service, Mr Philby carried out his duties ably and conscientiously and I have no reason to conclude that Mr Philby has at any time betrayed the interests of his country or to identify him with the so-called Third Man, if indeed there was one.

Similarly Sir Anthony Eden during the House of Commons Debate associated himself with Mr Morrison's statement that 'nobody at the Foreign Office, at any time, no senior or other official tried to cover up any form of disloyalty to the State'. For he, too, knew too little about Kim Philby.

N

# 21

# Burgess And Maclean Come Alive

At this point, then, there were six expatriates behind the Iron Curtain: Donald Maclean, Melinda Maclean, their three children and Burgess. Letters had come from some of them but little reliable news of where they were living or what they were doing.

Melinda, at that time the last of the grown-ups to arrive, was the first to write what became a new series of notes. As long as Melinda and the children were still in the West, any publicity stirred reporters and intelligence officers to new efforts and therefore hindered plans for Donald's family to join him. Now, however, since they had reached safe territory, the Russians had no objection.

Melinda's letter, written and addressed in her handwriting, was sent to Mrs Dunbar who was then staying with Mrs Sheers at 7 Avenue de Segur, Paris. The letter arrived early in November 1953. It was undated and bore no address. It had been written on cheap greyish writing paper and posted in Cairo on 24th October. In it Melinda begged her mother in somewhat stilted English to forgive her for the worry she had caused and pleaded with her to understand that feelings in her heart would not allow her to do otherwise than she had. She said she and the children were all right and well, sent love to her two sisters and ended with the words 'Goodbye but not for ever'—a phrase which could have meant merely that she would write again or that she had been given assurances that she would be allowed to revisit the West once more.

Then on Christmas Eve the same year, the *Daily Express* announced that Burgess had sent Christmas greetings to his mother Mrs Bassett. They came in a typewritten envelope which contained a letter in Burgess's handwriting. The note was dated November without specifying any particular day. There was no address. The envelope bore the postmark of a London SE1 office and was one of 502,000 letters posted there that day in the Christmas rush.

Colonel Bassett, Burgess's stepfather, was delighted and was quoted as saying: 'Rather a nice Christmas present. He says he is in very good health and he seems very cheerful.' The Foreign Office, to whom the letter had been shown, added: 'It gives no indication of Burgess's present whereabouts. It merely expresses his love for his mother. He wishes her a happy Christmas and New Year.'

Yet positive proof was still lacking that Burgess was in Moscow, was not in prison, but really earning his living. As recently as 5th October 1953 *The Times* quoted the Soviet Magazine *New Times* as saying:

The disappearance of the British diplomats Burgess and Maclean and Mrs Maclean has not the slightest connection with the Soviet Union. A great noise has been stirred up by the Press in a 'slander campaign' against Russia. Some British and American papers had inferred that the diplomats escaped for 'political reasons', carrying secret documents. It is an attempt to confuse international political events with the clear aim of arousing empty and even absurd suspicions.

The meaning, if anything, was that Burgess and the Macleans had not been encouraged by the Soviet Union to defect there, that they were not spies, and that anyone who said so was slandering the Soviet Union.

The nearest the British came to pin-pointing the whereabouts of the diplomats and Melinda was still the statement by Mr Selwyn Lloyd, then Minister of State, who had told Colonel Lipton in the House of Commons on 25th January 1954: 'If you were to presume they are behind the Iron Curtain you would probably be right.'

Then—more silence until Christmas Day 1954 when Mrs Bassett received another typewritten envelope posted in the East End of London, E14, not far from the Surrey Docks where the Russian ship *Beloostrov* had berthed on 22nd December.

When asked about this new letter, Mrs Bassett said:

It is in my son's handwriting, it is unmistakable. He said he was well. He wrote very affectionately. There is nothing in his letter to say where he is or what he is doing. He has obviously seen the British newspapers because he knew his letter last year had been received. In this second letter Guy says he wrote to me before Christmas 1953. I didn't get those letters. I don't know how many there were—he didn't say. This is the first time I have heard from him since last year. I could not have had a nicer Christmas present. I am not going to reveal the contents to anyone—after all, they are private and personal between mother and son. But the letter indicated that Guy is well and happy. I expect to hear from him again.

The letter was read to MI5 who took Colonel Bassett's word for what was in it. Perhaps they were losing interest.

But the newspapers were not. In January 1955 the *Sunday Pictorial* announced:

The address of Burgess and Maclean is c/o The Kremlin, Red Square, Moscow, U.S.S.R. (Telephone: Centre 67571). They are working for the Soviet Foreign Ministry. Their job is to advise Russian experts on propaganda before it is put out to the West. The *Pictorial* understands that at least fourteen MPs know how Burgess and Maclean disappeared and what they are doing now.

Captain Henry Kerby, the Tory Member for Arundel and Shoreham, who was once in the Diplomatic Service, told the *Pictorial*:

The Foreign Office has known for many months all there is to know about Burgess and Maclean. They know the exact movements of the two diplomats from the moment they left England to the time they reached Moscow via Prague. They know the identity of all the people who aided the two men when they made their getaway.

Captain Kerby said: 'I strongly deplore the fact that the Foreign Office still refuse to make a clean breast of the affair.'

Then in June 1955, Réné MacColl, one of the *Daily Express*'s most respected Foreign Correspondents cabled from Belgrade:

Donald Maclean and Guy Burgess are living just outside Moscow. I am able to say this definitely on the strength of a statement from a highly reputable Soviet source, made during the conference between Tito and the Russian delegation which has just ended in Belgrade.

Until now, no Russian has ever admitted that Maclean and Burgess had sought sanctuary behind the Iron Curtain, let alone Moscow.

When I was in the Soviet Union last year I asked scores of people about the missing diplomats. Everyone looked blank.

But now a Russian—and there is no doubt that he has access to official information—confirms that Maclean and Burgess are indeed living near Moscow.

'What are they doing?' Said the Russian: 'A special job.'

Then came the Petrov report followed closely by the British White Paper which quoted apparently with approval Petrov's report that on arrival in Russia, Burgess and Maclean 'lived near Moscow'. Petrov himself had gone further and said that Kislytsin who had handled Burgess's and Maclean's material in London and Moscow and participated in the plans for their escape, was appointed their welfare officer. He saw them installed in a comfortable house on the outskirts of Moscow and signed the authorizations for their food, drink and other extras.

It seems generally accepted, however, that after a very short stay and before the two diplomats settled permanently in Moscow, they endured a period of de-briefing—that is of cross-examination in Kuibishev (*alias* Samara) where, despite the splendid flats they had overlooking the river, it was, according to Burgess, just like Glasgow on a Saturday night in the nineteenth century, after which, as the White Paper conceded, they worked as 'advisers to the Ministry of Foreign Affairs and other Soviet agencies'.

However, in January 1956 some months after the White Paper had made its declaration, Harold Wilson published a statement about an interview he had had with Khrushchev during which he asked the Russian leader if he could tell him anything about Burgess and Maclean. Khrushchev replied: 'I have read about these men. I have not heard anything about them from Soviet officials. Nor have I met them. It stands to reason, then, that I cannot know what they are doing.'

It was understandable that the Soviet Union should deny all knowledge of Burgess's and Maclean's spying activities, because any admission could lead the British Government to retaliate by expelling Soviet Embassy officials who, in one degree or another, were all engaged on intelligence work.

On the other hand, Soviet denials that they knew anything at all about Burgess and Maclean were growing less and less credible and this in turn was likely to sour the atmosphere of the visit which Marshal Bulganin and Khrushchev were shortly to pay to Berlin.

It was in these circumstances that Sidney Weiland, Reuter's man in Moscow, together with Richard Hughes and the man from Tass, the Soviet news agency, received on Saturday 11th February a telephone call inviting them to meet Mr V. G. Seliverstov, the Deputy General Manager of Tass, in Room 101 of the National Hotel. *The Times* man was unfortunately already on the plane from Moscow to Helsinki, and it was already three hours beyond the normal deadline for the *Sunday Times*, but the meeting with Mr Seliverstov nevertheless got excellent coverage. Indeed, reporters who hurried past the blue-uniformed doorman, through the hall with its chandeliers, into the tiny lift with gilded doors, found in Room 101, screened by lace curtains from the hotel's late-night restaurant, a world-beating story. For waiting in Room 101 (which in reality was a television lounge, furnished with plush chairs and a sofa and used from time to time as an emergency bedroom) were two men, the taller of whom, wearing English-looking clothes and a dark red spotted bow tie, stepped forward and said: 'I am Maclean.' The other man, who was seen to give a noticeable wink at his audience, was, of course, Guy Burgess, and it was he who, with his experience in the Foreign Office News Department, showed himself the more self-possessed of the two and took charge of the short conference that followed, pulling from a briefcase copies of a three-page statement by Maclean and himself which he deposited on the small round table before him. Asked what work they were doing, Burgess said: 'We do not wish to be followed about the streets. If I said where we are working I am rather afraid of the initiative journalists might take.' And in a rather more significant passage which suggested that his freedom was still rather limited, Burgess said: 'I would like to send a message to my mother. I think of her constantly and I hope to write to her as soon as I can.' Those who knew of the close relationship between Burgess and his mother took this to mean that he was prevented from writing as often as he would have liked. Asked if he also had a message he would like delivered, Maclean said in his loftiest Foreign Office style: 'I will be communicating myself.'

Soon afterwards, almost before the correspondents had time to read the Burgess and Maclean statement, the two men walked out of the room. The conference was over. It was left to Tom Driberg in his book *Guy Burgess, A Portrait With Background*, to answer with Burgess's concurrence some of the questions the reporters would have liked to put. Burgess told Driberg in August 1956, six months after his press conference, that he was working most of the time for the Foreign Literature Publishing House, advising them which English works would repay translation. He said he also acted as a kind of freelance adviser to friends in many different government departments who rang him up unexpectedly to ask him to join one of their conferences. He worked only with English-speaking officials, he said, as his Russian, even after five years, was only just good enough to cope with day-to-day housekeeping.

According to Burgess, Maclean was working for the Foreign Languages Publishing House which translated Russian books into foreign languages. Thus both were engaged in the kind of occupation which could give no offence to British public opinion in the year of Bulganin and Khrushchev's visit to Britain.

Their statement, too, was issued, mainly in the interest of good Anglo-Soviet relations. (The *Daily Express* believed that it had been issued to counterbalance the good results of the talks which Premier Anthony Eden had recently had in Washington with President Eisenhower.)

The text of the statement read as follows:

Burgess and Maclean, former members of the British Foreign Office, wish to make the following statement: It seems to us that doubts as to our whereabouts and speculation about our past actions may be a small but contributory factor that has been and may again be exploited by the opponents of Anglo-Soviet understanding. Accordingly we have thought it best to issue the following statement:

We both of us came to the Soviet Union to work for the aim of better understanding between the Soviet Union and the West, having both of us become convinced from official knowledge in our possession that neither the British nor, still more, the American Government was at that time seriously working for this aim.

We had in the positions we occupied every reason to believe that such an understanding was essential if peace was to be safe. We had every reason to conclude that such an understanding was the aim of Soviet policy. We had had every opportunity to know and grounds for fearing the plans and outlook of the few but powerful people who opposed this understanding.

At Cambridge we had both been Communists. We abandoned our political activities not because we in any way disagreed with the Marxist analysis of the situation in which we still both find ourselves but because we thought, wrongly it is now clear to us, that in the public service we could do more to put these ideas into practical effect than elsewhere.

It was probably our action in necessarily giving up political activities by entering the public service that, falsely analysed, led the Foreign Office to say through its spokesman it 'believed' we had been Soviet agents at Cambridge. The Foreign Office can of course 'believe' anything it wishes. The important point, however, is that on this question we know, and it does not.

We neither of us have ever been Communist agents. So far the ground was common for us both. Details of our subsequent careers were completely different and had, therefore, better be dealt with separately.

As regards Maclean, he worked in London and in Paris, Washington, and Cairo as a regular member of the Foreign Service from 1935 to 1951 and as such was part of the machine which, with the exception of the war period, carried out a policy unacceptable not only to him but to many others.

He was by no means alone inside the Foreign Service in objecting to British foreign policy before the war, particularly as regards Abyssinia, the Spanish civil war, and Munich. But he was increasingly isolated in doing so after the war. It became more and more difficult to find anyone willing to think or speak of anything but the 'menace of Communism' or to understand the folly and danger of American policy in the Far East and Europe.

Further work in the Foreign Service was becoming impossible. In May 1951, there were clear signs that whatever future course he might work out for himself, the Foreign Office and security authorities had plans of their own. His telephone in his office and private house were used as microphones. Plain-clothes policemen followed him wherever he went and one of his colleagues was put up to act as provocateur.

Maclean therefore decided to come to the Soviet Union to do whatever he could to further understanding between East and West from there. The difficulty of leaving the country while being tailed by the police was solved by a meeting with Burgess shortly after the latter's return from the Washington Embassy to London. The latter not only agreed to make arrangements for the journey but to come too.

The risk of such a journey would have been too great for Mrs Maclean, who was shortly expecting a child. She and the children came to the Soviet Union in 1953.

As regards Burgess, when he decided to leave Cambridge, he joined the BBC (British Broadcasting Corporation). Subsequently, positions were offered to him which he accepted, first in a department of the secret service and secondly in the Foreign Office. Throughout, he sympathized with Soviet policy and became increasingly alarmed by the post-war trend of Anglo-American policy. Most alarming of all was its failure first to reach, and later even to seek to reach, a *modus vivendi* between East and West.

Neither in the BBC nor in the Foreign Office nor during the period that he was associated with the secret service and also MI5 itself did he make any secret from his friends or colleagues either of his views or the fact that he had been a Communist. His attitude in these positions was completely incompatible with the allegation that he was a Soviet agent.

This statement of Burgess's position is necessary to understand the situation which arose a week or so after his return to London from Washington in 1951. He went to see Maclean as head of the American Department of the Foreign Office. They found that their information and opinion about the political situation and the danger of war were in agreement.

What now happened was determined by the following facts. Burgess, who some months previously had himself initiated arrangements to obtain a new job with a view to leaving the Foreign Office, was faced with the fact that the Foreign Office had independently and subsequently decided that they would no longer employ him. It is, of course, obvious that no agent would take the initiative in arranging to leave the Foreign Office.

However, when the break came, Burgess was doubtful whether he wanted or could conscientiously do the new job he had been arranging.

Therefore, when Maclean told Burgess that he himself had decided that he could no longer work for the Foreign Office and its policies and suggested that they should both go to the U.S.S.R., Burgess had no difficulty in agreeing. There alone there appeared to both some chance of putting into practice in some form the convictions they had always held.

As a result of living in the U.S.S.R. we, both of us, are convinced that we were right in doing what we did. We are handing this statement to the Press.

The statement apparently made these points:

1. Both Burgess and Maclean had been Communists but not Communist agents.
2. They abandoned political activity, not Marxism, when they entered the public service.
3. After the war, Maclean found himself isolated in his disapproval of British Foreign Policy.
4. 'Telephones in his office and private house were used as microphones. Plain-clothes policemen followed him wherever he went, and one of his colleagues was put up to act as provocateur.'
   (But according to the White Paper he was not followed 'wherever he went', but only in London, and the colleague put up to act as provocateur was presumably Sir Roger Makins who had been told to see whether his work was satisfactory and reported favourably on it. Here, nevertheless, is the kind of argument which, if believed by Melinda, would have brought her racing to Donald's side.)
5. The reason Melinda did not come to the Soviet Union with Donald was that she was pregnant and not due to disloyalty to her husband or his views.
6. Burgess had never concealed from his colleagues in the U.K. that he was a Communist, an attitude which was incompatible with that of a Communist agent.
7. Burgess had arranged to leave the Foreign Office—a thing no agent would do—before they had decided to get rid of him.
8. Burgess's conscience prevented him from taking up 'the new job he had been arranging'—presumably the one he said he had been trying for on the *Daily Telegraph*.
9. It was Maclean who suggested that Burgess should come with him to the Soviet Union.
10. They had no regrets about the course they had taken.

But once again their names were linked together in the public eye in a manner that neither of them would have wished if they could have looked into the future.

Abroad, their reappearance was not received with rapture, and Cassandra—the *Daily Mirror*'s caustic columnist—referred to them as 'performing dogs'.

And the Royal National Lifeboat Institution refused to accept the fee which Burgess had asked the *Sunday Express* to donate in payment for the curtain raiser he had written to Bulganin and Khrushchev's visit to Britain.

# 22

# Third Man Overexposed

Despite the efforts of Burgess and Maclean, the visit of Bulganin and Khrushchev to Britain did not pass off smoothly, and there was one incident that could have completely wrecked the trip. For, on 29th April 1956, two days after the Russian party had left Britain on their way home, the Admiralty released the news that Commander Lionel Crabb of the Royal Naval Volunteer Reserve had failed to return from an underwater trial, and must be presumed dead. The Admiralty spokesman explained that Crabb had been engaged in a test dive which took place 'in connection with certain underwater apparatus for which he had been specifically employed', and that the incident had occurred 'in Stokes Bay in the Portsmouth area about a week ago'.

It did not pass unnoticed that 'about a week ago' would have been just when the Soviet Naval Squadron was visiting Portsmouth. But at first there was no reason to connect the two events. Stokes Bay was an area of shallow water outside, and away from, Portsmouth Harbour where the Soviet Squadron had been berthed, and, if Crabb had been testing some new British device, there might be good reason why the Admiralty had not been more specific in their announcement. Nevertheless, there was a scent of mystery somewhere, for, on 21st April, police acting under orders received from the Chief Constable, had suddenly descended on the Sallyport Hotel, Portsmouth, at which Crabb, with his friend, a Mr Smith, had been staying about a week before, and had ripped out the pages on which Crabb's name and address, and that of his friend had been recorded.

Prime Minister Anthony Eden had a bad time of it in the House of Commons on 9th May when he insisted that it was not in the public interest to give a complete explanation of the affair. Although, on 4th May the Soviet Assistant Naval Attaché in London, Mr N. P. Elissenko, had already declared that a frogman had surfaced near the Soviet cruiser *Ordzhonikidze* while she was in Portsmouth Harbour—a hint that the matter was not to be allowed to rest in obscurity. He also failed to mention one rather important detail, that the Soviet Government had sent a note of expostulation about the matter.

The Russian note was moderate in tone and said that the Soviet Government attached great importance to such an unusual event as the carrying out of frogmen tests alongside the Soviet ships on a friendly visit and would be grateful for an explanation.

After nearly a week Eden sent a reply which was published on 12th May. It stated that Crabb had been carrying out 'frogmen tests'; the Ministers responsible had no knowledge of Crabb's presence in the vicinity of the Soviet cruiser and he had received no authorization or permission to go there. Mr Eden regretted the incident.

Rear-Admiral Kotov, who had commanded the Soviet Squadron during its visit, was nevertheless sceptical. Writing in *Pravda*, he said that three sailors aboard the Soviet destroyer *Sovershenny*, had reported that at 7.30 on the morning of 19th April, they saw a diver, wearing a black, light-weight diving suit and flippers, floating on the surface of the water, face upwards. After one or two minutes the diver disappeared below the surface of the water near the Soviet destroyer *Smotryashchi*. Kotov added that he took the matter up with Rear-Admiral Burnett, the Commander-in-Chief Portsmouth and was told that no diver could have appeared where he was reported to have been seen, because the diving school at HMS *Vernon* was not then functioning and its staff were on holiday. Now, he said, he was being asked to believe that there was indeed a diver but that the British Government knew nothing about it.

A full scale debate in the House followed shortly afterwards in which Mr Zilliacus, the Labour MP for Gorton, Manchester, felt called on to suggest that Crabb might have been working for the American Secret Service. Mr George Wigg believed that the operation had been undertaken to prove that the Russian fleet was a menace to British interests, while diarist Richard Crossman accused the Government of 'odious hypocrisy' since nothing at all would have been heard of the incident if Crabb had been successful.

What had happened was that someone in MI6, as the organization charged with getting information on military and other resources of foreign powers, had authorized a project to discover whether, as reported, the Soviet cruiser was fitted with a hatch near the keel through which nuclear mines could be laid. The mission had failed, and thereby jeopardized the Prime Minister's peace initiative, publicly humiliating both him and the British intelligence services. And what made matters worse was that MI6 had tried to hush up the whole affair so that, although Khrushchev knew the details and had even made one or two half-humorous references to it at a dinner given in his honour at Greenwich on 20th April, the Admiralty was not in a position to share the joke until a week later.

Obviously something would have to be done to see that there were no more similar wildcat MI6 schemes in the future, and Eden's solution was to move a civilian, Sir Richard Goldsmith White, a security-minded trusty from MI5, over to take charge of MI6, a transfer which no doubt benefited MI6 but also finally forced master spy Philby to break cover and take refuge in Moscow along with Burgess and Maclean.

Philby's story has been fully recorded elsewhere, by himself in *My Silent War*, by Patrick Seale and Maureen McConville in *Philby, the Long Road to Moscow*, and by Bruce Page, David Leitch and Philip Knightley in *Philby, the Spy who betrayed a Generation*. But it is perhaps still worth recording some close parallels between his own life history and that of Burgess and Maclean. Like them, he went to Cambridge and while there became a theoretical Marxist. When he left the university with an economics degree in the autumn of 1933, he experienced Marxism at first hand in Vienna where the socialists recruited a private army and joined forces with the underground Communist movement in civil war against a series of Austria's right-wing governments.

Philby took lodgings in the working-class area of the city, and married Litzi Friedmann the daughter of his landlord.

Julius Hay, Hungary's best known playwright, a Communist since 1919 and an old friend of Arthur Koestler's, saw it all happen. In his memoirs he described Litzi (at twenty-three already married and divorced) as 'petite with a nicely rounded provocative figure and dark brown hair. She had the kind of femininity men find hard to resist, and against which a young Englishman who had previously seen her like only from the safe refuge of a Cambridge College never had a chance. Her bedroom was five steps away from his'.

Litzi was a dedicated Communist and Kim was soon shielding militants of all kinds from the police in the cellars and sewers of Floridsdorf, a working-class suburb where much of the fighting took place. When things became too hot for Litzi he married her and got her out of Vienna as the wife of a British subject.

He was almost certainly recruited as a potential agent in Vienna and, like Burgess and Maclean, soon afterwards dropped all public connection with the Communist party in order to infiltrate the Whitehall machine. He took a job with the *Review of Reviews*, a Liberal monthly magazine devoted mainly to summarizing the articles of other periodicals. He joined the Anglo-German Fellowship—certainly no Communist organization, and covered the Spanish Civil War on the Franco side for *The Times*; he was personally decorated by Franco for bravery. At the beginning of Hitler's war, he worked again for *The Times* as an accredited War Correspondent, and when France fell and the correspondents and the army were brought home, Philby was recruited into MI6, partly, he said, through the good offices of Guy Burgess who was already installed in a military annexe of the organization.

Once inside the woodwork of the Establishment, his progress was steady if not spectacular, and early in 1944 he was put in charge of a section formed to collect information on agents who would operate after the war in Soviet-controlled territory. In 1946 he was awarded the OBE in recognition of his distinguished services to British Intelligence and in 1949 he was offered and accepted the post of head of the MI6 organization in the United States.

In the meantime, he had made a clean breast to his superiors of the 'youthful indiscretion' he had committed by marrying Litzi, and with their knowledge, obtained a divorce from her to marry Aileen Furse, by whom he had already had several children.

Philby's chief value to his Russian paymasters while he was in the United States lay, of course, in his knowledge of the American intelligence network and it must have been a shock when he was recalled in disgrace from Washington in the summer of 1951.

It was all very well for Philby to claim that he sheltered Burgess only because he was an old friend. But it was hardly credible that someone with Philby's sources could have been host for so long to someone who was obviously such a security risk, and the Americans threatened to end all co-operation with the British MI6 if Philby were not sent home.

For some years he remained under a cloud. His resignation was accepted and he was awarded a gratuity of £4,000—to be paid in instalments—in lieu of pension. He was subjected to several searching interrogations, firstly by Dick White, at that time a senior official of MI5, then in November 1951 by Helenius Milmo, a King's Counsel who had worked in intelligence, and later by William Skardon, the man who had broken Fuchs. Finally he was examined by his own MI6 colleagues, including Sir John Sinclair the MI6 Chief. But no one succeeded in trapping him into an admission. In the meantime he found it hard to make a living. He had nothing to give the Russians and for some time it was not worth their while even to communicate with him. He took a series of unprofitable, even unsuitable jobs.

When Macmillan cleared Philby's name in the House of Commons, he might have done so as a matter of plain justice, for, as some of Philby's MI6 colleagues pointed out, Philby had now had the finger pointed at him by MI5 for four years without being brought to trial or even charged. And Macmillan could see for himself that no one at this stage was likely to learn anything more

by questioning Philby directly. But he must also have appreciated
the difference that lay in the philosophies of the two great intelligence organizations.

MI6 had always subscribed to the view, expressed by J. Edgar
Hoover, that: 'Arrest and public exposure (of a spy whose cover
has been blown) are steps to be taken only as a matter of last
resort.' At an early stage in their training, MI6 recruits would have
been familiar with the classic story of Colonel Alfred Redl who,
in the days before the Kaiser's War, achieved distinction as Chief
of the Counter-Espionage organization in the Austro-Hungarian
Empire while acting at the same time as the Russian Tsar's top
agent. When exposed just before the war, the Austrians invited him
to commit suicide, thereby renouncing any chance of discovering
how much damage he had done, or what lines of communication
he had used. They were far more interested in hushing up the whole
affair, and even the Emperor himself was kept in ignorance of it
for some time afterwards.

No one had yet invited Philby to commit suicide, yet there must
have been those who felt that MI5's tactics had been just as
unproductive as if he had been, and since MI5's techniques had
proved so unavailing, perhaps MI6 could do better. Philby was,
after all, respectable to the extent that he had been cleared by
Macmillan, even if not by MI5. He no longer knew anything of
importance that he could pass on to the Russians and it might yet
be possible to find a use for him in some not too sensitive area.
After a hand-to-mouth existence lasting several years, he would
probably be glad to work for the British, and it was far more
important to employ him than it was to leave him in idleness.

His loyalty could be tested by giving him 'chickenfeed', i.e.,
information of not too high security value which could be passed
on to Soviet agents in the hope that it would reveal their lines of
communication, thus giving him not only a second chance to prove
his loyalty—or his unreliability—but, more important, to expose
the agents who were controlling him, if they existed.

There is conflict of evidence about exactly what happened next.
According to Mr Donald Tyerman, who was then editor of the
*Economist*, a number of Philby's old friends approached him and
said that Philby was hoping for a job in the Middle East to carry
on the business established by his father, a desert explorer and
one-time adviser to the Saudi-Arabian Royal Family. At the same
time, the *Observer* got in touch with the *Economist* and suggested
that the two publications might employ Philby as a joint 'stringer'.
(A correspondent who although not a full-time member of the
regular staff, carries out assignments on request.)

According to David Astor, long-term editor of the *Observer*, the

Foreign Office came to him 'quite openly' to discuss Philby's future. They said that there had been so much gossip about Philby that he was now unemployable by them. But he had already served in the Middle East in Turkey, and had connections with the Arab world through his father's business. He had originally been a journalist and had worked for *The Times*. Would the *Observer* perhaps take him on?

Concurrently, the Foreign Office man gave Astor a very carefully worded assurance, according to which Philby had no further connection with British intelligence and would not become involved in any Government work.

Astor, wrongly as it turned out, took this to mean that Philby would have no further connection with secret service work—a very different occupation from 'Government work'.

In an interview with Roger Berthoud of *The Times*, Astor afterwards declared that he received a specific undertaking 'from the Foreign Office' that 'they would not use Philby as a spy'. And Tyerman said he had not known that the suggestion that the *Observer* should employ Philby had come from the Foreign Office. 'If I had known the Foreign Office had asked,' Tyerman told Berthoud, 'I would no more have employed him than if the CIA or KGB had asked.'

It was in these circumstances that Kim Philby arrived in Beirut in August 1956, alone, without his family, unsure whether he was trusted by either side. But in his role of reporter there was plenty for him to cover. Colonel Nasser's Suez Canal grab in 1956, the formation of the United Arab Republic, the overthrow of the monarchy in Iraq in July 1958, and the growth of Arab nationalism under Egypt's Nasser all needed interpreting. At first Philby lived in a house rented by his father in the hills above Beirut, visiting the city itself, and particularly the side table in the bar of the Normandy Hotel, only two days a week to collect material for his weekly stories.

Then he met Eleanor, the wife of a colleague, Sam Pope Brewer, the Middle East Correspondent of the *New York Times* who was also based on Beirut. Eleanor discerned in Philby a kind of old-world reserve and courtesy which seemed to set him apart from the brasher and less distinguished scribes. They became lovers, and after Philby's wife, whom he had left behind in the U.K., died and Eleanor had achieved a Mexican divorce, Philby embarked on his third marriage—at the Holborn Registry Office in London. The couple then moved to a penthouse flat with a spectacular semi-circular living-room with a panoramic view of the mountains and the sea (and easy access to the Soviet Commercial Mission close by).

Philby, as was to be expected, remained under some sort of

surveillance while he was in Beirut, and both British and American officials had been warned that he might have Communist affiliations, but, for several years, neither side seemed anxious to make use of his services. From mid-1960 onwards, however, a new MI6 Controller, a long-term friend of Philby's, arrived in Beirut and Philby seemed to become more active, possibly because the British side felt that he should by now be providing a flow of reports from his intelligence sources. (Also, as long as he was doing so little work for the British, the Russians would hardly think it worth while trying to contact him, as MI6 had hoped they might.)

So the Philbys gradually became more interested in giving cocktail and dinner parties for businessmen, professors, artists and Arabists who might have been regarded as useful sources.

Then came another development that forced everyone's hand. Over Christmas 1961, Anatoli Dolnytsin, the most important KGB officer ever to defect, came over to the West, and exposed some 200 Soviet agents. One of them was George Blake who, within a few months, received an exemplary prison sentence of forty-two years—a warning which Philby could hardly ignore—and another of those exposed by Dolnytsin was Philby himself.

Once the British knew for certain what Philby had hitherto refused to admit, there were several courses of action they could take. They could 'liquidate' Philby as a warning to others—which might have been the Russian way. But if a nation like Britain, unused to these methods, were to use them, there would always be the risk of a misfire and in any case Philby's death would not yield an extra tittle of information to British intelligence, and might even turn him into a martyr. Alternatively, Philby might be brought back to England for interrogation and trial. But Britain had no extradition treaty with the Lebanon, and Philby would therefore have to be abducted, an operation which, even if the Lebanese police tactfully looked the other way while it was being carried out, might be attended with risk. It would not be easy to bring Philby to justice under such circumstances and if he were interrogated even in prison, there was no guarantee that he would give away anything more than he already had. And another abortive attempt to cross-question an unco-operative Philby could only bring discredit—perhaps even a public inquiry into the working of the British intelligence services, which had already had a tousling over the Profumo affair.

Attempts were made to get Philby to come back to the U.K. voluntarily, as an innocent party, for questioning, but he demurred on the pretext of his responsibilities towards his wife and family. Eventually he was confronted with the evidence which the British now had, in the hope that this would lead to further admissions and titbits about the network of which he had formed a part. The probability is that he was offered immunity from harassment in return for co-operation. But none was forthcoming. Yet there could be no question of allowing Philby to remain in Beirut unmolested and unexposed. The British no longer wanted any part of him, whether employed by the *Observer* or unemployed. Two British agents sent specially from London, replaced the easy-going Controller who had been dealing with Philby, and from then on he seems to have become obsessed with fears that he was about to be badly beaten up, if not abducted, or handed over to the Lebanese police because of his failure to help MI5.

Already the strain of knowing that his cover had been blown was telling. He was drinking more heavily than before, staggering and falling down dead drunk at parties. He began to suffer from nightmares from which he would wake up struggling and calling for help.

He must have learnt somehow that the Armenian proprietor of a pastry shop over which he had been wont to meet his contacts had been arrested. He seemed afraid to leave the security of his home, although somehow he had to tell his Soviet friends that he could be of no further use to them and that he must seek asylum in the Soviet Union as soon as it could be granted.

He may even have been preparing the ground by laying a false trail when he wrote to his employers the *Observer* saying that two of his children would be returning to the U.K. this summer and that he would like to accompany them for a short spell of home leave. Surely the authorities, if they had read this, would forbear to question Philby in Beirut when they could do so under more favourable circumstances at home.

On New Year's Day 1963, which was also the date of his fifty-first birthday, he drank so much that he fell down in his flat, cutting his head so badly on a radiator that it needed twenty-four stitches. On 6th January he cut an appointment with his two colleagues from London. His nerve had been totally destroyed. He was waiting for the green light to appear for his passage to the Soviet Union.

On 23rd January, the day of a wild rainstorm in Beirut, Philby grabbed his raincoat and went out of the flat, saying that he would be back at six in the evening. But about an hour later he telephoned and left a message for Eleanor who was then in her bath. He asked her to meet him at the dinner to which they had both been invited at the house of Glen Balfour Paul, First Secretary at the British Embassy, and an old friend of Philby's father. He was to have arrived there at eight o'clock.

Instead, Philby set off for the Soviet Union, probably in the

Soviet freighter *Dolmatova* which sailed from Beirut unexpectedly without loading her cargo.

Like Melinda Maclean, Eleanor had at first no idea of what might have happened to her husband. He might for all she knew have fallen to his death over the sea wall or been run over while drunk or even robbed and killed. None of his colleagues liked to suggest that he had finally thrown in the towel and sought refuge in the Soviet Union. His wife received a note from him left for her at the Hotel Normandy, still a rendezvous where correspondents assembled to air their opinions over a morning drink. It said that she was not to worry, that Kim was all right and would write again soon. It asked her to put the word round that his paper had sent him off on a long tour of the Middle East area.

Like Melinda, Eleanor knew the name of the British Security Officer whom she was to get in touch with in such an emergency. She had the same wish to believe that her husband was not a spy. She had the same handicap of a British passport and dependence on the British authorities for a travel document for Philby's son, Harry, if she wished to leave Beirut.

Rather sooner perhaps than Melinda, she received evidence that Kim Philby wanted her in Moscow. In a message to her, Eleanor wrote, Philby suggested that she should book tickets at the British Overseas Airways Office in Beirut, but at the same time should fetch a duplicate ticket which would be waiting for her at the Czechoslovak Airways office, provided she gave them a clear ten days notice. She was asked to declare her proposed departure date by chalking it on a certain wall. If in any difficulties, she was to place a flower pot in the window of the flat where it could be seen from the street. If she did that, a Soviet agent would be with her within the hour.

But Eleanor was not yet ready to fall in with Kim Philby's proposal. She not only apprised the British of her husband's plans but identified from photographs shown her by the MI5 men a Russian agent who had called to see her.

None of this emerged publicly at the time but that summer, the CIA, unwilling to pander any longer to British inhibitions, boldly disclosed what they had learned of Dolnytsin's revelations—that Philby had indeed been a long-term spy while he was in the United States and declared without reservation that Philby was probably now in Moscow.

Once again the whole story blew up. The American public wanted to know why Macmillan had cleared Philby when their own security men, and especially General Bedell Smith, had been so certain that he was unreliable. His British newspaper colleagues asked why the Foreign Office had given him a new lease of life by recommending him to the *Observer* as worthy of trust? The authorities feared that the Russians were planning to produce Philby at a press conference and decided to step in first.

Early in July 1963 Mr Edward Heath, as Lord Privy Seal, was compelled to backtrack on the earlier assurances given by Mr Macmillan that no evidence had been found that Philby had warned Burgess and Maclean or betrayed the interests of his country or was the so-called Third Man.

Mr Heath now declared that, on the contrary, Philby had been the Third Man and had betrayed the interests of his country before 1946.

The suspicion that he might have done so from 1946 on was one that Mr Heath did not divulge to the Honourable Members—but he had already assured them in an answer given in March that Mr Philby, since his resignation, had had no access to any official information (except presumably from British Embassy Press Officers). 'Chickenfeed', if any, presumably was not 'official information'. Evidently Mr Heath accepted the view that MI6 had done the right thing in putting Philby back into circulation. At any rate, he considered it had been 'wise' that Mr Philby should be in employment.

Shortly after Mr Heath's statement, the Soviet Union announced that Philby had applied for and had been granted asylum and Soviet citizenship. And in September Eleanor Philby, with the help of officials of the Soviet Embassy in London, left on a visit to Moscow, backed by an assurance that she could leave the Soviet Union to visit her family whenever she wished. We shall meet her again in Moscow.

# 23

# The Last Days Of Guy Burgess

Of the three men who had sought sanctuary in Moscow, Burgess was the one who found most difficulty in acclimatizing himself to the Soviet environment. He was no longer a member of the élite class as he had once been in Britain. He had never been fascinated by the Russians, or even by their music or literature and he never troubled to learn their language, which precluded him from discussing the topics that interested him with those he would have most liked to influence.

He missed the Reform Club and its bar. He missed the establishment which he loved to taunt—and shock. And during his early months in Moscow he was deprived of male sex-partners simply because he did not know whereabouts in the city they could be recruited. He missed the scandal in high places which he had done so much to promote and which provided him with so many friends. Now, at last they were beginning to slip out of his grasp.

And he, Burgess, was forced to go underground by adopting a ridiculous Russian name—Jim Andreyvich Eliot—and journey across Russia with the travel document of a Soviet citizen, though he never became one. He was pathetically anxious for news from home and corresponded regularly with friends—Harold Nicolson was one of them—who were prepared to answer his letters. From time to time he was in touch with his stockbrokers. Before the war he had bought Rolls Royce shares; after the war he bought gold and did handsomely out of both. He obtained special concessions on dividends to which a British subject living abroad was entitled. Sometimes he ordered bow ties from London in Old Etonian colours of black and pale blue through the forwarding firm used by a Russian travel agency. He wore English clothes, some of which came from Tom Brown, his tailor at Eton, favouring dark blue suits with chalk stripes, topped with a camel overcoat when the wind was cold. Whenever possible, he got a hamper of goodies from Helsinki, Copenhagen, or better still London. He read the English papers, four days late, and kept up his subscription to the *Autocar*.

For the last six years of his life, Burgess lived in a south-west suburb of Moscow in Apartment No. 68 in a large, newly-built block of flats at No. 53–55 Bolshaya Perogovskaya Street, an avenue which leads towards the Lenin Central Sports Stadium. It was a normal three-room bachelor suite, with a fine view over the Novodevichy Monastery, and somehow Burgess managed to give shelter there to Tolya, an Alsatian dog and to a young guitar-playing electrician, also named Tolya, a permanent 'nephew' whom he had picked up, he said, in the street one evening. He also had a very large library with first editions—some signed—of his favourite British authors. Once more, an elaborately carved piece of wood-work stood at the head of his bed, and at various times he seems to have had a piano, or a small portable harmonium of the kind used in processions, on which he delighted to play the Eton Boating Song. His old friend Tom Driberg, who visited him in 1956 with a view to writing *Guy Burgess, A Portrait with Background*, took with him some reproductions of Renoir and Cézanne for Burgess's flat—as well as some nylon socks. He also had a *dacha* about forty minutes drive away at which he appeared to spend a fair amount of time, although, he said, it was situated in a security zone which made the entertainment of foreigners at any rate difficult.

His job, in so far as he had a regular one, consisted in recom-mending suitable works for translation into Russian. One of them was *Diplomacy*, written by his old friend Harold Nicolson, and two were by Graham Greene. But he was also called on for back-ground information or advice on any subject of which he might have special knowledge. In addition, he helped to edit the English edition of *Soviet Union*, a cultural paper on the Soviet life-style. He was said to have acquired considerable credit for forecasting correctly, after the Suez Crisis of 1956 and the resignation through illness of Anthony Eden, that Harold Macmillan and not R. A. Butler would be the next Prime Minister.

After this, the Russians, reflecting perhaps that nothing too awful had happened at the Burgess–Maclean press conference, allowed Guy a little more of the freedom for which he had been clamouring.

In the thaw which followed Stalin's death, he was allowed to write more letters and see more people. One of them was his mother, Mrs Eve Bassett, with whom he spent a holiday at Sochi on the Black Sea in 1956, sunbathing, riding in speedboats, and walking through palm-lined streets. Guy arranged it all. He bought her ticket, arranged for her foreign currency and wrote to tell her in a letter forwarded through the British Embassy Diplomatic Bag that the Russians approved of her visit and would give her a visa in London. 'She was always specially fond of Guy,' a friend told the newspapers about a week after she had left to meet her son. 'She spoiled Guy as only a devoted mother can, and has never ceased to believe in him. She maintains that Guy acted for the best and is not a traitor.'

A reporter who met her on her return early in August noted that she came back smoking a Russian cigarette and described her as a 'determined apple-cheeked little woman wearing a veiled hat of eggshell blue perched at a jaunty angle on her thin grey curls'. She mentioned Guy only to say that she had swum with him once and that of course he was a wonderful swimmer.

In 1961 Burgess told a reporter: 'I am more happy after ten years in the Soviet Union than I was after five.' Nevertheless, both earlier and later, he was sounding out the possibility of revisiting Britain.

In 1959 he told Douglas Clark of Beaverbrook Newspapers: 'I am anxious to go back to Britain. I want to make an early visit for personal reasons and particularly to see my mother.' But he would want assurances first. 'They have no evidence against me but I don't want to have to pay £10,000 to some barrister for my defence.' And about the same time he told George Hutchinson, then Political Correspondent for the London *Evening Standard* after dinner that, if allowed to come home he would agree to give no interviews without Foreign Office permission. In return he asked for an undertaking that he would be free to leave after a month. Burgess told Hutchinson that he was grateful to HMG in so far as they had taken no hostile action against him and added: 'I, for my part, have never said a lot of things I might have said in public.' He had also written a personal letter to Macmillan, asking for a safe-conduct, without getting a reply.

In 1960 he was again quoted as saying he would like to come to Britain for a holiday as long as he could be certain of getting back to the Soviet Union, adding for the record: 'It comes to everyone to feel that he had made a mistake and you can quote me on that.' (This did not necessarily imply that he had any regrets but merely, as he had said at his press conference, that in his innocence he had supposed that he would be helping the cause of world peace by seeking to influence the Whitehall machine from within rather than from outside it.)

In 1962, however, matters became more serious, for the Soviet Minister for Foreign Affairs in Moscow announced that Burgess and Maclean were free to leave the Soviet Union whenever they pleased and added: 'They are subjected to no kind of pressure to go or stay. We do not know anything about their intentions.' This added force to the rumours that Burgess, and perhaps Maclean also, might be expected to land in Britain at any moment—despite the fact that Burgess had always maintained that he was most anxious not to damage Anglo-Soviet neighbourly relations.

Rumours said they might be expected to arrive in Amsterdam on the 18th April 1962 on a KLM flight from Moscow; they would transfer to a British European Airways Flight, arriving at Heathrow at ten minutes past ten that evening. Detective Superintendent G. G. Smith of Scotland Yard's Special Branch acted quickly. He obtained as a matter of urgency a warrant allowing him to arrest the two wanted men or either of them if they landed in the U.K. even if they were in transit (it was thought that they might even be on their way to Cuba). The warrant was taken out in a closed court at Bow Street and signed by the Chief Metropolitan Magistrate, Sir Robert Blundell, but the news was released for publication.

Some crime reporters, lacking for once their usual sophistication, suggested that it had been a mistake to announce that warrants for the arrest of Burgess and Maclean had been taken out. But Sir Reginald Manningham Buller humoured them by saying that the Press would have found out anyway. He also maintained that, though the announcement of the arrest warrants might indeed prevent the two men from coming here, yet, if they did, the chances of arresting them would be increased.

It has sometimes been suggested that even by 1962 the authorities had not collected sufficient evidence to make a charge stick against Burgess under the Official Secrets Act, and that this was the reason why they were so anxious to discourage his return to Britain. But, in fact, there was plenty of evidence.

According to Section 1 of the Official Secrets Act of 1911 which was in force at the time: An offence is committed by any person who obtains, collects, records, or publishes or communicates to any other person any secret official code word or pass word or any sketch plan, model, article, note or other document or information which is calculated to be or might be or is intended to be directly or indirectly useful to an enemy. Under the same Act all official information is the property of the Crown.

In a technical sense, there was already information which Burgess had given to Tom Driberg for use in *Guy Burgess, A Portrait with Background*, published in 1956, on which action could have been taken—though the publishers had taken precautions to get the work cleared in advance. Apart from this, however, there was other information on Burgess's war-time work which he had given Driberg in an original draft which, at the authorities' request, was deleted and not published. And apart from all this, Burgess had told Randolph Churchill in 1959 that he had worked for MI5 before the war at the same time as Peter Hope was sent to check up on his work in Liechtenstein. These were indiscretions which could have got Burgess into rather more serious trouble.

In fact, however, the authorities' unwillingness to welcome Burgess to Britain stemmed from something different. As both Burgess and the authorities were very well aware, Burgess possessed a vast store of knowledge about the foibles and weaknesses of officials and others he had met during his none-too-respectable career. And the man who had already teased the authorities by claiming that he had been living off the immoral earnings of his mother would not be too careful of the reputations of non-relatives. Ridicule, if nothing worse, would result. And in addition, Burgess might play havoc by denouncing innocent men. And what purpose would be served by paying for the upkeep of Guy Burgess in prison in the U.K. when he was already under wraps in the Soviet Union?

As it happened, Burgess had just begun a three-week holiday in Samarkand at the time the storm broke. He hurried back, probably at the request of his Controller, to deny at a hastily summoned press conference in the Ukraine Hotel, Moscow, that he was about to make even a short trip to Britain. He would like to meet his mother, even in Stockholm, he said, but she was too ill to go there.

But in the event, Burgess was to die before his mother. Friends noticed a change in his appearance after he came to Moscow. His face had become fleshier, his hair thinner and grey. He admitted to one reporter that he had put on half a stone since he lived in the Soviet Union: 'You can't help it with the Russian food.' Whitney Straight, Chairman of Rolls Royce and an old Cambridge friend, who visited him in February 1963 noted that he was continuing to put on weight and losing hair. 'He still feels he is pro-British in the sense that he is still interested in what goes on here and is anxious for better relations between Britain and Russia,' Mr Straight reported.

But putting on weight was only part of Burgess's troubles. He had already had a spell in the Vishnevsky Hospital in 1961 where he was treated for ulcers and hardening of the arteries. He gave up smoking—for a time only. Then he had a heart attack. A lifetime's drinking, topped up with vodka and the Armenian brandy and the sleeping draughts he had always needed, was catching up on him. He began to spend more and more of his time waiting in his flat for the Soviet nurse who came, sometimes four times a day, to give him the injections he was now obliged to have. Sometimes he lay about from dawn to dusk on the bed without bothering to dress. He had given up the idea of going to the translation bureau. He refused to eat, and left untouched broth-and-dumpling lunches that his housekeeper Nadezhda prepared for him. He was smoking up to sixty cigarettes a day between slugs of Armenian brandy.

He had obviously been down-graded under the system of 'nomen-klatura', which determines what privileges, if any, shall be granted to government employees. He had lost the will to live.

Reporters, when they first heard that Philby had vanished from Beirut, had flocked to Burgess to ask if he knew anything. But Burgess was sure that Philby could not be in Moscow. 'I should have been the first person he would have got in touch with if he'd been here. And he hasn't and that's flat.' Later, when Burgess apparently disappeared from his flat, the correspondents felt sure that he had gone to meet Philby. Instead, he had been taken to the Botkin Hospital, to an iron bed in the general ward on the third floor, overlooking a tree-fringed courtyard. There, on 30th August 1963, he died in his sleep.

Donald Maclean was one of the first to know—but not from the Russian newspapers. He was rung up by Burgess's housekeeper. And he in turn sent word through the Soviet Embassy in London to Mrs Bassett, who expressed a wish that, after cremation, Burgess's ashes should be brought back to England to be buried in his father's grave.

Guy's brother, Nigel Burgess, flew to Moscow where he was met by Donald Maclean and a Soviet official.

In Moscow, the Soviet KGB had obviously gone through Burgess's effects with scrupulous care and had taken with them everything likely to be of assistance to MI5 or MI6. But they were careful to leave behind a sheet of paper on which Burgess's last wishes had been scrawled. They were respected by Nigel Burgess, to whom Letters of Administration were granted in respect of Burgess's British assets of £6,220.

Burgess wanted all his books and a third of his estate to pass to Kim Philby who, in turn, passed the money on to his children.

Philby, who had not been present at the funeral, turned up soon afterwards at Burgess's flat and was able to secure some of his effects as well: the portable organ, a little dressing-table that had belonged to Mrs Bassett, the carved bed-head and the comfortable plum-coloured wing chair that Burgess claimed had once belonged to Stendhal. Philby also secured most of Burgess's clothes, wearing some and, after having to wait some time for buyers, selling Burgess's shoes and overcoat.

Burgess's twelve-cylinder Lincoln car, left at the Embassy, had already been sold—for $35—and the Embassy, with a straight face, held on to the money as representing storage costs.

One of the last acts that Burgess had performed was to issue a denial that Philby could have been the Third Man. The truth, he said, was that Maclean had stopped his taxi in St James's Square and had been bumped into by a car carrying over-eager Special

Branch sleuths. 'He was on his way to lunch with me,' Burgess continued in an interview. 'It was this and this alone that revealed to Maclean that he was being followed. There was no Third Man, no unnamed diplomat, no Philby, who is supposed to have told me in Washington what was going on.'

Burgess would certainly have liked the chance to talk over old times with Philby and explain in person the real reason that made him fly with Maclean—whether this was due to him having lost his nerve or because he was acting under orders, or both. He may have already tried to do so during a mysterious call that he made to America on the day he left England, for which Hewit was afterwards called on to pay a bill of £7.

Philby was, after all, a very old friend. At a personal press conference which he gave shortly after Macmillan had cleared his name, Philby said he had been a genuine friend of Burgess's since undergraduate days, though he disapproved strongly of his actions. 'There are fair-weather friends and foul-weather friends and I prefer to belong to the second category,' Philby said. He refused to indulge in slinging mud at Burgess.

But there was no chance for the two to meet. Philby, of course, had only just arrived back in the U.S.S.R. at the time Burgess died and was probably still being 'de-briefed' by Soviet intelligence officers while events were still fresh in his mind.

The funeral took place a few days after Nigel Burgess had arrived in Moscow. It was apparently an ordinary cremation, but, at the end, a brass band emerged from behind the pillars and played the Internationale, whether as a Soviet custom or as a special tribute to Burgess or as a substitute for a sacred hymn was not clear. Maclean gave a short address in which he said of Burgess that 'he came to the Soviet Union with some idealism, which many people have not understood'. Burgess, he said, was a gifted and courageous man who dedicated his life to the cause of peace and the struggle for a better life for the people. A KGB colleague then added a tribute in Russian. The ashes were delivered to Nigel Burgess in an earthenware container marked with Russian characters and decorated on top with a miniature spike.

In an interview published on 4th September, Nigel Burgess said: 'A brother is a brother, no matter what he has done. I have always kept well out of the business. When it all blew up I naturally had very strong feelings but I've never mentioned them either to my brother or to the public. Until now I have succeeded in dissociating myself completely from him. I would not say I was ashamed of my brother. But I decided to break all contact with him. I have not even written once.'

Mrs Bassett, described as seventy-six and 'white haired with beautiful hands' allowed herself to be interviewed, too, while she smoked a Turkish cigarette. She said: 'An awful lot of lies have been written about my son. But I never have denied them and I never will. There is no need to deny them. Lies always defeat themselves in the end—they do, you know.'

Mrs Bassett told reporters that she had been ill and had not been outside the flat for a year. 'I have no information about my son. I have never talked about him and I never will.' She had no recent picture of Guy.

Asked if she knew that he had been ill, unhappy and homesick, she replied: 'I will not say what my son wrote in his letters.'

Burgess's ashes were duly taken to the Rev. J. C. Hurst, at that time Rector of the Hampshire village of West Meon, where they were interred on Saturday 5th October in an unmarked part of the Burgess family grave on a green grass slope overlooking the village. The villagers did not become aware of the fact until some time after the event had taken place, for, although the Rector did not consider it to be any concern of theirs, he took the precaution of performing the interment after dark.

# 24

# In Moscow, More Equal Than Some

Though Donald Maclean had pronounced the oration at the funeral of Guy Burgess, the togetherness which they had once felt over lunch at the Royal Automobile Club and later when motoring through the country lanes of southern England on that May evening of 1951 had evaporated.

And even the scarcity of expatriate Britons in Moscow did not lead them to seek each other's company. Terence Lancaster, at that time a special correspondent in Moscow, happening to meet Burgess at a cocktail party, asked him if he saw Maclean. 'From time to time,' replied Burgess. 'Not very frequently—about as often as I did in England.'

Melinda, once so intrigued by 'Roger Styles' over the dinner table at Tatsfield, was no longer interested. And according to one widely believed story, Burgess shocked Maclean's sense of decorum by urinating over the fireplace at a reception given by the Chinese People's Republic.

Their attitudes to life in the Soviet Union differed sharply. Burgess hated the Soviet bureaucracy; Maclean was himself a bureaucrat. Burgess would have liked to revisit Britain and said so. Maclean realized he could never do so. Burgess intermittently courted publicity and the company of newspapermen. Maclean had been deeply wounded by some of the articles about him in British newspapers, and had no desire for any more exposure.

'My family and I have made our lives here and all we want to do is to live in peace without any kind of intrusion,' he told one caller in a typical brush-off. 'But,' he added, 'I have taken great interest and have been amused by the progress of Lord Mancroft's Bill to haul reporters into court if they pester people.'

'Shut the door, shut the door,' he barked to his son on another occasion when he saw a newspaperman hovering outside. All that emerged from that particular interview was that Maclean was wearing an open-neck shirt, corduroy trousers and red carpet slippers, and that his son, Fergus, was wearing horn rimmed glasses over a crew cut.

Maclean had been equally emphatic if asked about his relations with Melinda. 'I have absolutely nothing to say on the subject. I have decided to say nothing and that means nothing.'

Such reticence is perfectly understandable, not only in Maclean but in anyone in the U.S.S.R. who realizes that continuous contact with the West is likely to damage his, or her, own relations with the Soviet hierarchy—and even those of his wife and family.

Maclean's standard of living is better than that of most people in his intellectual bracket, since his family were soon given exclusive use of a three-room flat with heating and running water in an accessible sector of the city. It is on the sixth floor of an eleven-storey block, elaborately decorated in the Stalin style. The road to it lies south of the river past the Ukraine Hotel along the Kutuzovsky Prospekt, towards the Minsk Highway, and it enjoys a view both on to the Moscow River and the nearby railway lines. But Maclean would probably earn a higher salary in the West.

Robert Denniston, the publisher, who visited Maclean in 1969 in connection with Maclean's book *British Foreign Policy since Suez,* saw him as a large man, a long-haired diplomat with a bit of a paunch, wearing a good suit but no tie. He noted that Maclean had now handed over his green Volvo car, which Melinda had earlier driven around the city, to a driver who took him to where-ever he wanted.

The interior of the Maclean flat was described in some detail by Eleanor Philby in her book *The Spy I loved.* She recalled it in 1964 as having good furniture plus some western bric-à-brac of the kind that you might see in Belgravia, London.

The drawing-room, according to Eleanor, was large and pretentious, but the chintzes were rather shabby. The flat had two bedrooms, one for Maclean's daughter, the other, slightly larger, used at the time by his two sons, then aged eighteen and twenty. Donald and Melinda were sleeping on divans in the sitting-room.

The family had some shopping privileges though not, of course, equivalent to those given to the Party leaders, whose goods are ordered by telephone and called for by the chauffeur, but substantial, if only because both Donald and his wife have access from time to time to foreign currency which can be converted and used for buying imported goods in the special Beryoska or hard-currency stores. Nevertheless, Melinda found that in the search for perfect equality, the shops sometimes ran out of such things as tomatoes and cucumbers; and fresh grapefruit was a find to be talked about. And it paid to carry about as much money as possible, so that if you noticed a store had received a consignment of some rarity—be it clothing, food or electrical goods—you could join the queue at once without having to go home or elsewhere to fetch the money.

The Macleans found that they could afford to take short trips to

Leningrad in the Red Arrow overnight express in which they could have a compartment each and drink champagne against a background of plush upholstery and pink lampshades. They were able to visit historically romantic areas of the Soviet Union—Novgorod, for example, and Pskov and Samarkand.

The Macleans were also awarded a *dacha*, or weekend retreat, in Shelkobo, in a part of the countryside closed to foreigners, where, in his early days, Maclean grew his own fruit, vegetables and flowers, besides having a share in a nearby community potato field.

In his social life, Donald appears to have retained the impression that he was still one of the élite, and Eleanor detected in him a certain 'unappealing conceit' which made her doubt whether they would ever become close friends. Maclean has no regrets about leaving the West—or if he had, was too proud or too reluctant to express them.

He feels that he has not been guilty of anything except disagreeing fundamentally with Foreign Office policy (and even this would not have troubled the Government if he had been a market gardener or a lift attendant instead of a diplomat). He likes working in the Soviet Union and has no intention of coming back to Britain without a safe conduct. It was a defence remarkably like that offered by Burgess, who said that he had done nothing injurious to the interests of his country, unless it is held that opposition to the Government's foreign policy must be contrary to the interests of the country. 'I have been a Marxist,' Burgess used to say, 'but in Britain there's no law against that.'

In 1960, Maclean's old friend, Mark Culme-Seymour, seeking export orders, happened to run into the Macleans in Leningrad and spent a weekend of sight-seeing and reminiscing with them there. Donald, according to Culme-Seymour, seemed to have lost some of his individuality. He seemed inhibited by Melinda and would, Culme-Seymour felt, have talked more freely if she had not been with them. Melinda 'seemed convinced that everything that is marvellous is Russian'. Donald did not seem so certain but she 'jumped down his throat' whenever he started to be critical. (She may have feared that Culme-Seymour would be interviewed when he got back to London.)

Like Burgess and Philby, Donald Maclean has been endowed with a new surname as resident in the Soviet Union—he was at one time 'Mark P. Frazer', but more recently acquired a Russian *alias* of Comrade Madzoevsky.

The job that Maclean was first given to do in Moscow was originally similar to Burgess's, only in reverse. For whereas Burgess concerned himself with arranging for English language books to be translated into Russian, Maclean was involved in the translation of Russian works into English. He has also worked as one of the editors of the English language political monthly *International Affairs* at the Foreign Language Publishing House, and more recently ran the British Desk in the Soviet Institute of World Economic and International Relations, which is one of the Institutes of the Soviet Academy of Sciences. Even at home, Donald himself had been attracted by the works of the classic Russian authors such as Chekhov, Tolstoy, Turgenev. Now he had the chance of sampling other less well known ones.

At weekends, Moscow offers family amusements or the zoo, or skating or ski-ing. Or the Macleans could stay snugly at home, where they had one of the earlier television sets for listening to plays, concerts, etc. (Since those days, the number of television channels in Moscow has increased to four, with most programmes in colour, some of them beamed by satellite.)

Donald clearly believed that great changes were to follow the end of the Stalin era. Of course Stalin had achieved a great deal but during the fifties there was to be an enormous change for the better—a return to the original ideals of the revolution.

He believed that the 1956 revolution in Hungary would have led to the restoration of Fascism there soon, if not at once, if Soviet tanks had not been used there in the same anti-fascist cause as they had been in the Spanish Civil War. Not all his old friends were able to share these views, and more than one thereafter stopped writing to him.

Apart from his specific job in Moscow, Donald has also done some freelance work. Shortly after his reappearance at his press conference in 1956, he wrote a piece for the *Daily Herald*, in which he argued that U.S. policy was based on preparations for war with the Soviet Union, whereas Soviet society was concerned with producing more, building more, and educating more. 'Making or threatening war doesn't come into the picture,' he wrote, adding that the Soviet Union offered a new civilization 'with which the people of Britain have no reason for quarrelling, but one with which far closer and friendlier relations could be established . . . I believe that it is up to us all to try to bring that about.'

There was also his book, *British Foreign Policy since Suez*, which his brother Alan (who had finally managed to carve out a highly successful career for himself in publishing) suggested to Hodder & Stoughton.

In the preface to the book, which Donald Maclean wrote on the thirtieth anniversary of the outbreak of Hitler's war, he described his treatise as an attempt to produce a slightly clearer picture of what British policy-makers had been aiming at and the factors by which they were influenced. His forecast of the future was one of an irreversible trend towards Communism throughout the world, with Britain in the unenviable position of having to choose between remaining a satellite of the United States in order to keep her nuclear capability or of dropping her relationship with the United States in order to gain entry to the Common Market.

His principal mistake seems to have been to suppose that the choice had already been made: 'Thus Macmillan and his colleagues when they prolonged the Anglo-American nuclear partnership under the terms of the Nassau Agreement of December 1962, apparently did not realize that, by doing so, they were driving the last nail into the coffin of their own project of joining the Six,' he wrote.

As Donald would have liked, his children have, for the most part, been educated in the Soviet Union, and one of the first pieces of news about them to reach the outside world was that Fergus, aged twelve, and Donald, aged ten, had been as 'Soviet Pioneers' to a holiday camp near the Sea of Azov. Both they and their sister, Melinda junior, known in the family as Mimsie, grew up bilingual, speaking Russian a good deal better than their parents.

Robin Denniston visiting the family in 1969 found Donald junior a handsome young fellow of twenty-three with a swarm of girl friends and a promising career as a chemical engineer. Mimsie had turned into an attractive blonde. After attending a specialized school of languages, she had just begun studying Spanish at Moscow University, with ambitions to become a literary critic. Fergus, whose friends have rechristened him Felix as more easily pronounceable had originally opted for mathematics, but switched to sociology and in September 1973 came to Britain, with the joint approval of the Foreign Office and Home Office, to study European medieval and modern history at University College, London. He had told inquirers: 'I do not want to discuss anything about myself or my family now or in the future.' Asked if his wife Olga and their little boy, Dimitri, liked England, he replied: 'I don't think there is anything I care to add.'

Though he could claim British nationality as a patrial, he received no grant and paid the full cost of his fees and accommodation. He took his degree in 1976 and at the time this was written was job-hunting in the U.K.

Some earlier writers about the Maclean family had assumed that Donald's drinking spells had been due to the double strains of having to carry out the unacceptable (to him) policies of the Foreign Office, while at the same time concealing the fact that he was working against them as a Soviet agent. But his record after he settled in Moscow seemed to show that even now that he was doing the kind of work that he had always hoped to do since his conversion to Marxism at Cambridge, the old psychiatric influences were still at work. He still suffered from the spells during which 'Gordon' the wild boar replaced the image of 'Sir Donald', the ex-diplomat.

The Russians are tolerant towards those who drink—indeed, the citizen who neglects to help a Russian drunk lying in the street is heavily fined, since the winter cold can be a silent killer. But when drinking interfered with official business, action is taken. Thus early in 1957 it was noted that Maclean was away from his place of work and taking a cure which was apparently complete by May that year when he appeared to see the Soviet State Symphony Orchestra conducted by Sir Malcolm Sargent. (A junior member of the Embassy staff sat next to him without recognizing him.)

Between June and November 1964 while Eleanor Philby had been allowed to revisit the United States to see her daughter, Philby became interested in Melinda who, although now a plumpish brunette, was still attractive. He had been offered the key of the Maclean *dacha* while the Macleans were on a motor tour of the Baltic states and went there to hunt for mushrooms. That autumn he presented Melinda with a fish-slice, ladle and scoop and provided her with a pre-birthday dinner at which caviare, veal *à la moutarde* (a Kim-cooked speciality) and chilled blueberries were among the dishes served.

Philby dined at the Maclean's house and played family bridge with them, using young Donald as a fourth. He took Melinda to the ballet and to lunch alone at the Ararat Restaurant, one of Moscow's best and noted for its Armenian cooking, nominally as a thanks-offering for Melinda's kindness in allowing the Philbys to use her sterling account in London; he intervened to get the Maclean's Danish parcel through the red tape of the Customs House and fixed the plumbing at the *dacha*.

But these attentions did not, apparently, meet with the full approval of Donald Maclean, who, in one of his classic moods, accused Philby of having acted as a double-agent, spying for the West as well as for the East in a manner unbefitting a good Communist.

As the end of 1964 approached, Melinda, always somewhat nervous and highly strung, became more and more tense and Philby claimed that she must be on the brink of a nervous breakdown. 'Gordon' the wild boar once more invaded the Maclean apartment, and Melinda told Eleanor Philby that Donald had become quite impossible and that she was refusing to sleep in the same room with him, and would move instead into the room of one of her sons, together with the telephone extension and a record player. And about that time, Philby informed Eleanor that Melinda was unhappy and that Donald was impotent, and that he must try to make the rest of her life happier. Melinda was now to take first place in his life, although she had no objection to Eleanor staying on in Moscow.

It is hard to be sure whether Maclean, now in his fifties, had once again shown signs of being unable to satisfy Melinda, or whether Melinda had been given permission to spy on Eleanor, with *carte blanche* to oust her from Philby's household as 'unreliable'. Eleanor had, after all, worked for the U.S. Office of War Information and the U.S. War Department, as well as denouncing that Soviet agent in Beirut. On the other hand, it might be that Philby had once more got the seven year itch, or had been told to rid himself of Eleanor.

At any rate, in the spring of 1965 when Philby went to the Maclean *dacha* for ski-ing, there was no Donald. Reports reached the West that Maclean was seriously ill and though Melinda denied this, she confirmed that Maclean had again been sent to a 'rest house'. And from May of that year there was no Eleanor either. She had left Moscow for good.

Kim Philby, of course, had come from a different mould to the one that fashioned Burgess and Maclean. It is true that, like them, he had been educated at a British public school (Westminster) and at Cambridge. And there were other parallels. But his father, whom he deeply respected, had spent most of his life in Arabia as adviser to King Abd al-Aziz ibn Saud and the Royal Family, and had worked in permanent opposition to Lawrence of Arabia and the British Foreign Office in so far as they backed the rival Hashemite family and set its leaders on the thrones of Iraq and Transjordan. Philby senior, who believed in appeasement, had been interned in Britain at the beginning of World War II, having been lured, it is said, to a cocktail party aboard a British frigate in Karachi and brought back to England, lest he carry the gospel of defeatism to the Arabian peninsula. Thus Kim never felt that either he or his family owed anything to the British Establishment. 'To betray you must have belonged,' he said on one occasion in self-justification. He had never belonged.

In an interview given over lunch to Roy Blackman of the *Daily Express* in 1967, Philby, in between mouthfuls of smoked salmon, sturgeon and chicken *à la Kiev*, said that he had made up his mind to enter the fight for Communism as long ago as June 1933 and was prepared to subjugate anything else to it. 'I would do it again if I were a young man in Britain today,' he declared. Surrender to the circumstances around him would have been a much greater strain than resistance to them, he believed.

Asked to say what he liked or disliked most about Britain, he showed a sturdy independence from his host by numbering 'expense-account lunches' and 'the Beaverbrook press' among his short-list of hates, but conceded that he sometimes missed Bitter Beer, and oysters and the occasional fine evening at the Oval or Lords.

In material terms, Philby came off better than either Burgess or Maclean, having been awarded a flat with four large rooms—a living-room, a study, a dining-room and a bedroom plus a washing machine with spin drier, a fridge, a vacuum cleaner and even an electric floor-waxer.

He could afford to eat regularly at leading Moscow restaurants such as the Metropole, the Prague, the Berlin, the Aragvi, specializing in Georgian cooking; or the houseboats on the Moscow river. He has no problem in getting tickets for the ballet or key ice-hockey or football matches, though he has been known to deplore the general standard of football in the U.S.S.R.

But, like Maclean, he occasionally suffers from unfulfilled needs, and when his son John visited him in 1969 for a six-week holiday, his father asked him to bring twelve bristle (as opposed to nylon) toothbrushes, a tin of curry powder, six tins of waterproof band-aid plasters, 250 feet of waxed paper, one pair of size nine slippers, and 14 ounces of saffron.

He endeavours to live in even greater obscurity than Maclean. He uses an assumed name and pretends, if accosted in the street, to speak no English. His flat is in a nameless block set in a nameless cul-de-sac in the area of Gorky Street, flanked on one side by a garden, parts of which are flooded in winter to make a skating rink. Gorky Street, which leads north-west from the centre of Moscow towards Leningrad is, incidentally Moscow's smartest shopping centre. It contains not only the famous Gastronom I, probably the only food store still known to some by the name of its former proprietor, Yeliseyevsky, but also houses Moscow's finest bakery.

Philby seldom attends diplomatic parties, on the pretext that too many over-perfumed women go to them. His social life is passed in safety, largely among other British defectors. These precautions are taken, he assured Eleanor, because his protectors fear that the British or the CIA are out to poison him or shoot him. But it is far more likely that the Russians insist on security in order to protect their own agents who come to see Philby. His one desire seems to be to continue to please them and to hear them say once again— with some truth—'We can never repay you for the work you have done for us.' For them he has cast away his countrymen, his friends, his children and, not least, three wives. No doubt it helped to consolidate his position when, in 1965, he was expelled from membership of the Athenaeum Club and from the Order of the British Empire.

From all accounts Philby and Melinda lived together for two years, between 1967 and 1969. But Melinda recently denied that she ever considered divorcing Donald, and by 1969 when Robert Denniston spent the weekend with the Macleans, the couple were once more on speaking terms (they still are), and were planning a holiday in Poland. Moreover Donald had gone on the water wagon, and was not drinking. He and Melinda were living about three hundred yards from each other, half parted, half not. And

that was still the position in May 1976 when Melinda applied to
the U.S. Embassy in Moscow for a tourist visa to see her 85-year-old
mother, formerly Mrs Dunbar but now Mrs Brohana, who was said
to be ailing.

Melinda's application for a visa put the U.S. State Department
in something of a fix. If they refused to grant one, they could be
accused of being insensitive, if not inhuman, and of flouting the
provisions of the Helsinki agreement which calls on all signatories
—and not only the Russians—to allow greater freedom of communication between families outside the Soviet Union as well as
inside. If, on the other hand, the State Department was seen to
welcome Melinda then the Soviet authorities might suspect the CIA
of being up to its old tricks.

Eventually, not without difficulty, Melinda got her visa and
reached the U.S. in July, but was so discreet that her presence there
did not leak out until more than four months later.

There were suggestions that the State Department was negotiating
with the Kremlin for Melinda to remain permanently in the U.S.,
on the understanding that there would be no reprisals on Donald
junior and 'Mimsie' or the grandchildren, although only Party
Members on the highest level could possibly have vouched for
such an arrangement. Nevertheless in December, matters had
reached the point where Melinda told the *Daily Express* Foreign
Correspondent in New York, Paul Dacre: 'I love America. After
all it's my home. Of course one thinks about the possibility of
coming back.' Her mother, about the same time said: 'Melinda
has never been so happy.'

Melinda spent the first six months of her holiday at her mother's
luxurious lakeside house on Cape Cod, Massachusetts, and when
the weather closed in just before Christmas, she moved to New
York, still, for her, the most exciting city in the world.

But, back in Moscow, her husband, Donald, seemed to be sure
that Melinda would not be staying permanently in America. At
any rate he told John Miller, a member of the *Daily Telegraph*
Diplomatic staff, who dialled Maclean's telephone number direct
from London in December, that, though she was on a lengthy visit
and no return date had been fixed, she would certainly be coming
back to the Soviet Union—perhaps before the Spring; an accurate
forecast as it turned out.

Perhaps Donald Maclean knew Melinda better than she knew
herself—or perhaps he suspected, or knew, that the State Department had assured the Kremlin that, if Melinda were allowed to
leave Russia, they would not offer her an American passport or
persuade her to seek asylum.

Again one wonders how dedicated to Communism or to Donald,

Melinda can be. She would certainly have enjoyed life as with wife of say the British Ambassador in Paris, a position which Donald might easily have reached. (It is now occupied by 'Nicho' Henderson, once one of Maclean's closest friends in Washington and thereafter in London.)

And she can hardly feel satisfied when, having renounced the freedoms of the West in order to be reunited with her somewhat discredited husband, she is now separated from him.

But, on the other hand, she has not lived in the U.S. for nearly thirty years, and then only temporarily after previous spells abroad. At sixty it is too late for her to turn back to the happy times she recalls of playing family card games with Harriet and Catherine. Her sisters, older now, have made their own lives, and, in the years to come, only Melinda's own children and grandchildren can offer the companionship she needs; and besides, the hardships of life in the Soviet Union which might once have seemed unbearable are tolerable now—perhaps more tolerable than the partial ostracism she might expect if she stayed in the West.

And she must surely have asked herself: 'Could I ever live with myself if I stayed in America and then heard that through some action of mine—misunderstood perhaps or even misreported— the KGB had decided to take away my son or daughter for questioning?'

In the end, her own mother, Mrs Brohana, whom she had come so far to see, realized that, just as her own first thoughts must be for her daughter's happiness, so Melinda Maclean's first care must be for the welfare of her son, daughter and grandchildren. So Melinda turned away from the offers, some of which she said mentioned fabulous sums, for her life story, and, not long before her visa expired at the end of February, booked a one-way ticket on the Aeroflot Russian plane for Moscow. As she left the departure lounge of Kennedy Airport New York, she said she was looking forward to paying a return visit to New York in perhaps two years. But she must have wondered in her heart of hearts whether it would ever take place—at any rate while her mother was still alive.

Meanwhile Philby had still not 'surrendered to circumstances', and, in one of his last adventures, as a wrinkled white-haired figure of sixty-three, he proposed marriage, and was accepted, (after a week's reflection, during which, if the KGB had not already promoted the marriage, their approval was sought) by Nina, a 43-year-old spinster of Russo-Polish extraction. Philby sought Nina's hand with some diffidence, he said, as he wondered what he could offer a woman twenty years younger than himself. His wedding gift to his bride was a full length mink coat.

# 25

# Facing Both Ways

Can someone you have known well and welcomed as a friend really be the traitor the police are looking for? And, in a Communist world, would this traitor have stood by his fascist friends? Or would he have denounced them to the secret police? Is it possible to think rationally about any betrayal?

So far as I know, no friends or relations of Burgess, Maclean or Philby has given convincing answers to these questions. A few have been candid enough to realize that, it is impossible for anyone to abandon a friendship without losing a part of his own personality. Some have idealized the motives of their former friends or said that they were misunderstood. Or they have argued that spies have two personalities, of which they chose to like one, the nicer one. Others have justified their relationship with the vanished diplomats, explaining why it was natural for them to have been taken in, or why, despite moments of doubt and their own sense of duty, they were never in a position to place their suspicions at the disposal of the authorities until the thirteenth hour.

On the surface, there was indeed room for doubt. For instance, the enduring impression left by Maclean on a literary friend who knew him well was of his two slightly misplaced front teeth, that gave him the appearance of an amiable rabbit—a rather ineffective, if amusing one, who was always getting thrown out of places, and another example of the two faces which Maclean offered the world occurs in Sir John Colville's memoir *Footprints in Time*. There we have Maclean, in white tie and tails at a pre-war dance, leaning against the pillars of Dudley House, expounding to a group of simpering débutantes, the merits of Communism. To one Miss who was bold enough to ask 'But why Donald if you feel like that do you come to this sort of party?' he replied that the more people do so, the quicker the system would be discredited. Who could have been sure whether he was in earnest, or giving a flippant reply to avoid a serious discussion, or just teasing? Particularly since with his rumpled shirt and hair over his eyes he was clearly tipsy.

Some of those in the public eye, particularly those in official positions, declared with conviction that whatever damage Burgess (or Maclean) might have done at some other period, it did not occur at the time when they saw them most frequently. Thus, Sir Roderick Barclay was able to say with sincerity that, although Maclean had worked under him in Paris in 1940 and again in Washington, he never saw him drunk or disorderly, and believed that his serious drinking became much more common at a later stage, especially when he was in Cairo. (The Ambassador in Cairo, on the other hand, considered that Donald's overstrain must have been brought on by overwork at his previous post in Washington.)

Sir Paul Gore-Booth, for whom Maclean also worked in Washington between 1942 and 1945, saw Donald often and 'thought I knew him well'. He saw Maclean as an attractive figure with a quite outstanding professional ability, to whom, when under pressure, he could turn over work with perfect confidence. Indeed, it was Maclean who helped Gore-Booth to recover from overstrain while in Washington.

Gore-Booth said he called later in 1950 on Maclean as Head of the American Department and was appalled to see his apparent disintegration. He concluded (later) that Maclean's obligations to the Russians had remained dormant during the war and were then being called in, although at the time neither officials nor the public were in the mood to believe that betrayals by such highly placed officials were possible.

Robert Kee, who knew Maclean during his last days in London, questioned, on the other hand, whether Donald had been active as an agent during his later years. Philip Toynbee, perhaps an even closer friend, consoled himself with the thought that although Maclean had deceived his friends, he had derived no satisfaction from doing so.

The relatives kept up their end too. Lady Maclean in an interview given shortly before her death said: 'I still hear regularly from Donald and his wife. They and my grandchildren lead a perfectly normal and ordinary life in Russia. They seem very happy. But I do not think they will ever come to Britain and I am too old for travel and could never stand the journey.' There were no recriminations either from her or from brother Alan, whose career in the Foreign Office had ended so abruptly after Donald's departure. Some other members of the Maclean family, not to speak of relatives on Melinda's side of the family, felt that their careers had to some extent been blighted, and privately said so.

Mrs Dunbar, however, devoted her energies to helping Geoffrey Hoare with his book *The Missing Macleans*, in which Melinda was presented in a highly favourable light—though not favourably enough for her mother who, in Geoffrey's words, wanted her daughter portrayed as a cross between a nun and a girl guide.

Mrs Bassett, as already noted, stood by her son to the end, and even Colonel Bassett did his bit. In an interview given in January 1955, before the White Paper had implicated Burgess as a Soviet agent, he said:

> My stepson may have had the wrong contacts. These contacts are often foisted on you. I never had the slightest suspicions of him. Lots of fellows of that sort do think that things should be put right somehow and I think that was probably at the back of their minds. I would not say they have not been doing a bit of good. We see a certain change in attitude lately. But we are absolutely in the dark except for what appears in the Press.

Harold Nicolson, speaking in 1959 in Colombo after Guy Burgess had imprudently revealed that they were still corresponding, rationalized his relationship after a different fashion. He said: 'Guy Burgess is a friend of mine. And when a friend is in trouble, I never let him down. I began writing about two years ago and have since done so regularly. I cannot accept in my own mind that Burgess is devoid of all loyalty to Britain. He just did not know enough at the time he fled the country. Guy did what he did in a moment of wild impulse.'

Philby's case was rather different from that of the other two defectors as we know the reactions of his wife after he left her for Melinda. She took the view that his good qualities as a devoted husband and a delightful companion were in part a reaction from the restrictions placed on him by the conditions of his work, which forbade him to be spontaneous or to trust anyone or pity them or to love them. Even so, Philby never thought it necessary to apologize for having landed her in a difficult situation in both Beirut and Moscow.

Philby gave another view of himself in a letter from Moscow. Miles Copeland, a former CIA adviser who had been a close friend of Philby in Beirut, and his wife, Lorraine, had been shocked by Philby's defection. Mrs Copeland wrote to Eleanor in Moscow: 'It is painful to think that during the years we all loved Kim and had him constantly in our homes, he was all the while laughing at us.' Philby's answer—a postscript to his wife's reply, was: 'My dear Lorraine, I hope you never have to learn, as I have, that one lives one's life on several planes, and when there is conflict between the plane of one's ideals and that of one's friends it is, believe me, no laughing matter.' Klaus Fuchs in his confession took the same stance when he said that in one half of his mind he could be friends with the people whom he was at the same time deceiving and even endangering.

There is little doubt that Burgess, Maclean and Philby and other pro-Soviet spies were originally motivated by idealism of the kind which led Julius Hay to say:

> I became a Communist in order that I might assist in making everybody in this world happy, in abolishing war for ever, in securing equal rights for all peoples whether great or small, in bringing prosperity to the whole of mankind and in depriving everyone once and for all of the possibility of exploiting others, oppressing others, and of making others unhappy.

Associated with this idealism was a passionate longing to believe that the perfect society could be contrived, and that the first steps were being taken in the Soviet Union. It has been said that revolutions are conceived not by those who are out of sympathy with the present, but by those who live in a society of their own imagination. But perhaps it would be more accurate to say that some revolutionaries live in a society that has been imagined for them, first within left-wing discussion groups, and then within the Communist cells to which they become attached. Their loyalty is drawn first towards international ideals promoted by the United Nations. Then their enthusiasm is grafted onto the world Communist movement and finally linked up with the local Communist party. The Party itself does not engage in espionage and, indeed, is forbidden to do so. But then it is in a position to put the new recruit in touch with party workers who can introduce him to nameless men and women with whom he can work on 'assignments', the very place and nature of which he may not even be told before he embarks on them. And the illegal atmosphere in which Communists traditionally work adds a spice of adventure which can be attractive to the novice.

Possibly, where a man has two personalities, one as a normal citizen, the other as an agent, the latter, formed with white-hot enthusiasm and tempered with discipline and fear, becomes the dominant influence—the cuckoo fledgling that eventually overcomes and ousts all its rivals. At any rate, few recruits at any time appeared to have reconsidered their position, taken up in the thirties. Once the recruit's mind has become locked onto a vision of Utopia, actions are of only two kinds—for the Party or against it.

Those whose enthusiasm leads them to want to renounce their own country and live in the Soviet Union are told—if they are considered recruitable as agents—that they would do a far more effective part in the drive for Communism if they stayed at home.

By this time the Communist conscience is at work—the one which reproaches the party member for keeping up friendships with someone who is not a good party member. Family ties have become a bourgeois characteristic—a fact borne in mind by Donald Maclean when he deceived his own family so successfully.

Equally, Burgess deceived his mother, of whom he was so fond, and was forbidden to tell her the truth, and Philby, likewise, was false not only to his mother and father who had originally recommended him for intelligence work, but to his wives and children.

Logically, if the Soviet way of life was the only right one, then, as Donald Maclean put it to a friend, spying—though perhaps a disagreeable duty which could be likened to the cleaning of public lavatories—was an obligation which had to be carried out. It was a mistake, however, Maclean thought, to consider spying as a glamorous profession or commercialize it in the James Bond style. Still less should the secret service be allowed to influence policy, whether it be in foreign affairs or military adventures or disarmament. But Maclean's fears about the glamorization of agents may well have been exaggerated.

Certainly the role of the lone agent is of less importance than it used to be. Individual spies are now only one part of a vast intelligence picture (although they usually claim that any information they provide is exclusive and exceptionally valuable). Sometimes even when valuable information has been provided, poor judgement or prejudice has led to its rejection. This is particularly the case where the policy of the government conflicts with the facts provided by the intelligence agency.

Espionage and counter-espionage can, as Maclean and Burgess realized lead to political tension. And cases have not been unknown when one intelligence agency has denounced another working in the same government in a kind of civil war.

A single mistake can put paid to an agent's career. A forged passport signed by a consul who has died or been transferred, or an inappropriate serial number can betray the most accomplished spy. A plane crash or car crash can disrupt arrangements for meetings arranged perhaps months ahead. Dead letter drops can be detected and taken over by the enemy. Or an agent, frustrated or discouraged by unsuitable assignments or lack of promotion, may defect to the other side, denouncing fellow agents which it may have taken his own side years to get into position. Another of the agent's limitations arises from the fact that much of the information the governments would like to have is far too technical for him to understand, and it is only once in a while that one can recruit a Klaus Fuchs or Nunn May. Certainly the United States now relies far more than it used to on satellite observation, atmospheric analysis and other indicators and less on conventional field agents, who require an extensive staff to control, monitor and pay them. Moreover, both sides have improved their counter-espionage and security measures, thereby increasing the risks that an agent will be detected before he has established himself.

In Britain, searching investigations are now made not only into the records of those seeking jobs in sensitive government offices or factories, but also into their characters, their habits, their hobbies, their families and their social life. And this 'positive vetting' continues throughout their career. Heads of Departments are now expected to get to know and report any serious failings such as drunkenness, financial instability, addiction to drugs, untruthfulness, homosexuality, loose living, or anything else, including Communist associations or sympathies, which might affect security. A Government tribunal appointed in 1963 also recommended that Heads of Departments should feel free to deny access to secret information to named Trade Unionists of Communist leanings. It declared that Trade Union officials should not be entitled to such information by virtue of their office.

Each Government department is now obliged to have a section responsible for physical and personnel security, covering officials from the lowest to the highest level. Care is now taken to see that rooms in which officers work singly when typing, duplicating or photocopying documents are not completely shut off in isolation but communicate with neighbouring offices through a door, window or hatch. Checks are now made on officers who stay late in the office or work at times outside normal office hours. Restrictions are more closely enforced on officers wishing to take documents home. Papers are less often on show during the day.

Abroad, it is now a standing rule in British Missions that any except chance contacts with Communist bloc citizens must be reported to a responsible official without delay.

And on balance? Undoubtedly for a time the Burgess–Maclean–Philby affair damaged the reputation of the British security services and their standing in the United States. It also gave added significance to a notion put forward in that light-hearted novel mentioned earlier, *The Conspirator* by Humphrey Slater, published in 1948, which suggested that the upper classes, too, could be subverted and led to betray their own country.

Slater's 'traitor' was Major the Hon. Desmond Ferneaux-Lightfoot, DSO, Grenadier Guards, who had been recruited into the Communist Party by a left-wing don while attending a course at Oxford. Desmond married Harriet Frodsham, a nice, simple, non-political girl, some years younger than himself and hardly out of the schoolroom, whom, he decided (as Donald might have decided about Melinda) could easily be trained to think as he did. He, too, believed in the inevitable triumph world-wide of the Communist system. Not many pages from the beginning of the novel we find him defending the real Dr Nunn May as a fighter for peace in the same way as Donald Maclean himself would have done. Desmond has friends in the British Embassy in Paris and succeeds in securing the text of a vital Anglo-American agreement which he passes on to his Russian friends, at a meeting in the basement of a house in Hampstead. He even goes to the same kind of restaurant patronized by Maclean and his friends in Charlotte Street.

Obviously, Slater could not have known in 1948 how the Maclean story would end, but his own *dénouement* was quite as bizarre. Harriet discovers that her husband is a spy and begs him to break away from the Communists; but Desmond, to protect himself, proposes to his NKVD friends that Harriet should be recruited into the network. The Russians, however, fear that she cannot be relied on, and they order Desmond to liquidate her. He tries to do so while on a shooting party, but misses, and she escapes.

When Desmond reports his second failure as a spy, there is a fresh crisis. The NKVD Colonel decides to denounce him to the British intelligence. Then, whatever happens, nothing is lost. If Desmond denies everything and is tried and convicted without betraying his comrades, then the British will execute him or put him in prison where he can do no harm. But if he turns King's Evidence and gives the authorities the full story, there will be a major scandal about treachery by the ruling classes—a convulsion which would shake the faith of other countries in Britain's reliability as an ally. And that is almost what happened when the truth leaked out about Burgess and Maclean.

Could the whole thing happen again?

Lunching one day with a highly placed Soviet official, I put it to him that the idealism that made Donald Maclean reject the conventionally successful career he could have had in the Foreign Office and choose instead the road to Moscow no longer existed in Britain. We had become too materialistic, I suggested, to be able to offer more recruits of the same kind. He agreed, adding that, unfortunately, the younger generations of every country in the world have become more materialistic. Understandably, he offered no suggestion as to where, if anywhere, replacements for Burgess and Maclean could still be found.

# Appendix

## REPORT CONCERNING THE DISAPPEARANCE OF TWO FORMER FOREIGN OFFICE OFFICIALS

### The full text of White Paper, Cmd. 9577

On the evening of Friday, 25th May 1951, Mr Donald Duart Maclean, a Counsellor in the senior branch of the Foreign Service and at that time Head of the American Department in the Foreign Office, and Mr Guy Francis de Moncy Burgess, a Second Secretary in the junior branch of the Foreign Service, left the United Kingdom from Southampton on the boat for St Malo. The circumstances of their departure from England, for which they had not sought sanction, were such as to make it obvious that they had deliberately fled the country. Both officers were suspended from duty on 1st June 1951, and their appointments in the Foreign Office were terminated on 1st June 1952, with effect from 1st June 1951.

2. Maclean was the son of a former Cabinet Minister, Sir Donald Maclean. He was born in 1913 and was educated at Gresham's School, Holt, and Trinity College, Cambridge, where he had a distinguished academic record. He successfully competed for the Diplomatic Service in 1935 and was posted in the first instance to the Foreign Office. He served subsequently in Paris, at Washington and in Cairo. He was an officer of exceptional ability and was promoted to the rank of Counsellor at the early age of thirty-five. He was married to an American lady and had two young sons. A third child was born shortly after his disappearance.

3. In May 1950 while serving at His Majesty's Embassy, Cairo, Maclean was guilty of serious misconduct and suffered a form of breakdown which was attributed to overwork and excessive drinking. Until the breakdown took place his work had remained eminently satisfactory and there was no ground whatsoever for doubting his loyalty. After recuperation and leave at home he was passed medically fit, and in October 1950 was appointed to be Head of the American Department of the Foreign Office which, since it does not deal with the major problems of Anglo-American relations, appeared to be within his capacity.

4. Since Maclean's disappearance a close examination of his background has revealed that during his student days at Cambridge from 1931 to 1934 he had expressed Communist sympathies, but there was no evidence that he had ever been a member of the Communist Party and indeed on leaving the University he had outwardly renounced his earlier Communist views.

5. Burgess was born in 1911 and was educated at the Royal Naval College, Dartmouth, at Eton and at Trinity College, Cambridge,

where he had a brilliant academic record. After leaving Cambridge in 1935 he worked for a short time in London as a journalist and joined the BBC in 1936 where he remained until January 1939. From 1939 until 1941 he was employed in one of the war propaganda organizations. He rejoined the BBC in January 1941 and remained there until 1944 when he applied for and obtained a post as a temporary press officer in the News Department of the Foreign Office. He was not recruited into the Foreign Service through the open competitive examination but in 1947 took the opportunity open to temporary employees to present himself for establishment. He appeared before a Civil Service Commission Board and was recommended for the junior branch of the Foreign Service. His establishment took effect from 1st January 1947. He worked for a time in the office of the then Minister of State, Mr Hector NcNeil, and in the Far Eastern Department of the Foreign Office. In August 1950 he was transferred to Washington as a Second Secretary.

6. Early in 1950 the security authorities informed the Foreign Office that in late 1949 while on holiday abroad Burgess had been guilty of indiscreet talk about secret matters of which he had official knowledge. For this he was severely reprimanded. Apart from this lapse his service in the Foreign Office up to the time of his appointment to Washington was satisfactory and there seemed good reason to hope that he would make a useful career.

7. In Washington, however, his work and behaviour gave rise to complaint. The Ambassador reported that his work had been unsatisfactory in that he lacked thoroughness and balance in routine matters, that he had come to the unfavourable notice of the Department of State because of his reckless driving and that he had had to be reprimanded for carelessness in leaving confidential papers unattended. The Ambassador requested that Burgess be removed from Washington and this was approved. He was recalled to London in early May 1951 and was asked to resign from the Foreign Service. Consideration was being given to the steps that would be taken in the event of his refusing to do so. It was at this point that he disappeared.

8. Investigations into Burgess's past have since shown that he, like Maclean, went through a period of Communist leanings while at Cambridge and that he too on leaving the University outwardly renounced his views. No trace can be found in his subsequent career of direct participation in the activities of left-wing organizations; indeed he was known after leaving Cambridge to have had some contact with organizations such as the Anglo-German Club.

9. The question has been asked whether the association of these two officers with each other did not give rise to suspicion. The fact is that although we have since learned that Maclean and Burgess were acquainted during their undergraduate days at Cambridge, they gave no evidence during the course of their career in the Foreign Service of any association other than would be normal between two colleagues. When Burgess was appointed to the Foreign Office Maclean was in Washington and at the time Burgess himself was

appointed to Washington Maclean was back in the United Kingdom awaiting assignment to the American Department of the Foreign Office. It is now clear that they were in communication with each other after the return of Burgess from Washington in 1957 and they may have been in such communication earlier. Their relations were, however, never such as to cause remark.

10. In January 1949 the security authorities received a report that certain Foreign Office information had leaked to the Soviet authorities some years earlier. The report amounted to little more than a hint and it was at the time impossible to attribute the leak to any particular individual. Highly secret but widespread and protracted enquiries were begun by the security authorities and the field of suspicion had been narrowed by mid-April 1951 to two or three persons. By the beginning of May Maclean had come to be regarded as the principal suspect. There was, however, even at that time, no legally admissible evidence to support a prosecution under the Official Secrets Acts. Arrangements were made to ensure that information of exceptional secrecy and importance should not come into his hands. In the meantime the security authorities arranged to investigate his activities and contacts in order to increase their background knowledge and if possible to obtain information which could be used as evidence in a prosecution. On 25th May the then Secretary of State, Mr Herbert Morrison, sanctioned a proposal that the security authorities should question Maclean. In reaching this decision it had to be borne in mind that such questioning might produce no confession or voluntary statement from Maclean sufficient to support a prosecution but might serve only to alert him and to reveal the nature and the extent of the suspicion against him. In that event he would have been free to make arrangements to leave the country and the authorities would have had no legal power to stop him. Everything therefore depended on the interview and the security authorities were anxious to be as fully prepared as was humanly possible. They were also anxious that Maclean's house at Tatsfield, Kent, should be searched and this was an additional reason for delaying the proposed interview until mid-June when Mrs Maclean who was then pregnant was expected to be away from home.

11. It is now clear that in spite of the precautions taken by the authorities Maclean must have become aware, at some time before his disappearance, that he was under investigation. One explanation may be that he observed that he was no longer receiving certain types of secret papers. It is also possible that he detected that he was under observation. Or he may have been warned. Searching inquiries involving individual interrogations were made into this last possibility. Insufficient evidence was obtainable to form a definite conclusion or to warrant prosecution.

12. Maclean's absence did not become known to the authorities until the morning of Monday, 28th May. The Foreign Office is regularly open for normal business on Saturday mornings but officers can from time to time obtain leave to take a weekend off. In accordance with this practice Maclean applied for and obtained leave to

be absent on the morning of Saturday, 26th May. His absence therefore caused no remark until the following Monday morning when
he failed to appear at the Foreign Office. Burgess was on leave and
under no obligation to report his movements.

13. Immediately the flight was known all possible action was
taken in the United Kingdom and the French and other Continental
security authorities were asked to trace the whereabouts of the
fugitives and if possible to intercept them. All British Consulates
in Western Europe were alerted and special efforts were made to
discover whether the fugitives had crossed the French frontiers on
26th or 27th May. As a result of these and other inquiries it was
established that Maclean and Burgess together left Tatsfield by car
for Southampton in the late evening of Friday, 25th May, arrived at
Southampton at midnight, caught the SS *Falaise* for St Malo and
disembarked at that port at 11.45 the following morning, leaving
suitcases and some of their clothing on board. They were not seen
on the train from St Malo to Paris and it has been reported that
two men, believed to be Maclean and Burgess, took a taxi to Rennes
and there got the 1.18 p.m. train to Paris. Nothing more was seen
of them.

14. Since the disappearance various communications have been
received from them by members of their families. On 7th June 1951,
telegrams ostensibly from Maclean were received by his mother Lady
Maclean, and his wife Mrs Melinda Maclean, who were both at that
time in the United Kingdom. The telegram to Lady Maclean was a
short personal message, signed by a nick-name known only within
the immediate family circle. It merely stated that all was well. That
addressed to Mrs Maclean was similar, expressing regret for the
unexpected departure and was signed 'Donald'. Both telegrams were
dispatched in Paris on the evening of 6th June. Their receipt was at
once reported to the security authorities, but it was impossible to
identify the person or persons who had handed them in. The original
telegraph forms showed, however, that the messages had been
written in a hand which was clearly not Maclean's. The character
of the handwriting, and some mis-spelling, suggested that both telegrams had been written by a foreigner.

15. On 7th June 1951, a telegram was received in London by Mrs
Bassett, Burgess's mother. It contained a short and affectionate personal message, together with a statement that the sender was embarking on a long Mediterranean holiday, and was ostensibly from
Burgess himself. The telegram had been handed in at a Post Office
in Rome earlier on the day of its receipt. As with the telegrams from
Paris to Maclean's family, there was no possibility of identifying
the person who had handed it in. The handwriting had the appearance of being foreign, and was certainly not that of Burgess.

16. According to information given to the Foreign Office in confidence by Mrs Dunbar, Maclean's mother-in-law, who was then
living with her daughter at Tatsfield, she received on 3rd August
1951, two registered letters posted in St Gallen, Switzerland, on 1st
August. One contained a draft on the Swiss Bank Corporation,

London, for the sum of £1,000 payable to Mrs Dunbar; the other, a draft payable to Mrs Dunbar for the same sum, drawn by the Union Bank of Switzerland on the Midland Bank, 122 Old Broad Street, London. Both drafts were stated to have been remitted by order of a Mr Robert Becker, whose address was given as the Hotel Central, Zurich. Exhaustive inquiries in collaboration with the Swiss authorities have not led to the identification of Mr Becker and it is probable that the name given was false.

17. Shortly after the receipt of these bank drafts Mrs Maclean received a letter in her husband's handwriting. It had been posted in Reigate, Surrey, on 5th August 1951, and was of an affectionate, personal nature as from husband to wife. It gave no clue as to Maclean's whereabouts or the reason for his disappearance but it explained that the bank drafts, which for convenience had been sent to Mrs Dunbar, were intended for Mrs Maclean.

18. Lady Maclean received a further letter from her son on 15th August 1951. There is no doubt that it was in his own handwriting. It had been posted at Herne Hill on 11th August.

19. Mrs Bassett, the mother of Burgess, received a letter in Burgess's handwriting on 22nd December 1953. The letter was personal and gave no information as to Burgess's whereabouts. It was simply dated 'November' and had been posted in South-East London on 21st December. The last message received from either of the two men was a further letter from Burgess to his mother which was delivered in London on 25th December 1954. This letter was also personal and disclosed nothing of Burgess's whereabouts. It too was simply dated 'November'. It had been posted in Poplar, E.14, on 23rd December.

20. On 11th September 1953, Mrs Maclean, who was living in Geneva, left there by car with her three children. She had told her mother, who was staying with her, that she had unexpectedly come across an acquaintance whom she and her husband had previously known in Cairo and that he had invited her and the children to spend the weekend with him at Territet, near Montreux. She stated that she would return to Geneva on 13th September in time for the two elder children to attend school the following day. By 14th September her mother, alarmed at her failure to return, reported the matter to Her Majesty's Consul-General in Geneva and also by telephone to London. Security officers were at once dispatched to Geneva where they placed themselves at the disposal of the Swiss police who were already making intensive inquiries. On the afternoon of 16th September Mrs Maclean's car was found in a garage in Lausanne. She had left it on the afternoon of the 11th saying she would return for it in a week. The garage hand who reported this added that Mrs Maclean had then proceeded with her children to the Lausanne railway station. On the same day, 16th September, Mrs Dunbar reported to the Geneva police the receipt of a telegram purporting to come from her daughter. The telegram explained that Mrs Maclean had been delayed 'owing to unforeseen circumstances' and asked Mrs Dunbar to inform the school authorities that the

two elder children would be returning in a week. Mrs Maclean's youngest child was referred to in this telegram by a name known only to Mrs Maclean, her mother and other intimates. The telegram had been handed in at the Post Office in Territet at 10.58 that morning by a woman whose description did not agree with that of Mrs Maclean. The handwriting on the telegram form was not Mrs Maclean's and it showed foreign characteristics similar to those in the telegrams received in 1951 by Lady Maclean, Mrs Maclean and Mrs Bassett.

21. From information subsequently received from witnesses in Switzerland and Austria, it seems clear that the arrangements for Mrs Maclean's departure from Geneva had been carefully planned, and that she proceeded by train from Lausanne on the evening of 11th September, passing the Swiss-Austrian frontier that night, and arriving at Schwarzach St Veit in the American Zone of Austria at approximately 9.15 on the morning of 12th September. The independent evidence of a porter at Schwarzach St Veit and of witnesses travelling on the train has established that she left the train at this point. Further evidence, believed to be reliable, shows that she was met at the station by an unknown man driving a car bearing Austrian number plates. The further movements of this car have not been traced. It is probable that it took Mrs Maclean and the children from Schwarzach St Veit to a neighbouring territory in Russian occupation whence she proceeded on her journey to join her husband.

22. There was no question of preventing Mrs Maclean from leaving the United Kingdom to go to live in Switzerland. Although she was under no obligation to report her movements, she had been regularly in touch with the security authorities, and had informed them that she wished to make her home in Switzerland. She gave two good reasons, firstly that she wished to avoid the personal embarrassment to which she had been subjected by the Press in the United Kingdom, and secondly, that she wished to educate her children in the International School in Geneva. It will be remembered that Mrs Maclean was an American citizen and in view of the publicity caused by her husband's flight it was only natural that she should wish to bring up her children in new surroundings. Before she left for Geneva the security authorities made arrangements with her whereby she was to keep in touch with the British authorities in Berne and Geneva in case she should receive any further news from her husband or require advice or assistance. Mrs Maclean was a free agent. The authorities had no legal means of detaining her in the United Kingdom. Any form of surveillance abroad would have been unwarranted.

23. In view of the suspicions held against Maclean and of the conspiratorial manner of his flight, it was assumed, though it could not be proved, that his destination and that of his companion must have been the Soviet Union or some other territory behind the Iron Curtain. Now Vladimir Petrov, the former Third Secretary of the Soviet Embassy in Canberra who sought political asylum on 3rd April 1954, has provided confirmation of this. Petrov himself was

not directly concerned in the case and his information was obtained from conversation with one of his colleagues in Soviet service in Australia. Petrov states that both Maclean and Burgess were recruited as spies for the Soviet Government while students at the University, with the intention that they should carry out their espionage tasks in the Foreign Office, and that in 1951, by means unknown to him, one or other of the two men became aware that their activities were under investigation. This was reported by them to the Soviet Intelligence Service who then organized their escape and removal to the Soviet Union. Petrov has the impression that the escape route included Czechoslovakia and that it involved an aeroplane flight into that country. Upon their arrival in Russia, Maclean and Burgess lived near Moscow. They were used as advisers to the Ministry of Foreign Affairs and other Soviet agencies. Petrov adds that one of the men (Maclean) has since been joined by his wife.

24. Two points call for comment: first, how Maclean and Burgess remained in the Foreign Service for so long and second, why they were able to get away.

25. When these two men were given their appointments nothing was on record about either to show that he was unsuitable for the public service. It is true that their subsequent personal behaviour was unsatisfactory, and this led to action in each case. As already stated Maclean was recalled from Cairo in 1950 and was not re-employed until he was declared medically fit. Burgess was recalled from Washington in 1951 and was asked to resign. It was only shortly before Maclean disappeared that serious suspicion of his reliability was aroused and active inquiries were set on foot.

26. The second question is how Maclean and Burgess made good their escape from this country when the security authorities were on their track. The watch on Maclean was made difficult by the need to ensure that he did not become aware that he was under observation. This watch was primarily aimed at collecting, if possible, further information and not at preventing an escape. In imposing it a calculated risk had to be taken that he might become aware of it and might take flight. It was inadvisable to increase this risk by extending the surveillance to his home in an isolated part of the country and he was therefore watched in London only. Both men were free to go abroad at any time. In some countries no doubt Maclean would have been arrested first and questioned afterwards. In this country no arrest can be made without adequate evidence. At the time there was insufficient evidence. It was for these reasons necessary for the security authorities to embark upon the difficult and delicate investigation of Maclean, taking into full account the risk that he would be alerted. In the event he was alerted and fled the country together with Burgess.

27. As a result of this case, in July 1951 the then Secretary of State, Mr Herbert Morrison, set up a Committee of inquiry to consider the security checks applied to members of the Foreign Service; the existing regulations and practices of the Foreign Service in regard to any matters having a bearing on security; and to report whether

any alterations were called for. The Committee reported in November 1951. It recommended, among other things, a more extensive security check on Foreign Service officers than had until then been the practice. This was immediately put into effect and since 1952 searching inquiries have been made into the antecedents and associates of all those occupying or applying for positions in the Foreign Office involving highly secret information. The purpose of these inquiries is to ensure that no one is appointed to or continues to occupy any such post unless he or she is fit to be entrusted with the secrets to which the post gives access. The Foreign Secretary of the day approved the action required.

28. A great deal of criticism has been directed towards the reticence of Ministerial replies on these matters; an attitude which it was alleged would not have been changed had it not been for the Petrov revelations. Espionage is carried out in secret. Counter-espionage equally depends for its success upon the maximum secrecy of its methods. Nor is it desirable at any moment to let the other side know how much has been discovered or guess at what means have been used to discover it. Nor should they be allowed to know all the steps that have been taken to improve security. These considerations still apply and must be the basic criterion for judging what should or should not be published.

## SOURCES

*Chapter 1*  This chapter relies on the account given in 'The Great Spy Scandal' compiled by Donald Seaman and John Mather of the *Daily Express* the newspaper which first broke the story of Burgess and Maclean's flight.

*Chapter 2*  The details of Melinda Maclean's domestic arrangements are based on *The Missing Macleans* by Geoffrey Hoare, Foreign Correspondent of the *News Chronicle*, who knew the Maclean family well.

*Chapter 3*  This relies in part on details from the late Tom Driberg's *Guy Burgess, A Portrait With Background* and on investigations into socialism at Cambridge in the early nineteen thirties by Bruce Page, David Leitch and Philip Knightley in *Philby, the Spy Who Betrayed a Generation* and by Patrick Seale and Maureen McConville in *Philby, the Long Road to Moscow*.

*Chapter 4*  The full account of Burgess's unsuccessful attempt to recruit Goronwy Rees appears in the latter's reminiscences *A Chapter of Accidents* which also contains other details of Burgess's life-style.

*Chapter 5*  For this I am indebted for information given by Sir Osbert Lancaster and Mr John Price, both of whom worked with

Burgess in the News Department of the Foreign Office. Some further details on Burgess are taken from Sir Harold Nicolson's *Diaries and Letters*.

*Chapter 6* For the particulars of Guy Burgess's misdemeanours in Washington I have relied on Squadron Leader F. J. Thompson's *Destination Washington*.

*Chapter 7* This is based mainly on 'off the record' interviews particularly as to the circumstances of Maclean's conversion to Communism.

*Chapter 8* The details of Melinda Maclean's early life are set out in Geoffrey Hoare's account in *The Missing Macleans*; the circumstances of the British Embassy withdrawal from Paris at the time of the fall of France are drawn mainly from Sir Roderick Barclay's *Ernest Bevin and the Foreign Office 1932–1969*.

*Chapter 9* The account of Maclean's life in Washington is based mainly on accounts given by those who served with him there in the Embassy. His value to the Russians at that time has been assessed by the U.S. State Department and later elaborated in the two biographies of Philby mentioned above.

*Chapter 10* For this chapter I have relied on the accounts given by Geoffrey Hoare, Philip Toynbee and Major A. W. Sansom, Security Officer at the British Embassy but also on a number of invaluable 'off the record' interviews with those involved.

*Chapter 11* This is based largely on 'off the record' interviews.

*Chapter 12* This relies mainly on published records of those involved in the Cold War—particularly *Men and Decisions* by Lewis Strauss and *The Traitors* by Alan Moorehead.

*Chapter 13* This is structured mainly on the Government White Paper 'Report Concerning the Disappearance of Two Former Foreign Office Officials' and also the account given by Cyril Connolly of Maclean's last days in London.

*Chapter 14* This is founded on Burgess's own account of his escape as told to Tom Driberg—cross checked with the reconstructed account in *The Great Spy Scandal*.

*Chapter 15* For this I am indebted to contemporary reports in the newspapers of the time, some of which were reproduced in *The Great Spy Scandal*.

*Chapter 16* The account of the Foreign Secretary's appearance in the House of Commons is founded partly on *Hansard* and the circumstances which led up to it on Herbert Morrison's autobiography and on contemporary accounts of the MacArthur controversy.

*Chapter 17* Melinda Maclean's holiday was extensively reported in the media as well as—with one significant omission—in *The Missing Macleans*.

*Chapter 18* Melinda Maclean's flight from Geneva was widely reported by national newspapers.

*Chapter 19* Vladimir Petrov and his wife Evdokia who defected from the Soviet Embassy in Canberra wrote their own story in *Empire of Fear* and in *The People*. Michael Bialoguski who helped to bring about their defection recorded the circumstances in *Petrov Story*. Other details in this chapter are derived from the Government's White Paper and from an interview given by the late Maurice Webb to *The People*.

*Chapter 20* The accounts of the debates in the Commons and Lords on the Burgess and Maclean affair and the 'Third Man' are based—though not exclusively—on *Hansard*.

*Chapter 21* The re-appearance of Burgess and Maclean is based on contemporary reports and also on their own written statement.

*Chapter 22* The details of the final settlement with Kim Philby are derived in part from the biographies mentioned above and from Eleanor Philby's autobiographical book *Kim Philby, the Spy I Loved*.

*Chapter 23* This is based mainly on interviews given by Burgess and Maclean in Moscow to visiting pressmen.

*Chapter 24* I am indebted to Eleanor Philby's *Kim Philby, the Spy I Loved* for some details of Maclean's drab existence in Moscow.

*Chapter 25* This chapter is derived mainly from official reports on Government Security, and 'off the record' interviews.

# Select Bibliography

Abse, Leo, *Private Member* (Macdonald, 1973).
Acheson, Dean, *Sketches from Life* (Hamish Hamilton, 1961).
——, *Present at the Creation* (Hamish Hamilton, 1970).
Barclay, Sir Roderick, *Ernest Bevin and the Foreign Office 1932–1969* (published by the author, London, 1975).
Bialoguski, M., *Petrov Story* (Heinemann, 1955).
Bulloch, John, *Akin to Treason* (Arthur Barker, 1966).
Caute, David, *The Fellow Travellers* (Weidenfeld & Nicolson, 1973).
Chapman, Guy, *Why France Collapsed* (Cassell, 1968).
Christiansen, Arthur, *Headlines All My Life* (Heinemann, 1961).
Churchill, Randolph, *The Rise and Fall of Sir Anthony Eden* (MacGibbon & Kee, 1959).
Churchill, Winston S., *The Second World War* (Cassell, 1948–1954).
Colville, Sir John, *Footprints in Time* (Collins, 1976).
Connolly, Cyril, *The Missing Diplomats* (Queen Anne Press, 1952).
Cooke, Alistair, *A Generation on Trial* (Rupert Hart-Davis, 1950).
Cookridge, E. H., *Shadow of a Spy* (Leslie Frewin, 1967).
Copeland, Miles, *The Real Spy World* (Weidenfeld & Nicolson, 1974).
Dalton, Hugh, *The Fateful Years* (Frederick Muller, 1957).
de Gramont, Sanche, *The Secret War* (Andre Deutsch, 1962).
Driberg, Tom, *Guy Burgess, A Portrait With Background* (Weidenfeld & Nicolson, 1956).
Dulles, Allen, *The Craft of Intelligence* (Weidenfeld & Nicolson, 1963).
——, *Great True Spy Stories* (Ginniger, in association with Collins, 1966).
Foote, Alexander, *Handbook for Spies* (Museum Press, 1949).
Gore-Booth, Paul, *With Great Truth and Respect* (Constable, 1974)
Hay, Gyula, *Born 1900* (Hutchinson, 1974).
Hinchley, Colonel Vernon, *The Defectors* (George Harrap, 1967).
Hirsch, Richard, *The Soviet Spies* (Nicholas Kaye, 1947).
Hoare, Geoffrey, *The Missing Macleans* (Cassell, 1955).
Horne, Alistair, *To Lose a Battle* (France, 1940) (Macmillan, 1969).
Hubatsch, Walther, ed., *The German Question* (Herder Book Centre, New York, 1967).
Koestler, Arthur, and others, *The God that Failed*, S.I.S. Studies in Communism (Hamish Hamilton, 1950).
Lehmann, John, *The Whispering Gallery* (Longmans Green, 1955).

Lehmann, John, *I am My Brother* (Longmans, 1960).

——, *The Ample Proposition* (Eyre & Spottiswoode, 1966).

Lucas, Norman, *The Great Spy Ring* (Arthur Barker, 1966).

McDermott, Geoffrey, *The Eden Legacy and the Decline of British Diplomacy* (Leslie Frewin, 1969).

——, *The New Diplomacy and Its Apparatus* (Plume Press, in association with Ward Lock, 1973).

Maclean, Donald, *British Foreign Policy Since Suez* (Hodder & Stoughton, 1970).

Macmillan, Harold, *The Tides of Fortune* (Macmillan, 1969).

Masterman, J. C., *The Double-Cross System* (Yale University Press, 1972).

Mather, John S., ed., *The Great Spy Scandal* (*Daily Express*, 1955).

Moorehead, Alan, *The Traitors* (Hamish Hamilton, 1952).

Morrison, Herbert, *Autobiography* (Odhams Press, 1960).

Muggeridge, Malcolm, *The Infernal Grove* (Fontana/Collins, 1975).

Page, Bruce, with David Leitch and Phillip Knightley, *Philby, the Spy Who Betrayed a Generation* (Penguin Books, 1969).

Petrov, Vladimir, and Evdokia, *Empire of Fear* (Andre Deutsch, 1956).

Philby, Eleanor, *Kim Philby, the Spy I Loved* (Hamish Hamilton, 1967).

Philby, Kim, *My Silent War* (Panther Books, 1969).

Purdy, Anthony, and Douglas Sutherland, *Burgess and Maclean* (Secker & Warburg, 1963).

Ransom, Harry Howe, *The Intelligence Establishment* (Harvard University Press, 1970).

Rees, Morgan Goronwy, *A Chapter of Accidents* (Chatto & Windus, 1972).

Sansom, Major A. W., *I Spied Spies* (Harrap, 1965).

Seale, Patrick, and Maureen McConville, *Philby, the Long Road to Moscow* (Hamish Hamilton, 1973).

Seth, Ronald, *Forty Years of Soviet Spying* (Cassell, 1965).

Slater, Humphrey, *The Conspirator* (Macmillan, 1948).

Spears, Major-General Sir Edward, *Assignment to Catastrophe*, Vols. I & II (Heinemann, 1955).

Spender, Stephen, *World within World* (Hamish Hamilton, 1951).

Strauss, Lewis L., *Men and Decisions* (Macmillan, 1963).

Strong, Major-General Sir Kenneth, *Men of Intelligence* (Cassell, 1970).

Sweet-Escott, Bickham, *Baker Street Irregular* (Methuen, 1965).

Tangye, Nigel, *Facing the Sea* (William Kimber, 1974).

Thompson, F. J., *Destination Washington* (Robert Hale, 1960).

Toynbee, Arnold, *Experiences* (Oxford University Press, 1969).

Toynbee, Arnold, and Philip, *Comparing Notes—A Dialogue Across a Generation* (Weidenfeld & Nicolson, 1963).

Toynbee, Philip, *Friends Apart* (MacGibbon & Kee, 1954).

Trevor-Roper, Hugh, *The Philby Affair* (William Kimber, 1968).

Trilling, Lionel, *The Middle of the Journey* (Secker & Warburg, 1975).

Werth, Alexander, *The Last Days of Paris* (Hamilton, 1940).
West, Rebecca, *The Meaning of Treason* (Macmillan, 1949).
Wighton, Charles, *Adenauer* (Frederick Muller, 1963).


## OTHER SOURCES

*Official Documents*

Report Concerning the Disappearance of Two Former Foreign Office Officials (White Paper). Command Paper No. 9577, September 1955.

Security Procedures in the Public Service (Radcliffe Report): Command Paper No. 1681, April 1962.

Official Secrets: Report of the Tribunal appointed to inquire into the Vassall case and related matters: Command Paper No. 2009, 1963.

Lord Denning's Report: Command Paper No. 2152, September 1963, covering the Profumo Affair and the Operation of the Security Service.


Newspapers and periodicals consulted include: *Daily Express, Sunday Express, The Times, Sunday Times, The People, Sunday Dispatch, Daily Telegraph,* Manchester *Guardian, Daily Mail, Daily Herald* and the *Hansard* records of Parliamentary debates.

# Index